Escape from Detroit

ESCAPE FROM DETROIT

THE COLLAPSE OF AMERICA'S BLACK METROPOLIS

By Paul Kersey

Dedicated to the memory of Coleman A. Young

Book Cover

The top image on the book cover is of "The Spirit of Detroit," a statue that was dedicated in 1958. In its left hand, the large figure holds a bronze sphere emanating rays to symbolize God.; in the right hand, is a family group that symbolizes all human relationships.

Detroit was roughly 70 percent white when this statue was dedicated. It rests outside the city's municipal center, which has subsequently been renamed for the first Black mayor of Detroit, Coleman Young.

The bottom picture is of the Joe Louis Statue, a giant Black fist that has come to symbolize "Black power" in a city that is 89 percent Black in 2012

In 1912, Detroit was less than 2 percent Black. *Escape from Detroit: The Collapse of America's Black Metropolis* is the story of what actually happened in a city that was once dubbed "The Arsenal of Democracy."

It is hard to believe that in the 1920s, Detroit had the tallest buildings in America and a thriving arts and culture industry. The cosmopolitan attitude cultivated in Detroit, with architects building towers that jettisoned into the sky at heights previously unseen in the entire world, earning the city the title of "The Paris of the West." Now, those largely empty buildings stand as a monument to 'what could have been' in a city that wasn't ravaged by unions, liberalism, or a natural disaster but was abandoned by its white majority population for the people that took over the city in the wake of the 1967 riots.

"The Mogadishu of the West" offers a warning to other American cities. In Black and white, this is the story of Detroit's collapse.

Introduction

The iconic Journey song *Don't Stop Believing* has an interesting line in the opening verse: "Just a city boy, born and raised in South Detroit…"

In bars all across the country, this song will inevitably play, immediately energizing patrons hoping to roll the dice, one more time.

Detroit will not get that chance.

The city of Detroit – 100 years ago nearly an all-white city; today 89 percent Black – is done. Finished.

Escape from Detroit: The Collapse of America's Black Metropolis is the story of what happened in *The Motor City* after the election of Coleman A. Young in 1973 as the city's first Black mayor. He ushered in an era where Black people in Detroit became the political powerbrokers of what was once the nation's fourth largest city.

It's fitting that disgraced former Detroit mayor Kwame Kilpatrick recently published his memoirs, for he was America's first "hip hop" mayor and presided over the city in the first part of the 21st century, before his career ended in shambles and shackles.[1]

Only in Detroit could a man like Kwame Kilpatrick get elected, but it took the election of Coleman A. Young and the systematic ethnic cleansing of whites from Detroit (yes, that's exactly what happened) via the threat of Black crime that allowed this to happen.

---

[1] http://www.freep.com/article/20080124/NEWS05/801240414/Kilpatrick-chief-staff-lied-under-oath-text-messages-show

8

Luke Bergmann wrote a book about his time following young Black men in Detroit who had taken to the entrepreneurial activity of peddling drugs in their community. He tells the story of the celebration of Detroit's three hundredth birthday celebration in 2001, where city leaders prepared to honor the past and prepare for the future:

> A pictorial time line produced by the Detroit 300 Committee was meant to mark significant milestones in Detroit's history. It begins with a bust of Antoine de la Mothe Cadillac (the 18th century founder of the city)... It includes notations of the first car in Detroit (1896), the opening of Henry Ford's plant in Highland Park (1913), and the initial organization of the United Auto Workers and its successful effort to gain concession from General Motor's management (1936). The time line, of course, does not omit Detroit's heralded period as the "Arsenal of Democracy" during World War II, when Ford produced all the armed services B-23 bombers at the Willow Run assembly plant west of Detroit.
>
> But the time line takes a curious turn here – or rather, skips a beat – to the present. Underneath a photograph of World War II-era B-24s lined up in an assembly hangar, the tercentennial committee gives us a view of the contemporary Detroit skyline, emphasizing the foreshortened, looming Renaissance Center.
>
> For the time line is a nearly effective effort to make the disappearance of sixty years of postwar history seem utterly natural. The reader is hardly encouraged to wonder, Did nothing happen between the end of World War II, Detroit's reign as the supposed Arsenal of Democracy, and the present?

Perhaps the most startling aspect of the omission of Detroit's postwar history is the absence of any acknowledgement that Detroit has become, by an overwhelming majority, an African American city. Looking at he tercentennial committee's brochure, one would have no idea that the city has a black cultural identity and was one of the most important centers of black political activity and power in the last decades of the twentieth century.[2]

The condition of Detroit in 2012 is a postwar acknowledgment of Black contributions to the city. The complete collapse of the city is directly correlated to the moment that Black people became the majority population of the city. As whites fled to the suburbs and rebuilt their city, Detroit was made into the image of its new majority population – what Bergmann calls "one of the most important centers of black political activity and power" at the end of the 20th century.

Dan Austin documented what "Black political power" means in his book showcasing the ruins of the city in *Lost Detroit*; Yves Marchand and Romain Meffre did the same in their book *The Ruins of Detroit*; and Andrew Moore published yet another book of photographs from Black-run Detroit in his book *Detroit Disassembled*.

Bergmann can look at any of these three books and see for himself the contributions of Black people over the past sixty years in Detroit.

Black America played no part in the building of Detroit; Black played almost an exclusive part in the destruction of Detroit.*

What happened though? How could a city that was 72 percent white in 1960 become only 57 percent white in 1970?

Kevin Boyle describes it well in his book *"The UAW and the Heyday of American Liberalism"*:

---

[2] Bergmann, Luke. *Getting ghost: two young lives and the struggle for the soul of an American city.* New York: New Press, 2008.34-35

...on July 23, a minor incident in Detroit's Near West Side ghetto, a routine police raid of an after hours bar, triggered the worst civil disorder of the twentieth century to date. By week's end, 43 Detroiters had been killed, over 1,000 had been injured, 5,000 left homeless, and over 7,000 arrested. Officials estimated that as many as 1,000 buildings had been destroyed, 2,500 businesses looted, and $134 million in property damaged. "it looks like Berlin in 1945, " Mayor Jerome Cavanagh lamented as he toured the riot scene."

In retrospect, the Detroit riot was predictable. Despite the Great Society's expansive promises, many of the city's African –Americans remained locked in poverty. Detroit's largely white police force had earned a reputation for brutality in the ghetto, and the city's vocal black power advocated had fueled the flames of discontent. [3]

Life magazine put Detroit on its August 4, 1967 cover with the title, *"Negro Revolt: The Flames Spread"*. Herb Colling catalogued the plundering of the rioters this way:

In a music store, looters clean out bins of jazz and sacred music. They leave the Lawrence Welk behind. Every piece of electronic equipment; guitars, amplifiers and phonographs have already been cleaned out. At a pawnshop, two men pry up the bottom of a security gate as another scrapes through on his belly. He reaches through the broken window and scoop watches in the display case. One-third of the liquor stores, and hundreds of small grocery stores, have been plundered. [4]

Even as Black people become the majority population – indeed, almost all the inhabitants of Detroit – poverty remained a consistent problem. Thomas Sugrue pointed this out, writing:

*

[3] Boyle, Kevin. *The UAW and the heyday of American liberalism, 1945-1968*. Ithaca: Cornell University Press, 1995. 228-229

[4] Colling, Herb. *Turning points the Detroit riot of 1967 : a Canadian perspective*. Toronto: Natural Heritage Books, 2003. 19

Racial preferences in government contracts also created a lucrative niche for African American-owned businesses. Detroit's first African American mayor, Coleman Young, much like his white predecessors, used city employment and city contracts to reward loyal supporters over the course of his twenty-year mayoralty (1974-1994). But in the private sector, companies and workers continued to resist affirmative action programs, and blacks have remained underrepresented in skilled an white collar work throughout the post riot years.

Patterns of segregation actually worsened in the 1970s and 1980s. Real estate steering and discrimination against blacks have persisted, as audits of brokers' racial practices have demonstrated. Whites remained reluctant to live in racially mixed neighborhoods, and even when middle-class African Americans moved in prosperous suburbs like Southfield, just north of Detroit, the white population has fled, creating new segregated enclaves.

Poverty statistics by census tract for 1970 and 1980 reveal a growing concentration of poverty in certain sections. The black neighborhoods that had housed the poorest third of the city's black population in 1950 and 1960 were even poorer in 1970 and 1980. [5]

White people fled Detroit because of high-rates of Black crime; because of the *fear* of Black criminality. When restrictive covenants were declared unconstitutional in 1948, the city's fate was sealed.

Escape from Detroit is exactly what the white people - whose ancestors built the city - did when it became illegal to protect the integrity of your community through the law.

Detroit in 2012 is a direct look at what happens when white flight is replaced with Black power.

It's really that simple.

---

[5] Sugrue, Thomas J.. *The origins of the urban crisis: race and inequality in postwar Detroit : with a new preface by the author*. Princeton: Princeton University Press, 2005. 268-269

—

The lesson of Detroit is a warning to every city in America. It is my belief the best days for this nation are still ahead of us, if only we can confront the reality of Detroit's demise.

The motto of the city is fitting: It will rise from the ashes.

A re-birth of not just The Motor City, but the American spirit can rise from the ashes of Detroit, if we understand the lessons of the city's collapse.

It is for this reason *Escape from Detroit: The Collapse of America's Black Metropolis* was written.

"Don't stop believing."

- Paul Kersey
  March 30, 2012

Table 1:Detroit Black population and housing growth 1900 - 2001[6]

Year	Total Population	Black population	Black total (%)	Black total increase (%)	Black home-owners (%)
1900	285,704	4,111	1.4	-	16.1
1910	465,766	5,741	1.2	1	-
1920	993,000	40,838	4.1	7	-
1930	672,000	120,066	7.7	14	15.0
1940	1,568,662	149,119	9.2	53	14.7
1950	1,623,452	300,506	16.2	67	33.6
1960	1,849,568	482,229	28.9	102	39.0
1970	1,670,144	660,428	43.7	112	-
1980	1,511,482	758,468	63.0	32	53.1
1990	1,203,369	777,916	75.7	11	-
2000	951,270	775,772	81.5	3	53.4

Before we begin our journey through Detroit post-1967, understand the reality of the racial demographics throughout the city's history. Yes, the city was roughly 98 percent white 100 years ago. *In the space of one man's lifetime it has changed to nearly all black.*

---

[6] Shaw, Todd Cameron. *Now is the time!: Detroit black politics and grassroots activism.* Durham: Duke University Press, 2009. 41

Table of Contents

Sorry Rush Limbaugh, it's not Liberalism: 100 Years Ago, Detroit was almost 100 Percent White. Now, it's 80 Percent Black

Roughly 100 years ago, the Titanic (D) hit an iceberg and sank to the bottom of the icy Atlantic ocean. Thinking the boat was unsinkable was part of the hubris of the engineers who designed it and the careless navigation of the ship's captain. **

At that same time, Detroit, Michigan was a growing city of 465,766 people, almost 99 percent of them being of European descent. They built a city - with the auto industry as the backbone of the economy - that became known as "The Arsenal of Democracy" and "The Paris of the West."

Hundreds of thousands of Black people would move north during this time period and seek fortune and stability for their families in what become known as The Motor City, and also gravitate to places like Chicago, Milwaukee, St. Louis, and Cleveland. This was known as "The Great Migration," though history will one day call it by a different name: "The Black Undertow Effect".

2012 Detroit is a much different picture than what 1912 Detroit looked like, and not once in Dan Austin's *Lost Detroit: Stories Behind the Motor's Majestic Ruins* (a pictorial account of Detroit's mighty buildings left to the ravages of the new rulers of the city) does he allude to the inconvenient truth that the city is now 82 percent Black. The Whites who built Detroit, toiled in its factories, kept the city streets safe for children and nurtured small businesses; all vacated the Motor City for the suburbs; thus rebuilding what they fled when the Black Undertow became too unbearable.

Detroit's population fell to 713,777 in 2010, the lowest since 1910, when it was 466,000. In a shift that was unthinkable 20 years ago, Detroit is now smaller than Austin, Tex., Charlotte, N.C., and Jacksonville, Fla.

"It's a major city in free-fall," said L. Brooks Patterson, the county executive of neighboring Oakland County, which was also hit by the implosion of the automobile industry but whose population rose by almost 1 percent, thanks to an influx of black residents. "Detroit's tax base is eroding, its citizens are fleeing and its school system is in the hands of a financial manager."

But a major factor, too, has been the exodus of black residents to the suburbs, which followed the white flight that started in the 1960s. Detroit lost 185,393 black residents in the last decade.

"This is the biggest loss of blacks the city has shown, and that's tied to the foreclosures in the city's housing," Mr. Frey said. Because of the Great Migration — when blacks flowed from the South to the North — and the loss of whites, he said, "Detroit has been the most segregated city in the country and it is still pretty segregated, but not as much." At one point, the city was 83 percent black.

Many blacks moved to nearby suburbs, but census data shows that even those suburbs have barely held their own against population loss. [7]

As Black people flee the still dead Frankenstein-monster that is Detroit, they move to the safe Whitopia's that will inevitably be in turn vacated by white people fleeing the crime and depreciated property values that follow the Black refugees of The Motor City.

But when did this actually start to occur? The book *Violence in the Model City: The Cavanagh Administration, Race Relations, and the Detroit Riot of 1967* by Sidney Fine:

---

[7] http://www.nytimes.com/2011/03/23/us/23detroit.html

It was crime and its association with blacks that triggered a major crisis in race relations in Detroit in 1960. Four days after the Civil Rights Commission concluded its hearings in the city, the *Detroit News* noted in an editorial that although blacks constituted 26 percent of the city's population, they were responsible for almost 65 percent of its serious crimes. Asserting that the black community bore "a share of responsibility" for this fact, the *News* complained that the black leadership had "not pressed as hard" on this issues as it should have. "A wave of murders, rapes and purse snatching," with blacks identified as the perpetrators, culminated that same month in the murder of a white nurse's aide, a twenty-eight-year-old mother of three.[8]

Twenty-six percent of the population, yet responsible for 65 percent of violent crime: is it any wonder why white families started heading for suburbs of Detroit and tried – in vain – to keep Black families from being their neighbor?

---

[8] Fine, Sidney. *Violence in the model city: the Cavanagh administration, race relations, and the Detroit riot of 1967.* Ann Arbor: University of Michigan Press, 1989. 15

You see Black crime has always been bad in America. This is why white people didn't want to live around Black people then and why laws were erected in the south that convinced Black people to participate in "The Great Migration" north that culminated with Democrats in Michigan in 1972 giving the nod to Alabama segregationist George Wallace in the primary.
Yes, you read that right.

Finally it culminated in white people abandoning Detroit to the ravages of the Black Undertow, blacks who promptly elected Coleman Young - the city's first Black mayor - and watched as The Motor City started a collapse unprecedented in human history that confirmed Black people can't maintain the civilization they are handed. The collapse of Detroit is best described as a continual aerial bombardment of the city with Black people serving as the munitions.[9]

It should be stated here that Detroit's International Airport is named after Coleman Young, the Black mayor of Detroit who presided over Detroit is a reminder not of what liberalism does to a city (Pittsburgh has been rated as the best place to live in America and it has never been a bastion of conservatism), but what Black people do to a city, a county, or a country that has been immolated because of the power of white guilt in the face of Black incompetence.

As the concept of Structural Inequality shows us, even Disingenuous White Liberals (DWLs) now admit that Black people can't sustain the infrastructure of a city they have inherited because of white flight.

Detroit, a city that was nearly 100 percent white but one century ago, is now on the verge of being taken over by the state of Michigan (much as Black-run Washington D.C. was once taken over by an act of Congress because Black people were running the city into the ground) in a moment that confirms one thing: the Black Undertow is the greatest threat to the future security, prosperity, and existence of the United States of America.

The New York Times admitted what the concept of the Black Undertow has done to Detroit, and will inevitably do to Whitopia's

---

[9] http://detroit.blogs.time.com/2009/12/02/coleman-young-revisited/

surrounding the city with this op-ed by Sugrue, in a piece that should have been named "A Dream that Never was to be":

> AT first glance, the numbers released by the Census Bureau last week showing a precipitous drop in Detroit's population — 25 percent over the last decade — seem to bear a silver lining: most of those leaving the city are blacks headed to the suburbs, once the refuge of mid-century white flight.

> But a closer analysis of the data suggests that the story of housing discrimination that has dominated American urban life since the early 20th century is far from over. In the Detroit metropolitan area, blacks are moving into so-called secondhand suburbs: established communities with deteriorating housing stock that are falling out of favor with younger white homebuyers. If historical trends hold, these suburbs will likely shift from white to black — and soon look much like Detroit itself, with resegregated schools, dwindling tax bases and decaying public services.[10]

Why can't Black people sustain a city and maintain public services? Why does Sugrue admit that - just like Detroit - where ever Black people end up they will only replicate what they left?

How many other major cities have been overwhelmed by this phenomenon? Memphis? Charlotte? Birmingham? Philadelphia? Cleveland? Chicago? St. Louis? Atlanta? Newark? Baltimore? Montgomery? Milwaukee? Harrisburg? Buffalo? New Orleans? What about Prince George's County, with Washington D.C. quickly becoming a Stuff White People Like (SWPL) playground?

Folks, Rush Limbaugh would have you believe its "liberalism" that has ruined Detroit, as he told Fox News this recently:

---

[10] http://www.nytimes.com/2011/03/27/opinion/27Sugrue.html?_r=3

In an appearance on Fox News Channel aired on Thursday night's "On the Record with Greta Van Sustren," conservative talk show host Rush Limbaugh explained, in no uncertain terms, how to fix Detroit, where unemployment and poverty are rampant. His solution: End liberalism.

"Get rid of every liberal in government," he said. "What is the one constant in Detroit, all of these years? Been run by liberals. Liberal ideology. Liberal economics. Liberal belief system. Detroit, other places: A microcosm of where Europe is, and where we are headed — unchecked, unstopped liberalism. For those of you who like the Democrat Party, that's where we are headed. There hasn't been any opposition there, not of any strength or power. Take a look. That's the one thing that is constant. It was the same thing in New Orleans, post-Katrina. What's the one thing that was constant there? All run by liberals. All run by Democrats."[11]

What does that even mean? The connection between New Orleans collapse (plus rampant crime) and Detroit's is Black people! New Orleans and Detroit aren't two of the most dangerous cities in the world because of liberalism, they are two of the most dangerous cities in the world because of Black people. "Liberlism" dosen't explain why hospitals in Cincinnati and Baltimore are used as trauma-training centers for military surgeons preparing to go overseas to war zones; because Black people have turned these cities into war zones that are far worse than what our troops see overseas.[12]

Wait, *The Baltimore Sun* did just publish a celebratory article for the city posting the fewest murders since 1977. Thank God we have harsher sentences on Black criminals, the real reason crime has dropped (barely) recently.[13]

---

[11]   http://dailycaller.com/2011/12/30/rush-on-how-to-fix-detroit-get-rid-of-every-liberal-in-government/#ixzz1iLVGaojj

[12]   http://stuffblackpeopledontlike.blogspot.com/2011/10/war-zone-usa-black-undertow-provides.html

[13]   http://www.baltimoresun.com/news/breaking/bs-md-ci-year-end-crime-20120101,0,6012046.story

Detroit's collapse is 100 percent racial. Just look at the breakdown of population from 1910 (nearly all-white) to now (nearly all-Black). Just check out p. 23 of Thomas Sugrue's *The Origins of the Urban Crisis: Race and Inequality in Postwar Detroit* to see a racial breakdown of Detroit from 1910-1970. Better yet, look at the data we have provided above.

There is no inequality in Detroit; it's just that Black people can't maintain the civilization (buildings, infrastructure, economy, businesses, tax-revenue, school system) that white people left them.

It wasn't liberalism that killed Detroit, Mr. Limbaugh. It was the city actually being run by Black people.

And, no, just because *The USA Today* states that Detroit is resurgent doesn't make it so. Nor *BusinessWeek* parroting the same theme either.[14]

We will know that Detroit is making a comeback only when Coleman Young International Airport is stripped of its namesake, for he represents the very Organized Blackness that helped bring about the disastrous Black Riot of 1967 that sealed the fate of the city.

---

[14]http://www.businessweek.com/magazine/detroits-resurgence-12222011.html

---

Media asks "Is Iowa too white for first Presidential Caucus?" We ask "Is Detroit too Black for Civilization?"

"Is this heaven?," asks the ghost of Shoeless Joe Jackson in *Field of Dreams*. That same question is asked by his father, right before they finally have a catch together.

The United States of America once looked like Iowa (the state is 91 percent white; in 1964, America was 90 percent white). Now, the Iowa State Fair is home to "beat whitey night," an event that is being replicated all across the country with nary a peep from anyone in a position of power.

One Hundred years ago, Detroit was nearly 100 percent white. Today, Detroit is 82 percent Black and on the verge of bankruptcy. The civilization blacks inherited has died on their Watch, with this fitting story putting an exclamation point on that statement:

> Detroit Police Department precincts and districts may no longer be open to the public 24 hours a day.
>
> Beginning Monday, precincts and districts will be closed to the public from 4 p.m. until 8 a.m., officials said. As part of the plan, several job assignments will be eliminated and those officers will end up on the street, Detroit Police Cmdr. Steve Dolunt said.
>
> "I think it's going to work," he said. "I think it'll get the officers more involved" with citizens.
>
> Detroit Police spokeswoman Sgt. Eren Stephens said Chief Ralph Godbee Jr. will address "the new procedures regarding Front Desk Operations" at 1 p.m. Thursday.[15]

---

[15] http://www.freep.com/article/20120103/NEWS01/120103049/Detroit-police-precincts-limiting-hours

This story confirms that the Detroit of 2012 -- already one of the most violent and dangerous in all of the world -- is in a far worse state than that depicted in 1987's *Robocop.*

Consequently, the following story (published in both *The Christian Science-Monitor* and the *US News and World Report*) shows that Disingenuous White Liberals (DWL) like NBC's Andrea Mitchell hope that all of America one day looks like Detroit:

> Is Iowa too white to be politically representative of the United States as a whole? That question arises because NBC correspondent Andrea Mitchell on Sunday implied that it was.
>
> While interviewing GOP strategist Mike Murphy, Ms. Mitchell made this comment: "The rap on Iowa – it doesn't represent the rest of the country. [It's] too white, too evangelical, too rural."
>
> Conservative critics have leaped on Mitchell for injecting her opinions into the discussion. To be fair, however, she was clearly citing "critics" who say such things – and they do. In fact, she was almost directly quoting from a New York Times article of Dec. 17, which made much the same point while discussing Iowa's relative economic stability.
>
> "As the first state to take part in the Republican nominating contest, Iowa has long been criticized as too much of an outlier to be permanently endowed such an outsize influence in shaping the presidential field," wrote the Times' A.G. Sulzberger. "Too small, critics say. Too rural. Too white."
>
> It is the "white" part of this that may be raising the most hackles among conservatives. They point out that in 2008 then-candidate Barack Obama won the state and its seven electoral votes, after all.

Well, this is easy to check, isn't it? And at first glance there is something to the criticism of Iowa as racially unrepresentative of the US. According to the US Census Bureau, Iowa is 91.3 percent white. The US as a whole is 72.4 percent white. Iowa's population is 2.9 percent black, as opposed to 12.6 percent for the US as a whole. Latinos make up 5 percent of the state versus 16.3 percent of the US.[16]

Fitting that that 12.6 percent of the United States helps make life inhospitable in places like Birmingham, Alabama; Baltimore, Maryland; Newark, New Jersey; and Milwaukee, Wisconsin. Fitting that that 12. 6 percent of the population engaged in massive riots over Air Jordan's during Christmas 2011 that cost $180 a pop, when most rely on EBT/Food Stamps, TANF/Welfare, Section 8 Housing, and other entitlements to merely survive.

Fitting that that 12.6 percent of the population has been responsible for turning Detroit, once one of the shining examples of human achievement and ingenuity, into the Detroit of 2012: a macabre example of what happens to any city, county, or country that transfers from white rule to Black.

Black people had nothing to do with the building of Detroit; they have everything with its collapse.

Iowa's relative economic stability is predicated upon the fact that it is almost all-white; Detroit's economic instability is predicated upon the fact that it is almost all-Black.

We call the latter the Visible Black Hand of Economics. Here's *The New York Times* on the oddity of a state that is actually efficiently run, because it avoids having Black Undertow cities that are a drain on the economy:

---

[16] http://www.usnews.com/opinion/articles/2012/01/03/is-iowa-too-white-to-kick-off-the-presidential-selection-process

As the first state to take part in the Republican nominating contest, Iowa has long been criticized as too much of an outlier to be permanently endowed such an outsize influence in shaping the presidential field. Too small, critics say. Too rural. Too white. But this election cycle, there is another particularly relevant way in which the state does not represent the nation as a whole: it is too economically healthy.

Iowa, one of several Midwestern states that largely sidestepped the reckless rise of the housing market and the crash that followed, has remained relatively stable through these difficult years. Buoyed by a booming agriculture sector, the state is enjoying lower unemployment, greater income growth, steadier home sales and fewer foreclosures than most others. [17]

---

[17]   http://www.nytimes.com/2011/12/18/us/politics/economy-rules-gop-message-but-iowa-differs.html?pagewanted=all

In the 2010 movie *The Crazies*, it took a military pathogen unwittingly unleashed in an Iowa town's water supply to destabilize the (almost all-white) population, turning them into maniacal murderers. Looking at the homicide rate of Detroit (or for that matter any town with a sizable Black population) we can't blame a military pathogen on the lawlessness there.

"Is this heaven?," asks the ghost of Shoeless Joe Jackson in *Field of Dreams*. That same question is asked by his father, right before they finally have a catch together.

When one visits Detroit, the question doesn't even need to be asked: You are entering hell on earth, a city Dante himself would never dare visit.

So the media can ask "Is Iowa too white for first Presidential Caucus?" We'll ask at SBPDL this simple question: "Is Detroit too Black for Civilization?"

Judging by the rate that middle class Black people are fleeing Detroit, where structural inequality is too much of a burden for Black people to overcome, the answer is a resounding, emphatic "yes."

How Did it Come to This? WaPo Sheds Tears Over the Inevitable Collapse of Detroit

The coming collapse of Detroit represents a watershed moment in American history. A mere 100 years ago, Detroit was nearly 100 percent white.

Beyond the horizon, these white citizens envisioned a magnificent city, with opulent buildings, grand theaters for entertainment and a thriving economy that would be the envy of the world. If you build it, they will come.

From the southern United States flowed "The Great Migration," as Black people saw that same horizon and realized they could never build an infrastructure for a city near the grandeur of Detroit. For that matter, no record exists of any city that Black people have ever built with an economic infrastructure or low crime rate that didn't receive massive subsidization or entitlements from a government or charitable organization or was under Military occupation.

Today, Detroit is 82 percent Black, a rotting shell of its former self.

Black people inherited an existing infrastructure that white people abandon due to unsavory social *Climate Change*. In an embarrassing op-ed for *The New York Times*, Thomas Sugrue wrote these words about white flight from Detroit:

> Those who left the city cited various reasons: desire for a little green space, new housing, better schools, freedom from crime. Few of them acknowledged the racial motive behind white flight, that words like "freedom from crime" were code for moving away from blacks.[18]

---

[18] http://www.nytimes.com/2011/03/27/opinion/27Sugrue.html?_r=4

It's not just Detroit that white people have abandoned and with it the hopes of dreams of their ancestors who toiled, saved, and hoped for a brighter tomorrow for their children then the one they had. "Freedom from crime" means freedom from the Black Undertow, who are responsible for the majority of the crime in the United States of America. "Better schools" can only be found in school districts not relying on Superman to save the day.

If only white people would admit this reality, there would never be another Detroit; there would never be another Clayton County (Ga.); there would never be another Jefferson County, Alabama; there would never be another major city or county where "Structural Inequality" would be the excuse for Black people's inability to maintain what was left to them, which equates to white people 'willing' the real estate knowing full well that economic death and ruination will only follow this gesture.

On New Year 1912, white people in Detroit celebrated a future filled with endless possibilities; on New Year 2012, Black people in Detroit celebrated in an endless drunken stupor while two members of medical emergency personnel in a broken-down ambulance sat frozen in horror and prayed for rescue while gunshots from revelers kept them behind the locked-doors of the immobile vehicle.[19]

Now, The Washington Post reports the impending Civil Rights fiasco in a city where freedom failed once the Black Undertow assumed control:

> As a Michigan panel considers whether a state-appointed emergency manager should take over Detroit's debt-laden budget,[20] some residents and leaders are arguing that the move would disenfranchise black voters.

[19] http://www.occidentaldissent.com/2012/01/06/black-new-years-2012/

[20]   http://www.washingtonpost.com/national/with-detroit-in-dire-straits-mayor-invites-big-thinking/2011/02/07/ABL6NwQ_story.html

"How come all of the jurisdictions put under emergency management are majority African American? Has anybody noticed that?" asked Rep. John Conyers (D), who has represented Detroit for 47 years. "There seems to be a racial aspect, a racial component of the application of this law."

Under a newly strengthened law allowing the governor to appoint emergency managers over local governments, appointees are now running other financially bereft cities with large black populations — including Benton Harbor, Pontiac, Ecorse and Flint. If Detroit is added, a sizable proportion of the state's black residents will be living under emergency managers.

Michigan Gov. Rick Snyder (R) said that he has no interest in running Detroit and wants the city to be responsible for itself.

"Our role is to be a supporting resource," Snyder said in a video he released last month. "My goal is to avoid appointing an emergency manager, because that's a failure point."

But if the city meets certain conditions, appointment of an emergency manager is the next step under state law.

Snyder understands he is stepping into a political minefield if an emergency manager is appointed, said Bettie Buss, a senior research associate at the Citizens Research Council of Michigan, a public policy think tank. "There is no upside for the governor to appoint an emergency manager of Detroit, but the city is facing a crisis," she said.

Mayor Dave Bing (D) said at a city council meeting Thursday that the city's cost-saving measures are beginning to work, the Associated Press reported. He presented an update that highlights savings from 1,000 imminent layoffs, overdue payments from the Detroit Public Schools district and a corporate tax increase he says will mitigate a cash shortfall. He has also said his negotiations to rework the city's union contracts are progressing.

Detroit owes bondholders, retirees, and other debtors more than $14.1 billion, according to a research council report.

The state law allows emergency managers to sell off city assets, restructure debt and break union contracts. But the managers also usurp the powers of local elected officials.

"It is the civil rights issue of our time. I didn't vote for an emergency manager. I voted for a mayor. I did not give up my right to vote on the whims and fancies of a law that we believe is unconstitutional and immoral," said the Rev. Wendell Anthony, pastor of Fellowship Chapel and a civil rights activist in Detroit. "We view it as another step in the direction of voter suppression and vote oppression."[21]

Rep. Conyers, the answer to your question is simple: Black people lack the ability to overcome the horrors of "Structural Inequality" nor do they have the acumen to sustain an economy, education system, public works infrastructure, or attract outside investors (save the Salvation Army).

It's not just Detroit. It's any city that once was the envy of the world. We could have been on Mars, but we had to erect a new Detroit in the suburbs; we had to erect a new Atlanta in the suburbs; we had to erect a new Cleveland in the suburbs; we had to erect a new Philadelphia in the suburbs; we had to erect a new Los Angeles in the suburbs; we had to erect a new Chicago in the suburbs that were ultimately abandon to the rising Black Undertow, all subsidized with entitlement money (TANF/welfare, EBT/Food Stamps, Section 8 Housing, and free lunches for their neglected children and free daycare at public schools) from predominately white tax-payers.

Rep. Conyers, you have been an elected official for almost half a century. You have presided over the collapse of Detroit, elected to Congress to represent a district that resembles Mogadishu of 2012 more than it does the Detroit of 1912.

---

[21] http://www.washingtonpost.com/politics/possibility-of-emergency-manager-in-detroit-prompts-civil-rights-concerns/2012/01/04/glQATFqYdP_story.html?hpid=z4

Fitting for a man who in 1967, during the heat of the Detroit Riot, tried to persuade Black men and women to stop their lawless ways and was promptly shouted down by the Mahogany horde. One Black person even climbed onto the car Conyers stood upon and tried to wrestle the bullhorn he was using to address the Black crowd away from him.[22]

He learned there was no use in trying to be the "Uncle Tom" for Detroit from this encounter.

There was a time when majority Black Washington D.C. was considered the worst run government in America. Guess what? White people took the city from democratically elected Black representatives who were scaring away investors and whites who would "Gentrify" the city. The Washington Post reported this in 1995:

> Congress today approved legislation to create a financial control board for the District of Columbia, a measure that would effectively end home rule for the city for at least eight years. President Clinton is expected to sign the bill into law shortly.

> Like similar boards established to guide New York, Philadelphia and other cities through earlier fiscal crises, the five-member financial control panel, whose members are to be appointed by Mr. Clinton, would have vast authority over municipal spending, financial planning, borrowing, hiring and contracts.

> It would also have authority to overrule decisions of Mayor Marion S. Barry Jr. and the City Council, a power that would give unelected officials the largest influence over the District since limited home rule was granted by Congress more than 20 years ago.

> Further, the legislation all but kills the campaign of statehood for the District, a leading goal of the city's Congressional delegate, Eleanor Holmes Norton.

---

[22] Locke, Hubert G.. *The Detroit riot of 1967,*. Detroit: Wayne State University Press, 1969. 38

34

The board, the only authority that would be allowed to borrow money from the Federal Treasury on the District's behalf, is viewed by its creators in the House and the Senate as a means of salvation for a city facing insolvency by next month, a deficit that could reach $722 million in this year's budget of $3.2 billion and a continuing decline in municipal services.

"For the city, it is the ultimate way to start revitalizing itself," said Representative Thomas M. Davis 3d, a Virginia Republican whose House subcommittee drafted the legislation. "It has to become financially stable, and this is the first step."

After weeks of resisting demands by Congress to reduce the size of city government and add to the cuts he had already made in spending, Mayor Barry said that as a result of the legislation, he felt "excited and positive" about the District's future.

"We are going to have the best-run city government with the best citizen services in the nation," he said in a statement issued by his office.

The Mayor made no reference to the new reduction in his role other than to say, "My administration will respond vigorously and enthusiastically to this next period of home rule."

For Mr. Barry, the legislation provides political cover, since he can now justify any painful spending cuts by declaring that the board insists on them.
The Senate passed the bill on Thursday, adding several amendments to a version earlier passed by the House, which approved the Senate's changes today.[23]

---

[23]http://www.thefreelibrary.com/The+worst+city+government+in+America-a06977500

The final nail in the coffin of Black-run Detroit is being put in place. Black-run Washington D.C., where financial mismanagement, corruption, high crime rates, horrible schools, and economic stagnation was ultimately saved by white people usurping freedom from elected [duplicitous] Black officials in the mid-90s. [24]

The Wall Street Journal put together a list of the best-run and worst-run of 2011 and the list broke down along racial lines again. Majority Black cities, where high rates of crime are endemic, ensure that you are on the worst list. Remember, your elected officials come from this class too.[25]

So, with the impending collapse of the city once dubbed "the arsenal of Democracy" we can safely surmise that freedom truly failed once Detroit's future was in the hands of Black people.

There's your answer Rep. Conyers. Then again, you should have known Black people were incapable of running a city when the wheels of your government leased Cadillac Escalade were stolen in front of your home:

> First, the son of U.S. Rep. John Conyers (D-Detroit) was forbidden from using dad's taxpayer-leased Cadillac Escalade. Now, it looks like nobody else will be driving the fancy SUV real soon either, not after a thief stole the wheels off of the vehicle.

> According to news reports, a Conyers staffer confirmed that the wheels had been stolen yesterday while the vehicle was parked in front of the congressman's home on the west side of Detroit.[26]

---

[24]http://www.washingtonpost.com/wp-srv/local/longterm/library/dc/mismanage/manage20.htm

[25]http://247wallst.com/2012/01/05/best-and-worst-run-cities-in-america/

26

http://www.mlive.com/news/detroit/index.ssf/2011/03/car_trouble_for_cony ers_wheels.html

---

Detroit must never be rebuilt. It must remain as a monument to the folly of egalitarian thinking, courtesy of Utopian-visioned Disingenuous White Liberals (DWLs) who refused to acknowledge that the fate of ALL major American cities is similar to that of The Motor City once they go black. (or give in to the Black Undertow or ceed the city to a black population, etc)

Detroit must be allowed to go back to nature; a cautionary, despondent reminder that race is not a social construct, but a biological fact. So that in 2112, school children can fly into the renamed International Airport in Detroit and trek into the abandon ruins of a city that 200 years earlier was on the cusp of greatness; that 100 years was on the brink of disaster

And it will be here, where these children will no longer be taught to hate their race (as they are now), but to remember the disaster that was only averted when their ancestors stopped allowing their guilt to outweigh their anger.

Detroit's collapse is 100 percent racial, for the same reason that Pittsburgh's ascension is 100 percent racial.

Our guilt outweighs our anger; for the future, we must understand that it is all predicated upon our anger outweighing our guilt.

The collapse of Detroit is 100 percent racial, and the thunder for the rest of America is just getting ready to roll in.

Structural Inequality? New Study Claims Black People in Detroit Can't Sustain Infrastructure Left Behind by White Flight

Climate Change, courtesy of the Black Undertow is the Visible Black Hand governing economics. *Climate Change* is why majority Black cities and counties can't sustain a local economy, save Check Cashing, Pawn Shops, Liquor Stores, Fast Food joints, and Hair Salon/Barbershops) that Adam Smith could never have foreseen.

There are those who would blame white people for every problem in this nation— even white flight itself. White flight is just a natural defensive mechanism to escape the Black Undertow and the crime, property value drop, dereliction of infrastructure, and decimation of the business district that follows this group.

In the coming weeks, Detroit will be taken over by the state of Michigan. Even though white people built a world-class city, full of architectural marvels that rivalled those found anywhere else on the planet, the Black people who inherited Detroit after the calamitous race war of 1967 (and the subsequent white abandonment of the city) have been unable to maintain even a modicum of what they were unceremoniously bequeathed. *The Los Angeles Times* bashed white people for the failure of the city, when it was white people ingenuity that was responsible for the greatness of Detroit in the first place.[27]

2011 Detroit is a direct representation of its majority population, which happens to be 82 percent Black. The ruins of the city, neglected and rotting monuments courtesy of a people who then rebuilt what they abandoned in the white suburbs surrounding Detroit, are to the Black inhabitants of the town what those strange heads on Easter Island where to the Europeans who first encountered them.

Your average Black inhabitant of Detroit has no understanding for how these architectural marvels were ever erected, nor could they - if trained by the top mechanical, industrial, electrical engineers and architects - ever hope to reproduce them. They can't even sustain them.

---

[27]   http://articles.latimes.com/2011/mar/27/opinion/la-oe-martelle-detroit-20110327

The haunting pictures of the empty Michigan Central Station; the staggering details on the facade of the Metropolitan Building still apparent despite the graffiti and trash found on the inside; Lee Plaza, once home to the elite of Detroit, now home to the elite of homeless Detroit; the Grand Army of the Republic Building, a castle erected in 1900 for veterans of the Civil War, now sits boarded up to keep out the descendants of freed Black people whose freedom has failed Detroit; the Broderick Tower, built in 1927, is the tallest skyscraper in America that has been deserted.

Like the post-apocalyptic world found in the book *The Earth Abides*, the Black people in Detroit show precious little concern for sustaining any of the city's former marvels. They find it hard to believe that people actually built them. Like the Sphinx in Egypt, Black people in Detroit sit in wonderment, gazing at some of the aesthetically - unequaled in the world for their majesty, even in their depressing state - magnificent buildings and wonder what they were once used for. Why were they even built?

It wouldn't be so bad if Detroit was the only city in America like this, but any city or county that the Black Undertow overwhelms inevitable fails.

In the south, you have Birmingham (72 percent Black), which was once one of the world's great cities. It has since been rebuilt in the white suburbs surrounding the city. With Vulcan looking on, the Black Undertow, which inherited Birmingham from whites after they fled the city, has decimated the hopes and dreams of the city founders and helped lead to the bankruptcy of Jefferson County, the largest municipal bankruptcy in American history.[28]

Well, two researchers at Michigan State just published a study that blames, you guessed it, white flight for the demoralizing results of the Black Undertow's leadership over cities and counties they inherit. In *ENVIRONMENTAL REVIEWS & CASE STUDIES: More Cost per Drop: Water Rates, Structural*

---

[28] http://stuffblackpeopledontlike.blogspot.com/2011/11/jefferson-county-declares-bankruptcy.html

Inequality, and Race in the United States—The Case of Michigan (published in the Cambridge Journal)[29] we learn that white people will always shoulder the blame for the problems befalling Black people:

White flight from urban centers often means minority residents are left to pay to maintain aging water and sewer systems, a new study finds.

This "structural inequality" is not necessarily a product of racism, but does mean that racial minorities pay systematically more than white people for basic municipal services.

"This study demonstrates a disturbing racial effect to the cost of basic services," says Stephen Gasteyer, assistant professor of sociology at Michigan State University. "People of color have the fewest opportunities to leave urban centers and are left to pay for the crumbling legacy of a bygone economic era."

For the study, reported in the journal *Environmental Practice,* researchers analyzed Census data on self-reported water and sewer costs in Michigan and found that urban residents actually pay more than rural residents, a finding that refutes conventional wisdom.
Perhaps more importantly, water and sewer services cost more in areas with greater proportions of racial minorities.

Detroit is the "poster child" for this problem, Gasteyer says. The city has lost more than 60 percent of its population since 1950, and the water and sewer infrastructure is as much as a century old in some areas. Billions of gallons of water are lost through leaks in the aging lines every year, and the entire system has been under federal oversight since 1977 for wastewater violations.

---

[29] http://www.esaim-m2an.org/action/displayAbstract?fromPage=online&aid=8466344&fulltextType=RA&fileId=S1466046611000391

"A fair proportion of Detroit's large low-income population cannot afford the burden of rate increases meant to offset infrastructure repairs, leading to tens of thousands of customers getting their water turned off every year," Gasteyer says.
Water and sewer lines are aging throughout the country. According to the U.S. Environmental Protection Agency, hundreds of billions of dollars will be needed to repair deteriorating systems over the next 20 years.

Paying for those upgrades likely will be a major issue in shrinking cities such as Cleveland, Pittsburgh, St. Louis, and Birmingham, Ala., Gasteyer says.

"Everything is wearing out, and we are going to have to grapple with how we pay for these so-called liquid assets that need to be upgraded. At the same time, we need to be cognizant of who may be paying an unsustainable burden as those rates go up."[30]
[]
Wow. What an amazing study! By the way, Pittsburgh has been rated the nicest place in America to live. It's not shrinking. Detroit and the other cities Gasteyer mentioned are, but not Pittsburgh.

Structural inequality? White people have abandoned world class cities across this nation to the Black Undertow. Inevitably, Black people lack the ability to sustain the infrastructure they are handed over in the transition of power.

Why can't the Black engineers just fix these water pipes? Why can't the elected officials set aside money to pay outside engineering firms to do this? It is because Black people can't sustain an economy to raise revenue to pay for upgrades to public utilities.

However, it is this line that smells fishy:

[30]http://www.futurity.org/society-culture/do-minorities-get-%E2%80%98hosed%E2%80%99-on-water-bill/

"This study demonstrates a disturbing racial effect to the cost of basic services," says Stephen Gasteyer, assistant professor of sociology at Michigan State University. "People of color have the fewest opportunities to leave urban centers and are left to pay for the crumbling legacy of a bygone economic era."

Gasteyer obviously hasn't looked at what happened when white people left Africa, specifically the Congo, or what happened to Rhodesia after the capitulation to Actual Black Run Zimbabwe (ABRZ) or in South Africa. Black people can't sustain the basic services that white people created worldwide. White people (and even Black people in Detroit) flee the Black Undertow in the Motor City because of the crumbling effect that Black people have on the the urban center.[31]

People of Color (PoC) in urban centers can only go so far as public transportation will take them, hence the decision by city leaders in Whitopia's to keep out bus systems and light-rail into their towns.

Black people can't sustain a city swimming pool, let alone plan to maintain a city's infrastructure that they have no part in building nor paying for. So those members of the Black Undertow shouldn't be forced to pay for their basic services either:

31

http://online.wsj.com/article/SB10001424052748704292004575230532248
715858.html

"These people are going to end up rioting about this," says Sheila Tyson, a community activist in Jefferson County, Ala. "If they let this stuff happen they are going to get the biggest riot the South has ever seen . . . I can see it coming."

That's a pretty serious prediction. What could possibly start a riot that big?

She's talking about the likelihood of Jefferson County increasing its water and sewage bill rates.

Oh. Is it really all that bad?

"If the sewer bill gets higher, my light might get cut off and if I try to catch up the light, my water might get cut off. So we're in between. We can't make it like this," says Tammy Lucas, a Birmingham resident who has been affected by a "financial and political scandal that has brought one of the most deprived communities in America's south to the point of what some local people believe is collapse," reports the BBC.

Lucas' monthly water and sewage rate has managed to quadruple in the past 15 years. Currently, her bill is $150 a month, which she pays for by using her $600 social security check.

When a federal judge forced Jefferson County to upgrade its outdated sewer system, officials decided to finance the project with bonds.

"Outside advisers suggested a series of complex deals with variable-rate interest . . . Loan payments rose quickly because of increasing interest rates as global credit markets struggled, and the county could no longer afford its payments," Bloomberg reports. That's why Jefferson County residents have seen a *329 percent* increase in their rates over the past decade and a half—the county has been trying to finance these new facilities.

The sewage system was supposed to cost $300 million. However, since the project started in 1996, the costs have risen to *$3.1 billion* after various problems and a series of bond and derivatives deals fell through in 2008.

"This is not even a race issue, if I'm telling the truth," said Tyson. "It's just so happens that it's affecting black people. It's a class issue. They don't give a doo-doo about poor people period."
So what does the "community activist" think should be done to fix the problem?

"Somebody from Washington D.C. needs to come down here and take these sewer bills to where they are affordable for the people in these districts. Injustice – that's all this is. They need to come down here and fix it," Tyson said.[32]

Riots? Black people already riot in Birmingham. It's a well-known fact that tens of thousands of Black people in Fulton County (home to Atlanta) never had to pay their water bills. They never have their water turned off either and rack up thousands of dollars in unpaid bills that the Black political elite never have these model citizens pay.

And why should they, when the cost can be redistributed to the white taxpayers in Buckhead and other white enclaves through higher property taxes?

---

[32]   http://news.yahoo.com/alabama-residents-furious-over-rate-increases-let-stuff-202403568.html

Freedom Failed: And the Thunder Rolls into ABRA Detroit

You can't see the lightning strikes. Not yet. You can see the horizon, far in the distance, starting to light up with increasing brilliance. There's rumblings, signifying approaching thunder. But it's still far-off, right?

Some are aware of the impending storm; most are afraid to admit it exists, preferring to ban all talk of unsavory topics in a so-called "Free" Republic; others have decided all that matters is lowering taxes for millionaires and billionaires, pursuing any and all avenues for reaching this objective; others -we call them Disingenuous White Liberals (DWLs) - have decided that the approaching calamity is a time to go all in on the "right vs. left" rhetoric.[33]

None of this will matter once the storm hits, for, like Hurricane Katrina, all that will be left in its wake is the unvarnished truth that those on both the politically-acceptable left and right work feverishly to hide: Detroit's collapse through financial mismanagement, depleted tax-base, shuttered businesses and completely broken local economy is due 100 percent to being the crown jewel of Actual Black-Run America (ABRA).

BRA doesn't mean that America is run by Black people; it means America - at every level of society - is run for the benefit of Black people, to the detriment of everyone else.

ABRA means, literally, that Black people control all levels of society in a given geographic area (be it city or county).

In BRA, freedom is denied to, well, everyone who isn't Black. In ABRA, most white people have completely fled the city or county, leaving behind Black people to tend to running the government, courts, schools, city services, and sustaining an economy.

Examples of ABRA would be Clayton County in Georgia, Prince George's County in Maryland, Baltimore, Birmingham, Memphis, Newark, and, who can forget, Detroit.

And it is Detroit - on the heels of Jefferson County (home to 72 percent Black Birmingham) declaring the largest municipal

---

[33]   http://www.thegrio.com/money/state-of-michigan-may-step-in-to-run-detroit.php

bankruptcy in American history - that *WILL* soon run out of money and declare the same.

People always like to say that the hope rests in the children, but with the sons and daughters of Detroit's leaders producing the worst 2011 NAEP scores in both reading and math of any big city in America, the future so bleak in that city you'd literally have to possess the atomic energy of the sun to see grounds for optimism.[34]

Any ABRA city or county shows that freedom failed, with property value plummeting amid the exodus of citizens looking for "good schools" and a safe place to raise a family. Businesses immediately fold, with a large part of the remaining citizenry subsisting on government entitlements (EBT, TANF/Welfare, Section 8 Housing) and having no discretionary income to spend on luxury items. Or even 'needs' most of the time.

ABRA Detroit's collapse has DWLs worried, most notably those at MSNBC:

> The potential takeover of the city of Detroit by an "emergency manager" under a controversial Michigan law was the topic of the night on MSNBC Thursday, with the Rachel Maddow and Ed Schultz shows tackling the topic.
>
> In Pontiac, emergency manager Louis Schimmel responded to a WJR radio host's question of whether he is a tyrant, by saying "I guess I'm the tyrant in Pontiac, then."
>
> According to an analysis by Chris Savage, a Democratic activist who runs the blog **Ecectablog**, when you count the cities and towns that have already been taken over by emergency managers, and cities like Detroit that are under review, 50.7 percent of blacks in Michigan are "on the verge of having no meaningful local democracy," Maddow said.
>
> Maddow said the story of Michigan's emergency manager law "could be the most important and most under-covered story of the year," a belief Maddow said she shares with Schultz.

---

[34] http://detnews.com/article/20111207/SHOWCASE/112070318/

48

During his show, Schultz talked to Rev. Alexander Bullock of Rainbow Push Detroit, who called the emergency manager law "the end of democracy."
Pointing to what he called racial implications of the law, Schultz highlighted one Detroit city council member's description of the emergency manager as a "master...someone to control the plantation." And he noted that Michigan congressman John Conyers is calling on the Justice Department to investigate the law, which Conyers said could perpetuate discrimination.

Bullock referred to the emergency managers authorized by the law as "emergency dictators."

"We thought the end of democracy is in Michigan," Bullock said. "The end of democracy is in Michigan. Michigan is the new Mississippi."[35]

---

[35] http://newsone.com/nation/thegrio6/is-the-man-trying-to-take-over-detroit/

50.7 percent of Blacks in Detroit are on the verge of having no "Democracy," because the concept of freedom has failed? White people were forced to leave Detroit in the late 1960s after brutal Black rioting made raising a family there a impossible task. One can only hope that the end of democracy in Michigan is at hand, for Detroit is an example of what ABRA will eventually do to any other city in America that goes that direction.

Thus the slow ceding of Detroit into ABRA began, culminating in the city becoming synonymous with corruption, crime, decadence, dereliction, and America's irreversible decline. But that decline is immutably tied to both the universal, dogmatic enforcement of BRA and the hundreds of cities and counties where actual ABRA exists.

Black people had the opportunity to take Detroit to new heights once white people left; Black people had the opportunity to sustain Detroit once white people left. Instead Black people once again reminded the rest of America what happens when a town goes ABRA... it fails. (Deleted)

Democracy isn't ending. Something more powerful is at play. Just as in the waning of the Soviet Union, most within the Iron Curtain no longer believed the lies of the state, a growing number of those held captive - and without Democracy in America - by BRA know that Detroit's collapse is 100 percent racial.

Those on holding positions of power on both the "right and the left" will refuse to admit this, knowing their seat at the 21st Century Nobility Table -- reserved only for traitors to Real America -- would be at jeopardy if they reneged on the promise for publicly joining the ranks of *Those Who Can See*.

One Detroit council member had the audacity to say the state takeover of ABRA Detroit would turn it into a "plantation," but Walter Russell Mead's blog on *The American Interest* states:

"Plantation"? "Plantation" is a colloquialism for a prosperous place where white people live good and make money from the back-breaking labor of black people.

Detroit is a place where the predominantly black population doesn't work but receives handouts from white middle and upper-middle class taxpayers in the form of food stamps, welfare, health benefits, etc. Rather than being prosperous, the whole thing is collapsing. "Plantation"? OK, you can start calling me a racist now. Just remember, I wasn't the one who made this a racial issue."[36]

Rachel Maddow would still find a way to spin this truth into blaming white people for the fall of Detroit because *not enough* money was spent on Black people.

Pontiac, Michigan (51 percent Black) is one of those towns that has been taken over by the state of Michigan. Home to Pontiac Silverdome (built for millions upon millions, but sold for half-a-million dollars) the city is another reminder that freedom failed:

If you don't feel like sugar-coating it, the emergency manager—Pontiac is one of three Michigan cities currently run by one—*is an admission that democracy occasionally doesn't work.* Michigan introduced an emergency "financial" manager law in 1990, as a way to straitjacket cities that were failing.[37]

---

[36]   http://blogs.the-american-interest.com/wrm/2011/12/03/detroit-on-the-brink/

[37]http://www.slate.com/articles/news_and_politics/politics/2011/11/pontiac_mich_can_a_technocrat_succeed_where_democracy_failed_.html

That the experiment of ABRA in Detroit ends so... so much like what happens when colonialism ends in Africa will not be addressed by the managerial elite who work to keep BRA moving forward.

But to *Those Who Can See*, the impending financial takeover of ABRA Detroit by the state of Michigan will be another reminder that freedom failed. And you'd be shocked at the number of *Those Who Can See*.

You can hear the rumbling. For those who ready, ABRA Detroit is about to be struck with a lightning bolt of truth that no sob story from MSNBC can help overcome.

Freedom Failed.

Once More Into the Breach: USA Today Proclaims Detroit's Comeback Offering Little Evidence in the Process

USA Today has published a hilarious cover story on the recovery in Detroit, a city that recently celebrated earning the illustrious honor of being America's Most Dangerous City, all courtesy of that city's primary inhabitants, Black people. Just ask the family of Greg McNichols.[38] Or Ross Capicchioni.[39]

Sadly, this article doesn't mention that Detroit is home to the worst school system in the civilized world, where EVERY student gets a free lunch so as not to stigmatize those who are part of the free lunch program.

---

[38] http://www.myfoxdetroit.com/dpp/news/ronnie_dahl/freddie-young-accused-of-killing-detroit-landlord-greg-mcnicol-20110516-wpms

[39] http://www.ebaumsworld.com/video/watch/81903838/

No mention of the RoboCop statue that the new immigrants to the city (primarily Disingenuous White Liberals) wanted to erect, a minor concession to hipster sensibilities that pales in comparison to the gold chairs at the public library the Black leadership splurged on. Nor does it mention that the failed Black leadership of that more than 80 percent Black city has forced the state of Michigan into taking over the school system and -- potentially -- the entire city.[40]

The article only peripherally mentions that Detroit has halted trash pickup and police patrols to only 20 percent of the city. This number represents just a tad less than the percentage of students who graduate from the high schools each year.[41]

No, here's what the article states:

> For years, this blue-collar city has been synonymous with the ills suffered by the decline of great American cities — crime, poverty and abandonment.

> These days, people think about Detroit a little differently.

> A new spirit is heard in the euphoria for its professional sports teams: The Tigers are in the American League Championship Series, while the Lions are 4-0 for the first time since 1980 — and playing on *Monday Night Football* for the first time in a decade.

> That spirit is celebrated in an Emmy-winning Super Bowl ad that touts the city's working-class roots. It's felt in the resurgence of the auto industry, which has seen sales rebound with new products and improved technology three years after almost collapsing.

---

[40] http://spectator.org/archives/2011/09/21/wards-of-the-state

[41] http://articles.businessinsider.com/2010-12-13/news/30065559_1_mayor-dave-bing-police-patrols-street-lights

"There's a tendency to think about Detroit as this Rust Belt, throwaway city," says Susan Mosey, president of Midtown Detroit Inc., whose group is offering financial incentives for people to move into the city. "All this has reframed that conversation. ... There is a moment in time for Detroit." Who ever thought the words "imported from Detroit" — tagline of the Super Bowl ad — would be cool?

People here say it's not just Detroit's image that's changing. They say after years of decline, the city finally is taking baby steps forward.

Several major companies, including Quicken Loans, Blue Cross Blue Shield of Michigan and DTE Energy, have moved operations downtown. More artists and young people are moving to the city's center.

In July, Detroit showed the largest one-year increase in home values of 20 major cities: a 1% uptick, according to the S&P/Case-Shiller index of property values. That comes after being down 46% from the city's peak in 2005.

"The car companies have stabilized. ... The sports teams are on the rise. We have a long way to go, but there are so many positive signs," says Grammy-nominated recording artist Kem, a native Detroiter.

Even Hollywood is taking notice. Four movies featuring metro Detroit locations are in the cineplex or opening soon. Among them: *Real Steel*, starring Hugh Jackman, and *The Ides of March*, starring George Clooney.

City leaders say the improvements do not hide the hard realities. Detroit lost 25% of its population during the past decade, the largest drop of any U.S. city with more than 100,000 people.

The city that in 1950 had a population of 2 million has about 702,000 residents, 38% of whom live in poverty. The region's unemployment rate is 14.4%, among the nation's highest.

The city is just coming out from under a scandal involving its former mayor, Kwame Kilpatrick, whose antics were material for late night comedians. Kilpatrick went to jail for lying in court about an affair with his chief of staff and also faces federal corruption charges. Several of his cronies are going to prison for bribery and other offenses.

The city was so distracted by the scandals that efforts to move forward got little traction, says City Council President Charles Pugh.

Now, he says, the sports teams' wins and other successes are helping Detroiters feel proud of their town again.

"It's a welcome reprieve from the reality of life in a big city," he says. "It's a reprieve from how do you solve the next problem."

The city's mayor, former Pistons basketball star Dave Bing, says the sports high is helping the city as more people crowd downtown restaurants, bars and hotels.

But, he says, "I don't want to get too giddy just yet. We are still treading water."

He says the city struggles to provide law enforcement, garbage pickup and lighting, to all corners of its 140-square-mile area.

Ken Lucas, Dearborn High School football and wrestling coach and a lifelong resident of suburban Dearborn, home to Ford's headquarters, says the wins are a morale boost.

"Everybody's hurtin' around here except the big honchos, and it gives you a little light at the end of the tunnel," he says. "You save a little bit, miss vacation to go to a Tigers game, go to a Lions game and take your son down there."

Gary Bailey says the Tigers' success embodies the spirit of a town that works hard.

"You see the excitement of the people," says Bailey, an insurance agent. "This is a tough town. It's a gritty town. I've lived here my whole life, and I'm still working. I'm not going to retire."

Even though they live in suburban Detroit, he and his wife of 50 years, Beverly, stayed downtown at the Marriott Renaissance Center for two of the games against the Yankees. They soaked up the scene at local bars, such as Cheli's Chili Bar, a popular spot owned by former Red Wings player Chris Chelios.

The excitement for the Tigers and Lions spills out to strangers who high-five each other on the street and cheer when they spot each other's team jerseys.

"Any real Detroiter views the team as their own," says Chuck Johnson, sports media director for Detroit public schools. "It's a 'we' situation. Right now, the teams are winning, so we are winning. Detroiters have always been resilient. That's what we see in these teams."

The Lions are one of only two NFL teams, along with the defending Super Bowl champion Green Bay Packers, with perfect records. They haven't lost a game since December 2010, when they played the Chicago Bears, the team they'll meet again here Monday night. Not bad for a team that in 2008 became the only one in NFL history to finish 0-16.

The Lions will play Green Bay in the traditional Thanksgiving Day game, which for the first time in years will mean something.

"It not only makes you feel good, it allows us to improve the city's image, one panning shot of Detroit on TV at a time," Pugh says.

'This is what we do'

"Detroit" has always been interchangeable with the American auto industry. Five years ago, Detroit's General Motors, Ford and Chrysler were headed for perdition. They were stagnating, could not compete with foreign automakers and cut 120,000 jobs. GM and Chrysler borrowed money from the government to stay afloat. Ford mortgaged the company.

Today, all three are making money, with strong sales in pickups and SUVs in September, and they are going on the offensive with new products.

"The image change for Detroit in the last three years probably has been more than any of us in the industry anticipated," says Jesse Toprak, vice president for industry trends and analysis at TrueCar.com, a car pricing and research company.

Not long ago, the auto-buying cognoscenti disdained Detroit and favored foreign brands. That attitude is uninformed, Toprak says. Detroit cars, overall, are "head to head with imports," he says.
"The real quality gaps between domestics and imports have almost vanished," he says, and considering "how much car you get for your money," Detroit vehicles tend to be better values than foreign-brand rivals.

Chrysler's "Imported from Detroit" ad campaign has generated a lot of buzz for Detroit cars — and the city. The ad featured Detroit native and rapper Eminem driving past factories, abandoned buildings and city landmarks.

"What does a town that's been to hell and back know about the finer things in life?" an announcer asks. "This isn't New York City. Or the Windy City. Or Sin City. And we're certainly no one's Emerald City."

"This is the Motor City. And this is what we do," Eminem closes.

"That commercial stood for the new Detroit," says Mike Bernacchi, a marketing professor at the University of Detroit Mercy. "There was no denial of what Detroit is. It says we've been knocked down, but we're not knocked out. ... The commercial brought that conversation to the country."

Most of the lost auto jobs are gone for good, but a few thousand are returning, and more are being preserved as the United Auto Workers and the car companies finalize new four-year contracts. A study by the Center for Automotive Research, an organization supported by foundations and car companies, shows that in Michigan there are 22% more auto-related jobs than there were when Detroit automakers hit bottom in 2009.

And Detroit is becoming an environmental leader.

GM's Chevrolet Cruze Eco is the highest-mileage gasoline car available, matching highway mileage ratings for small diesel cars. Ford converted a factory in nearby Wayne, Mich., that once made big SUVs to make Focus compacts and, soon, some hybrids and electric vehicles. Chrysler will build in the USA high-gas-mileage, four-cylinder engines for a line of cars developed by its majority owner, Fiat.[42]

---

[42]   http://www.usatoday.com/news/nation/story/2011-10-09/detroit-comeback-lions/50713354/1

So what have we learned? That the overwhelmingly white residents of Detroit's suburbs enjoy watching sports -- especially winning sports teams. USA Today reported that Detroit lost 25 percent of its population over the past decade, in a mad dash by residents to avoid living anywhere near Black people.[43] Take a look at the extreme levels of segregation in Detroit here[44], courtesy of University of Wisconsin-Milwaukee demographers.

Detroit still has no major grocery chain and the average price of home in 2009 was only $7,000. Wait, what is 1 percent of $7,000? $70 bucks!! What a dramatic rise![45]

The Wall Street Journal pointed out that these numbers were hardly worth celebrating, though any good news for Detroit is emphasized to counter the constant stream of negativity courtesy of Detroit's majority population (and its elected Black government officials).[46]

Here's an article from the WSJ detailing the horrible reality of touting Detroit as the best city for home pricing data (or the only source for positive news), which fails to mention how the Black Undertow has brought massive depreciation to home values in Atlanta and Cleveland:

---

[43]   http://www.usatoday.com/news/nation/census/2011-03-22-michigan-census_N.htm

[44] http://www4.uwm.edu/eti/integration/detroit.htm

[45]

http://www.businessweek.com/the_thread/hotproperty/archives/2009/03/the_median_home.html

[46]

http://online.wsj.com/article/SB10001424052970204010604576597131207120672.html?mod=WSJ_RealEstate_LeftTopNews

Maybe it's those Eminem Chrysler ads.

The S&P/Case-Shiller home price data came out this morning and only one of the 20 major city indexes showed a gain in February over the previous month: Detroit!

When Detroit headlines the housing data, you know it's not particularly awesome. And while Detroit did post a price rise, home prices in the Motor City remain about 30% below 2000 price levels. Yowzers. Atlanta, Cleveland and Las Vegas also have home price levels below the 2000 mark.

"There is very little, if any, good news about housing. Prices continue to weaken, trends in sales and construction are disappointing," says David M. Blitzer, Chairman of the Index Committee at S&P Indices.[47]

Like Philadelphia, capable Black people (the Black middle class) are fleeing the ruins of Detroit.[48] Ruins that were once the envy of the world - upon their erection by a much different people than who currently occupy the city - where commerce, innovation and a thriving economy were ultimately overwhelmed by the Black Undertow. *USA Today* is right about the decline of Detroit: crime, poverty, and abandonment. The city was abandoned by white people who long ago left for safe suburbs (that were built and maintained by the escaping refugees of Detroit), who attempting to evade the Black crime and the encroaching Black Undertow.[49]

Poverty? Black people can't sustain a national grocery chain in Detroit, which tragically shows that Black people have no buying power nor have the sense of community to sustain a business.[50]

There are mini-Detroit's all across the southern region of the United States (or wherever Black people have congregated in numbers great than 25 percent of the overall population). How will they ever make an economic comeback, when they lack sports teams for white suburban fans to cheer for and spend money supporting?

A thriving squatters renaissance has taken root in Detroit, where more than 100,000 abandoned houses (because people don't want to live among the Black Undertow, uprooting their lives to escape it) are now home to citizens who might just spark the next wave of innovation in that city.[51]

---

[48]

http://online.wsj.com/article/SB10001424052748704292004575230532248715858.html

[49] http://www.time.com/time/magazine/article/0,9171,844818,00.html

[50]   http://www.newser.com/story/61977/retail-exodus-speeds-detroits-fall.html

[51] http://www.businessinsider.com/vacant-detroit-homes-squatters-2011-8

Or so says *Business Insider.*[52]

The New York Times published an article saying that young, innovative white people (Stuff White People Like whites) were beginning to move into The Motor City, hilariously stating that these student loan debt-laden, liberal arts degree holding, latte swigging, Apple product hoarding, bike-riding goofs will be the saviors of the city.[53]

No matter what companies like Quicken Loan (who receive heavy tax breaks from the city and have virtually no overhead when acquiring unwanted commercial real estate in Detroit) who relocate to Detroit hope to accomplish, they will have to hire people from outside the city if they hope to stay successful.[54]

You still have more than 700,000 Black people in Detroit, the same ones who helped make the city the most dangerous in America; the same people whose children are paid to go to school and still put up some of the worst scores and lowest graduation rates in the nation; and no national grocery stores.

---

[52] http://www.businessinsider.com/detroit-crawls-from-the-trenches-to-reclaim-spot-as-a-city-of-innovation-2011-9

[53] http://www.nytimes.com/2011/07/03/fashion/the-young-and-entrepreneurial-move-to-downtown-detroit-pushing-its-economic-recovery.html?_r=2&pagewanted=all

[54]
http://www.freep.com/article/20111010/BUSINESS06/111010004/Quicken-Loans-Detroit-mayor-Dave-Bing-welcome-1-500-workers-downtown?odyssey=tab%7Ctopnews%7Ctext%7CFRONTPAGE

Detroit vs. Pittsburgh: The Difference between 'Most Miserable' and 'Most Liveable' is Skin-Deep

The Motor City gets dumped on a lot. Recently rated by *Forbes* as the Most Dangerous City in America,[55] Detroit also happens to be one of the most monochromatic. The core of the city (roughly 808,000) is 92 percent Black, where no major grocery store chain dares open for business. The suburban area - where the white people who work in Detroit and fled from the Black Undertow -live and politically control - is 82 percent white, complete with flourishing school systems and a robust economy.[56]

Detroit was rated as The Most Miserable City back in 2008 by *Forbes* and has since remained in dubious contention for that honor (competing with other Black Undertow cities like Cleveland and Memphis), probably because the Black population subsists entirely on government handouts, Disingenuous White Liberal (DWL) charity, and $1000 houses, which brings down the average Black family net worth.[57]

How did Detroit go from one of the most remarkable cities in the world - when it was all white - to, well, the Detroit of today? Thomas Sowell and other conservatives would have you believe it was all about liberal policies and socialism, yet those same policies have helped a country like Norway flourish. Innovation and entrepreneurial activities are commonplace in Norway, similar to the commonplace high rates of illiteracy, crime and corruption among elected officials found in Detroit.

It's a safe bet that none of the top neighborhoods to trick or treat in (according to Zillow.com) will be in Detroit (though many of the worst neighborhoods commonly featured in *First 48* will be), because maintaining a sense of community - where parents feel safe to send their kids out into the night to collect candy from neighbors - isn't something high on the list of Black people.

---

55   http://realestate.yahoo.com/promo/americas-most-dangerous-cities-2011.html

56

http://www.oregonlive.com/news/index.ssf/2009/01/in_a_changing_world_portland_r.html

57   http://www.forbes.com/2008/01/29/detroit-stockton-flint-biz-cz_kb_0130miserable.html

---

Just look at Prince George's County to see how the elite Black families live, courtesy of federal government employment (or should we say, mandated levels of over-representation of Black people as federal or state bureaucrats). You see, government can work, but when federal and state agencies become bloated with unnecessary employees on their payroll, accountability takes a back seat to coerced diversity.

But back to Detroit. People blame the loss of jobs and the stagnation of hope on the decimation of Detroit and its gradual collapse into an *Earth Abides* scenario. In reality, Detroit represents the ultimate *Life After Black People* for all to see (to borrow from the *Life After People* show on The History Channel). Detroit offers an unfolding drama into what happens when Climate Change - necessitated by white flight and the crippling effects of the Black Undertow taking control - turns a once thriving economy into the ultimate embodiment of what transpires when Black-Run America (BRA) reaches its logical conclusion.

But.. but.. but... Detroit lost so many jobs! Poverty causes crime! Lack of access to quality education dooms children to a life of misery (actually, it rewards them with a life provided entirely by taxpayers, either in jail or through welfare, EBT, Section 8 housing, etc.). In Detroit, students are paid to actually show up for classes (and everyone eats for free, courtesy of the taxpayer). School systems routinely have Teach for America-trained Crusading White Pedagogues (CWP) attempting to fight back the evil forces of nature with nurture and nearly unlimited funds, provided once again by the taxpayer.

Yet the population of Detroit has shown little to no motivation for innovation, save for the Coon Man selling his Raccoon, providing a melancholy raconteur for the demise of The Motor City.[58]

Exit Detroit, stage left. Enter Pittsburgh, stage right.

The Steel City, where a steel town girl once worked hard for her money. Sadly, much of those steel jobs disappeared when free trade agreements made purchasing and importing steel more

---

[58]   http://stuffblackpeopledontlike.blogspot.com/2009/06/171-wasting-raccoon-in-detroit.html

profitable then having an industry in Birmingham or Pittsburgh.[59]

Instead of waxing nostalgically for past glories and blaming the loss of an industry for the demise of an entire city, the citizens of Pittsburgh refrained from violence and turning their city into the Most Miserable and Most Violent in America and instead have diversified the economy through innovation and turned Pittsburgh into The Most Livable in America[60]; The Best City in America to Move to[61]; and The Economist rated Pittsburgh as The Best City in America.[62]

All accolades that will never be associated with 90 percent + Black Detroit, but are associated with one of the least diverse and most monochromatic cities in America, Pittsburgh is shockingly white - like Norway - and faced the same problems that Detroit did; the gradual erosion and loss of its primary industry. But because Pittsburgh was overwhelmingly white, the citizens were able to rally around a community and rebuild. Because white people fled the violent Black Undertow in Detroit - deciding that building new cities around the dying inner core of Detroit was a better proposition then raising children where trick or treating was an impossibility - you had the reverse of Pittsburgh.

[59] http://en.wikipedia.org/wiki/History_of_Pittsburgh#Collapse_of_steel

[60] http://www.forbes.com/2010/04/29/cities-livable-pittsburgh-lifestyle-real-estate-top-ten-jobs-crime-income.html

[61] http://postgazette.com/pg/11248/1172311-455.stm

[62] http://www.post-gazette.com/pg/09161/976252-53.stm

If you traded the population of Detroit with the population of Pittsburgh, instantly Pittsburgh is doomed. Just as quickly, Detroit recovers in a matter of months, with the overwhelmingly white suburban areas realizing that Detroit is safe once again. The city is rebuilt, schools work again, and the government is staffed with adults who care about the long-term consequences of their actions and decisions, instead of the short-term motivated Black politicians.

A paradox exists though: How can the Economist Intelligence Unit rate Pittsburgh the best place to live in America[63] when it lacks racial diversity?[64]

When there are few Black people (hence low crime rates)? How can a place that is so hideously white - and for that matter, a large thriving metropolis - work? Does Pittsburgh in 2011 resemble Cleveland in the 1950s? Detroit in the 40s and 50s? Birmingham before BRA took over? Or does it just resemble what America once looked like - even Los Angeles and San Diego - and offer a glimpse at what once was, and what could be again?

Yes, yes it does:

---

[63] http://www.dailymail.co.uk/news/article-1359195/Pittsburgh-best-place-live-says-Economist-Intelligence-Unit.html

[64] http://old.post-gazette.com/pg/11248/1172311-455.stm

It would be hard for any metropolitan area to be whiter than Pittsburgh.

It's so hard, in fact, that of the 100 largest metro areas in the United States, only one has a smaller share of blacks, Hispanics and Asians -- the Scranton-Wilkes Barre region of northeastern Pennsylvania.

A new Brookings Institution report released last week, examining 2010 census data on how Americans identified race and ethnicity, found that southwestern Pennsylvania is whiter even than the Amish country around Lancaster, the Mormon population center of Salt Lake City, Midwest agrarian capitals such as Des Moines, Iowa, and far more isolated places like Boise, Idaho.

It is not stunningly new data for this former melting pot -- findings from the 2000 census were much the same -- but what might be eye-opening is that the pace of change toward greater diversity is even slower here than for all those places above, as well as the rest of America.

The report called "The New Metro Minority Map,"[65] by demographer William Frey, found that the 87 percent white population of greater Pittsburgh -- Allegheny, Armstrong, Beaver, Butler, Fayette, Washington and Westmoreland counties -- is exceeded only by Scranton's 89 percent. The report noted 8 percent of metro Pittsburgh's population identified themselves as black, 2 percent as Asian and 1 percent as Hispanic.[66]

---

[65] http://www.brookings.edu/papers/2011/0831_census_race_frey.aspx

[66] http://old.post-gazette.com/pg/11248/1172311-455.stm

It's fitting to remember that the illegal immigration of the United States - which will end - is being fueled by the desire of white people to abandon Black Undertow cities for new suburbs, built by cheap labor from Mexico. Or from white people escaping California, where the crushing burden of paying for large Mexican families makes raising their own families impossible, and moving to Idaho, Arizona, Montana, or Texas.

But there stands Pittsburgh, one of the top cities in the world. Though it lost its steel industry, the cities inhabitants adapted, innovated and thrived.[67]

It didn't descend into violence and become the punch line for comedians the world over (somewhere in China, a comedian just told a joke about Black Detroit), it turned into a city that is attracting top talent and expats from failed cities and states in America.[68]

A tale of two cities; Pittsburgh and Detroit. One offers a glimpse of *Life After Black People*, a once mighty city ravaged by a weapon more destructive then an atom bomb (the mandated and enforced notion of egalitarianism). The other, is but an aberration, a city in 2011 America that resembles what all of America looked like before the Civil Rights Revolution enshrined BRA as the law of the land.

It's never been about what, as in the case of Detroit vs. Norway. It's about who, as in the case of Pittsburgh vs. Detroit.

---

[67] http://pennysleuth.com/looking-back-at-the-pittsburgh-steel-industry/

[68]   http://pittsburghfuture.blogspot.com/2010/03/thirty-years-later-steel-industry-still.html

Where would you rather live? In a city where taking your kids trick or treating mean possibly running into spooks who will shoot you for a Starburst or Reese's Peanut Butter Cup, or where you can take your kids trick or treating and see white families dressed as spooky characters engaging in Steel town fun?

Detroit vs. Pittsburgh: The Difference between 'Most Miserable' and 'Most Livable' is Skin-Deep. It's simply one city being nearly all-Black, and the other being nearly all-white.

To borrow a line from *Flashdance*, *what a feeling* stating a truth that so few dare state.

Tintin in the Detroit: The Horror, the Horror!

One of the more anticipated movies of 2011 is *The Adventures of Tintin*, the tale of the boy journalist and his trusty canine companion Snowy. It appears that a few people are up in arms at one of the early stories published in a more ignorant and unenlightened time period, *Tintin in the Congo*, which has the audacity of depicting Black people as, well, Black people:

> The Campaign for Real Education has condemned his publishers as "over the top" for deciding to package one of his early adventures, Tintin in the Congo, in shrink-wrap and with a warning about its content.

> Its criticism comes within weeks of the worldwide release of Steven Spielberg's new film about the boy reporter and his dog Snowy.

> George Remi, the Belgian artist better known as Herge, first published his tale of derring-do in Africa in 1930. When he re-worked it in 1946 he removed several references to the Congo being a Belgian colony.

> But the book still contained a number of images that were perceived as racist. One of these showed a black woman bowing to Tintin and saying `White man very great…White mister is big juju man`.

Over the decades Herge's work was excluded from reprints and became synonymous with racism that in 2004 a spokesman for the Democratic Republic of Congo's government responded to criticism by a Belgian foreign minister by saying: "It's Tintin In The Congo all over again."

Three years later the Commission for Racial Equality claimed the book depicted "hideous racial prejudice" and said it should be removed from sale.

The then Borders chain of bookshops agreed to move it to the adult graphic novels area of its shops, and Waterstones followed suit.

Nick Seaton, secretary of the Campaign for Real Education, is perturbed by the restrictions being placed on the book's sale in the run-up to the release of the Spielberg film The Adventures of Tintin.

"Most parents will think this is over the top," he claimed. "As long as children understand times have changed it seems ridiculous to separate this book into the adult section

"Much of children's literature is extremely graphic and sexually explicit these days and no one seems to bother about that."

He added: "It is another example of political correctness gone mad. All these silly attempts at censorship do not do a lot of good.

"It is a bit like the restrictions on Kipling because of his old fashioned values. Bookshops have to be responsible about things like this, but it can go too far and this is ridiculous."

The book's publisher, Egmont UK, said it recognised that some readers may be offended by the content.
A spokesman said: "This is why we took the unusual step of placing a protective band around the book with a warning about the content and also included an introduction inside the book by the original translators explaining the historical context.

"Whilst being frequently requested by fans and collectors who had seen it available in other languages, the work contains scenes which some readers may find offensive."

The warning reads: "In his portrayal of the Belgian Congo, the young Hergé reflects the colonial attitudes of the time...

"He depicted the African people according to the bourgeois, paternalistic stereotypes of the period – an interpretation that some of today's readers may find offensive."[69]

Of course, Disingenuous White Liberals (DWLs) must do everything in their power to keep negative depictions of Black people from entering the consciousness of the average American (or, in the case of the European Union, the average European). Even if that means banning a harmless children's story in the process, though luckily those who read Unamusement Park had a much better tour guide of the Congo than Tintin ever did.[70]

Our question for those DWLs who would ban unflattering stories and images that barely scratch the surface of what transpired (and the depravity of life in what is now loosely called the Congo) in deepest, darkest Africa, is what to make of major American cities where the Black Undertow has been left firmly in control.

What to make of Detroit? Could you imagine the hilarious stories and dangerous adventures that Tintin could find in deepest, darkest Detroit? All he'd have to do is ride the public transportation into the heart of darkness at the Rosa Parks Transit Center (you can't make this stuff up) and he'd see behavior that isn't even found in The Congo:

> People who catch the bus in Detroit may be waiting a while Friday morning. About 100 Detroit Department of Transportation bus drivers are at work, but are refusing to drive their buses.

---

[69]   http://www.telegraph.co.uk/culture/books/booknews/8866991/Tintin-banned-from-childrens-shelves-over-racism-fears.html

[70]   http://unamusementpark.com/2011/08/welcome-to-the-jungle-unamusement-park-explores-the-congo-part-1/

WWJ's Scott Ryan spoke with Henry Gaffney, spokesman for the D-DOT bus drivers union AFL-CIO Local 26, who said this was not an organized maneuver by the union. Gaffney said it's a matter of bus drivers fearing for their safety, citing an incident that happened Thursday afternoon.

"Our drivers are scared, they're scared for their lives. This has been an ongoing situation about security. I think yesterday kind of just topped it off, when one of my drivers was beat up by some teenagers down in the middle of Rosa Parks and it took the police almost 30 minutes to get there, in downtown Detroit," said Gaffney.

Speaking live on WWJ, Mayor Dave Bing spokesman Stephen Serkaian said they are working hard to resolve the matter and get drivers back on the road.

"We're working diligently to work with the union and encouraging the drivers to get back on the buses and get on the street," said Serkaian.

Gaffney said bus safety is an ongoing problem.

"If it's to the point where if the driver is not safe on the bus, then the passengers are not safe, then the citizens are not safe. You know, what about them too? We have no security, you can't get the police, nobody is doing anything to protect us. And I've been begging the mayor and the council for two years to do something to help us," said Gaffney.

But, Serkaian said there are discussions in the city right now to improve bus safety.

"It is a concern. We want to protect drivers and passengers alike. We used to have police presence on the buses. We're talking about the prospect of perhaps trailing buses with police cars. Nothing has been decided, it's all in discussion right now," said Serkaian. "It's a short-term and a long-term matter... It's all about money and it's all about funding, and our transportation system is already stretched to the max."

WWJ's Vickie Thomas was at a deserted Rosa Parks Transit

Center in downtown Detroit, which is typically booming with passengers and buses alike.

Saharah X. was waiting at the center for 30 minutes before flagging down a cab.

"They just try to find a way not to do their job. And then they got innocent old people, there an old lady on a cane sitting outside over there, that's dangerous. And she got to walk? Wow. I mean, what is the world coming to? No love, no nothing. Everybody's just thinking about themselves. Think about other people some," she said.

Richard Moses, who rides the bus every day, was waiting a bus stop along Woodward Avenue when a D-DOT supervisor rolled up in an SUV and basically told him to find another form of transportation Friday morning.

"They said there's no D-DOT buses running at this time and they don't know when any will be starting back up. I just got off work, I work midnights. Luckily, I got dropped off right here or else I would have been sitting on 8 Mile and Woodward, and I've got to go all the way to Livernois and Warren," said Moses.
Serkaian said they're asking stranded riders who are waiting for the bus to get to school and work to hang on and be patient.

"We understand their frustration, we feel their pain. We simply have to ask folks to be a little bit more patient while we try to resolve this matter," he said.[71]

---

[71] http://detroit.cbslocal.com/2011/11/04/d-dot-drivers-refuse-to-run-routes-bus-riders-stranded/

For those wondering, Black teenagers attacked bus drivers in Detroit, just like Black teenagers are engaging in Mahogany Mob attacks all across the country. The bus drivers are "scared for their lives" because of Black people attacking buses (rumors of spears found at the scene are unconfirmed).

How's that comeback for Detroit coming, *USA Today*? And all you conservatives blasting "liberal" policies for the downfall of Detroit: public transportation works swimmingly in Boulder, Denver, Seattle, Portland, and San Francisco: it's not a matter of what, but who.

In the case of Detroit, a city that is roughly 82 percent Black, should now be called The Congo of the Detroit River.

Public transportation can work; but only in cities that lack a percentage of Black people. In the case of Detroit, Atlanta, Philadelphia, Birmingham, Cleveland, etc., public transportation is a sunk cost. In the case of Portland, public transportation is a wonderful way to get around the city (but isn't Portland more liberal than Detroit?).

Tintin would have some high adventures in one of the former great cities of the world, traversing the ruins of the city and visiting former buildings, libraries, train stations, and factories where life was once vibrant, replaced with the shattered dream of racial equality. Each broken window, never replaced, in Detroit is a reminder of the nightmare unleashed by DWLs that plagues many of America's major cities.

What Tintin would see in Detroit would make his *Tintin in the Congo* seem like a scene out of *The Wiz*: he would see the reality of what happens when white flight gives way to Black Undertow rule. That, my friends, is an adventure not even Tintin would be prepared to take. Not even Tintin's dog Snowy would want to go on that adventure.

For all those who say colonialism is racist, isn't gentrification just another form of this pernicious practice?

Our Favorite News Story of All-Time: Rachel Maddow Profiles Detroit High School for Pregnant Girls

In twenty years time, only one news story will be needed to successfully inculcate young students of why Black-Run America (BRA) was doomed to fail. Only one.

Courtesy of Detroit, the town that illustrates beautifully (and tragically) what happens when white flight and Black empowerment mix, you have the story of Catherine Ferguson Academy[72] - a school for more than 300 pregnant or new mothers that are also high school students - closing:

> Catherine Ferguson Academy is unlike any other school in the country. It has been educating teen mothers since 1988. A high graduation and college acceptance rate, the alternative Detroit public school is set to shut its doors for good, following massive budget cuts and a lack of financial support from the private Charters system.[]Earlier this week, in an effort to save their school, current and alumni students staged a sit in which quickly ended when local authorities arrested the girls.[73]

---

[72]   http://www.annarbor.com/entertainment/food-drink/driving-downtown-detroits-wide-avenues/

[73]   http://www.thegrio.com/education-1/a-school-for-pregnant-teens-closes-in-detroit.php

---

Rachel Maddow used her show on MSNBC in an attempt to bring sympathy to this closing academy and the plight of the pregnant girls shown the door in Detroit. Many of the students were arrested in protesting the closing of the school.[74]

We know that Detroit is headed for economic collapse. The entire state of Michigan and its Black population are headed in the same direction. You can search our archives here and see that we have written about Detroit on numerous occasions.

Here's a 2004 story on Catherine Ferguson, a school that is 90 percent Black and virtually every student gets a free lunch (what about the babies?):

> This year the school was named a Breakthrough High School by the National Association of Secondary School Principals. One of 12 schools nationally to win the distinction, Catherine Ferguson earned it based on the following criteria: At least 50 percent of the school is minority; 50 percent of the student body qualifies for free and reduced-price meals; and at least 90 percent of students graduate and are accepted to college.
>
> The academy had no problem meeting the requirements — with 94 percent black students and 5 percent Hispanic, and more than 90 percent eligible for free or reduced lunches, every year Catherine Ferguson achieves a 90 percent graduation rate; 100 percent of those who graduate (85 last year) are accepted to two- or four-year colleges, most with financial aid, says the school's principal, G. Asenath Andrews.
>
> "Kids transform themselves here," Andrews says. "We're just a pot and kids jump in and turn themselves from lead into gold."

---

[74] http://www.myfoxdetroit.com/dpp/news/ronnie_dahl/protesters-arrested-at-dps-catherine-ferguson-academy-20110415-wpms

Every year, enrollment is first come, first served for as many as 400 students and 200 babies. There is no academic requirement; most of the girls are in the process of dropping out when they enter. As many as 20 percent drop out every year, Andrews says. (The 90 percent graduation rate is based on students who make it through the senior year.)

Andrews says the difference at her school is personal attention to each student. While Detroit public schools average 35 students for every teacher, Catherine Ferguson has an 18 to 1 ratio. Each student is assigned to a homeroom teacher whom she stays with until she graduates.

The homeroom teacher is responsible for looking after the student, the "first line" before issues head to the principal's office. When the kids don't show up or don't do their homework, a teacher asks, "Why? Where are you? What's going on?""What we know about schools that are successful is that kids feel involved," Andrews says. "I couldn't work in a school where the teachers didn't care. If there's a problem with a student, I'll go to her house, to her neighborhood."

Catherine Ferguson coaches every student on friendship, respect and loyalty as well as parenting skills. The school offers on-site services, including food stamps, an immunization clinic, dental services, and parenting/family literacy and counseling classes.
Also, students can take a three-week summer school program at Queens College in Canada, as well as other off-site study programs. To graduate, students must do an internship in a professional setting.

The one-stop education and social-service center is a great boon to Fior Marmol, 19, a young runaway who had a baby at age 15.
"When I graduate in January, I'm going to go to Central Michigan University,"
Marmol says. "I want to get a four-year law degree and learn two other languages. I already know English and Spanish. I want to go into the CIA [Central Intelligence Agency].

It wouldn't be far-fetched to conclude that Andrews possesses magical powers of persuasion. While Detroit public schools are bleeding students and dollars, prompting the recent announcement that the district will close 40 schools and cut 4,000 jobs to shore up a $200 million two-year deficit, Catherine Ferguson, somehow, every year, obtains about double the funding per student of the average Detroit public school. Andrews is tight-lipped about her budget and how she makes it work, except to say that the school is district-funded and gets dollars for special-needs students.[75]

---

[75] http://www2.metrotimes.com/editorial/story.asp?id=7026

Something smells incredibly fishy about this whole story. When you watch Maddow's news piece, notice the horses and gardens. This story has everything that liberals love: a school named after a slave, with an enrollment of almost all Black girls that are pregnant or have just given birth, and the illusion of success at the cost of hundreds of millions of dollars.[76]

We aren't sure what a Great School Rating means, but on this site, the school gets a 1 out of 10.[77]

It's obvious that Detroit is going back to nature, as the city is slowly overrun by vegetation in a scene reminiscent of *Earth Abides*.[78]

These types of strange news stories from Disingenuous White Liberal (DWL) reporters - like Maddow - are going to be ubiquitous in the coming months as austerity measures begin to dismantle BRA piece by piece.

This story of Catherine Ferguson Academy closing - and the unsuccessful privatization of the school through chartering - is an example of the free market at work. Any wonder why Black people don't like Ron Paul or the Austrians at Lewrockwell.com?

If you let the free market dictate things, it's obvious that no financial incentive or return on investment (ROI) can be calculated by privately funding Catherine Ferguson Academy.

The collapse of BRA is upon us and it's not going to be pretty. Detroit Public Schools have no money and attempts to make people empathize with the plight of Catherine Ferguson Academy are silly and non-productive. No one forced these girls to have sexual relations and get pregnant:

---

[76]   http://bigeducationape.blogspot.com/2011/05/detroit-schools-fight-for-catherine.html

[77]   http://www.greatschools.org/michigan/detroit/1269-Ferguson-Academy-For-Young-Women/

[78]   http://www.grist.org/article/food-farming-in-Detroit-schools-of-chard-knocks

The DPS faces a $327 million deficit out of a budget of $1.187 billion. A conventional student in the DPS costs $7,600 to educate, which is the highest in the state by far. But the DPS also has several "specialty" schools where the per-pupil cost is much higher. One of them, Catherine Ferguson Academy, exclusively educates teen mothers. [79]With free daycare and other amenities, it costs the school $12,619 per pupil to educate its students.
You want to shut it down to save money? I understand. But how many of these girls will never complete high school if you do that? And what will become of them, and their babies, as a result?[80]

Only a nation completely dedicated to Black-Run America would fund such a school, even though they claim to have a 90% graduation rate and 100% college and higher education acceptance upon graduation. How is that even possible?[81]

Something fishy is going on in Detroit and one day the books will be opened and an independent audit of the city will occur. Then, and only then, will we get to know just how big of a lie (and cost) the Catherine Ferguson Academy represented in BRA.

---

[79] http://detnews.com/article/20110527/SCHOOLS/105270383

[80]

http://apps.detnews.com/apps/blogs/watercooler/index.php?blogid=2386#i xzz1Okpk2J5K

[81] √

A RoboCop Statue in Detroit? Just Build Delta City in its Ruins

"Old Detroit has a cancer. That cancer is crime."

The words of the fictional CEO of Omni Consumer Products (OCP) at the start of 1987's *RoboCop* don't do the real Detroit of 2011 justice. Those who fled the city have created prosperous suburbs where crime rates are diminutive compared to a city that never saw a real-life RoboCop materialize and worse, one that real cops and firefighters live far away from:

These brave women and men already work in the city of Detroit — and now, Mayor Dave Bing wants police officers to live in the city as well.

Bing has been vocal about his desire to get police officers to move back into the city, and now he's taking action by announcing a new incentive plan to get them to live where they work.

Currently, 53 percent of Detroit Police officers commute to work from the suburbs, and Bing says the number is even higher for firefighters.

As part of a pilot program called "Project 14" Detroit cops and firefighters who live in the suburbs will be offered renovated homes in the city for as little as $1,000.

Mayor Bing said this is one step in a plan to revitalize Detroit.

"Project 14 is one approach that my administration is deploying to take two challenges facing Detroit — public safety and vacant homes — and turn them into an opportunity for neighborhood revitalization," Mayor Bing said.[82]

---

[82]   http://detroit.cbslocal.com/2011/02/07/mayor-pushing-police-to-live-in-detroit/

RoboCop is a fine 1980s film that brought the gritty reality of Detroit to the screen much better than *Home Improvement* did in the 1990s (though the criminals in the movie were almost all-white, just like in the early 1990s film The Crow).[83]

We have documented Detroit's collapse on multiple occasions and will continue to point out that a city's inhabitants are primarily responsible for the state of and quality of life in their city, whether good or bad. Detroit – a town Black people can't give up on – is collapsing into a condition that matches its citizens' own ennui.

With its 90 percent plus Black citizenry unopposed to the idea of once proud city completely falling apart under their watch, Detroit is in need of salvation. (Picture essays on the cities collapse are a case study in what happens [84]when the population that built and sustained a city evacuate for safer lands).[85]

Time wrote a heartbreaking cover story[86] on Detroit and wondered if the town would survive. Delta Airline's in-flight magazine, *Sky,* recently profiled the city and the two articles seem to profile an entirely different subject.[87]

[83] http://www.theatlanticwire.com/features/view/feature/Why-Are-There-So-Few-Black-Supervillains-2657

84

http://www.time.com/time/photogallery/0,29307,1864272_1810098,00.html

[85]   http://www.guardian.co.uk/artanddesign/2011/jan/02/detroit-ruins-marchand-meffre-photographs-ohagan?intcmp=239

[86] http://www.time.com/time/nation/article/0,8599,1925796,00.html

[87] http://msp.imirus.com/Mpowered/book/vds11/i2/p94

Just two years removed from being *Forbes* most dangerous city, the town *Sky* magazine profiles resembles a Detroit of 70 years ago whose citizens have long since sought refuge in the suburbs.

The only way to save Detroit is to replace the population that engendered and then watched over its complete demise with the population that fled and created prosperous suburbs. The Black population that destabilized the city is even fleeing now.[88]

Detroit has a population that exhibits little innovation, creativity, ability to graduate from high school and, well, read.[89]

Or even to erect a statue to the eponymous fictional character from *RoboCop*:

> Philadelphia has its Rocky statue, but do not look for Detroit to celebrate its connection to RoboCop any time soon.
>
> Detroit Mayor Dave Bing, who has taken to the Internet to solicit ideas for the city's revival, said on Monday there were no plans for a RoboCop statue to honor the 1987 science fiction movie based on Detroit. The question had come in via Twitter.
>
> "There are not any plans to erect a statue to RoboCop," Bing wrote on his Twitter account. "Thank you for your suggestion."
>
> Bing touched off an immediate wave of Twitter messages from fans of the movie who hope he will reconsider, and others amused that he had even responded.
>
> "Some people just don't get it," grumbled one message on Twitter. Another wrote: "If I were mayor of Detroit, my top priority would be a RoboCop statue."[90]

88

http://www.mlive.com/news/detroit/index.ssf/2009/09/black_flight_the_new _white_fli.html

[89] http://roissy.wordpress.com/2011/02/17/the-creativity-stagnation/

[90] http://news.yahoo.com/s/nm/20110208/us_nm/us_robocop

Though the mayor of Detroit publicly stated he is against building a RoboCop statue, citizens created a Web site soliciting donations and utilized crowdsourcing and social network sites to build public support and collect money for the project.[91]

It worked.[92] *Stuff White People Like* (SWPL) white people collected the money, believing that their art project could restore Detroit and turn it overnight into Portland.[93]

These goofy Disingenuous White Liberals (DWLs) mean so well, collecting money to build a statue of a character from a movie they saw as children. It's so -- artistic![94]

Never will one of these people criticize the dominant population of that city who turned a thriving metropolis into the laughing stock of the world.
Such is stupefying power of Black Run America (BRA).

Building this statute makes these SWPL white people feel special, important:

[91] http://detroitneedsrobocop.com/

[92] http://www.sfgate.com/cgi-bin/blogs/hottopics/detail?entry_id=83280

[93] http://www.citysbest.com/detroit/news/2011/02/16/affirmative-detroits-robocop-statue-is-funded/

[94]

http://www.dailytech.com/RoboCop+Statue+to+Be+Erected+in+Detroit/article20937c.htm

The surprisingly quick campaign to raise at least $50,000 to build a larger-than-life statue of RoboCop in Detroit shouldn't stop with the crime-fighting cyborg, the fund-raisers said Wednesday.

"If we raised this much money for RoboCop, imagine what others can do for the city," Detroit artist and fund-raiser Jerry Paffendorf said. "We could raise money for other art projects and for schools and neighborhoods."

In just six days, a group of local artists and sci-fi fans exceeded the fund-raising goal Wednesday with more than $53,000 in donations, an amount that could rise substantially by the March 29 deadline. The group received more than 1,500 donations from around the globe, with an average contribution of $17.[95]

Detroit does need *RoboCop*. In the movie he was embedded with three primary directives:
Serve the public trust, protect the innocent, and uphold the law.

Detroit is the most corrupt city in America, so if a real-life RoboCop were patrolling the streets all of the directives would require the imprisonment of most of the elected officials there. How would RoboCop deal with those citizens who don't snitch? How would he protect the innocent?

Soon the city of Detroit will become the latest location of Gotham City in the third Christopher Nolan *Batman* movie. Filming this movie in a third world city will save the production money, but what will it do for Detroit? What will building a RoboCop statute – a project of SWPL white people – do for the city?[96]

95

http://www.freep.com/article/20110217/NEWS01/102170475/1133/Sports2 1/RoboCop-statue-campaign-lesson-saving-Detroit?odyssey=nav%7Chead

[96] http://theamericanjingoist.net/index.php/2011/01/20/detroit-a-third-world-city/

Detroit does have a cancer. The entire United States of America has a cancer. It's called Black Run America (BRA) and this concept derails any legitimate discussion of race. RoboCop couldn't save Detroit now.

Perhaps actually building Delta City on the ruins of old Detroit is the only positive idea left.

To paraphrase the movie, "Real Detroit has a cancer. That cancer is Black crime."

It should be noted that the *Rocky* franchise made $565 million at the box office, while the three *RoboCop* films made a combined $109 million (an average of $94 million per *Rocky*). Perhaps Detroit does deserve a B-movie statue, while Philadelphia rightfully has a statue dedicated to the Italian Stallion.

Hey, people want to come see the Rocky statue. Who would want to go to Detroit, even with a RoboCop statue?

A *RoboCop* statue only detracts from reality, which is something DWLs do on a daily basis.

$1,000 for a chair? For a Library in Detroit?

There are a lot of tasteless stories about Detroit that attempt to explain that cities dramatic fall into obscurity, irrelevance and hilarious pursuit of continually being a national joke. What follows is a perfect example of the Nigga Rich mentality combined with complete control over the allocation of financial resources in Detroit:

A Livonia furniture dealer is defending the Detroit Public Library's purchase of lounge chairs that cost $1,092 and have become a symbol of extravagance for a system considering closing 18 branches.

The Allermuir brand chairs normally retail for $1,984 apiece and are popular with municipalities, schools and universities, said Paul Gingell, who is the company's Michigan sales representative.

He said Detroiters deserve to sit comfortably in the chairs, which are part of a $2.3 million renovation of the main library's south wing. The rehab set to open soon includes two alcohol-burning fireplaces that cost $5,000 apiece and 24 pendant light fixtures that cost $531 each.

"How about the young mother with several children that looks forward to a weekly trek through the snow/sleet to improve their reading skills and are hopeful that a spot near the fireplaces will be open, because the warmth provided is greater than what they experience at home?" Gingell, of W. E. Gingell Associates Inc., asked in an email.

"How about the elderly person that the highlight of (his or her) week is to find a book or newspaper and snuggle into a comfortable chair near a window?"

The library didn't buy the 20 chairs from Gingell.

But even administrators say the purchase was a mistake.

The system faces an $11 million shortfall and could close 18 of 23 neighborhood branches and lay off as many as 191 of 333 workers. The south wing overhaul grew from a $300,000 update.[97]

---

[97] http://detnews.com/article/20110426/METRO/104260351/Library-feeling-heat-over-buying-$1K-chairs#ixzz1LKiWGZxC

When the Federal Government wants to hide actual purchases and create a false paper trail, they 'claim' to spend $30 on a hammer, $50 on a toilet seat. The Black people in charge of Detroit find no such need in hiding such opulent gifts purchased on taxpayer dime and see the investment of $1,000 into chairs for a public library a solid financial maneuver.

That wasn't the only wasteful purchase:

> Documents show a $2.3 million overhaul of part of the Detroit Public Library's main branch included eight stainless-steel trash cans that cost a total of about $8,900.

> The Detroit News reports Thursday the spending is detailed in documents it obtained. The renovation of the South Wing has come under criticism as the library considers closing neighborhood branches and cutting jobs to deal with budget problems.

> Michael Wells, president of UAW Local 2200 representing 120 library staffers, says the cost for trash cans is "exorbitant."[98]

---

[98]   http://www.myfoxdetroit.com/dpp/news/local/detroit-library-rehab-included-costly-trash-cans-20110428-mr

Detroit has an illiteracy rate of 50 percent, so a multi-million dollar renovation of a public library makes absolutely no sense, especially when half the city can't read. Of course, it is well-known the president of the Detroit School Board - Otis Mathis - is illiterate.[99] (Deleted)
A movie was made back in the mid-2000s called *A Day Without a Mexican*. It was a spoof of what life would be like in California if all Mexicans disappeared.

A Day Without White People is a movie that doesn't need to be made. A real-life drama (comedy?) that chronicles such a fictional narrative is unfolding in Detroit, Michigan. The script could be classified as either horror, comedy or mock-u-mentary.

Either way, we still think they should build a *Robocop* statue. If a chair cost $1,000 bucks in Detroit, we imagine they could spend a few million on such an erection.

If you recall, Michigan has passed a "Financial Martial Law" bill:
Supporters say the bill gives the state a way to step into distressed municipalities and schools before they collapse. It also gives emergency financial managers broad authority to end employee union contracts, and to nullify elected boards and councils.

The bill's sponsor, Republican Rep. Al Pscholka, said Tuesday that it would give the state the power it needs to dig important institutions out of financial holes. "For years we have allowed cities and schools to be on the verge of bankruptcy without any intervention," he told Reuters. "When the state finally does arrive, in many cases we find the financial records in disarray and leave emergency managers with very few good options to balance the books."

Republican Sen. Jack Brandenburg last week said emergency managers would be deployed only in communities that need "financial martial law."[100]

---

[99] http://www.time.com/time/nation/article/0,8599,1925681,00.html

[100] http://www.politico.com/news/stories/0311/51396.html

Detroit is another city that will collapse as Black Run America (BRA) implodes on itself. The "Financial Martial Law" was passed because at some point soon the Nigga Rich spending going on in Detroit will come to a horrible end.

Detroit Public Schools President Otis Mathis and that scene from "There's Something About Mary"

There's something about Detroit Public Schools President Otis Mathis:

> *One day after facing accusations of fondling himself, Detroit Public Schools President Otis Mathis wrote a letter to colleagues today blaming "ongoing health problems" for his "poor judgment."*

The letter, which attempted to rescind his resignation he submitted Thursday, doesn't explicitly address accusations from Superintendent Teresa Gueyser that he touched himself during a private meeting.

But Mathis acknowledged that he "made inappropriate actions toward a professional employee of the board" and promises to remove himself from personnel decisions involving her.

"I am following up with my doctors because I need to pursue treatment, and because I want to make sure that what happened doesn't ever happen again," Mathis said. "However, I do not need to resign in order to take care of my health."

The letter to colleagues came the same day board Vice President Anthony Adams today released a two-page letter from Gueyser accusing Mathis of fondling himself during a meeting this week. She called it his "usual habit" during one-on-one meetings. She said she tries to ignore it.

94

"On many occasions, I have asked him not to touch himself," she wrote in the letter dated Wednesday.

Mathis attended the board's 5 p.m. meeting today, but sat in the front row of the audience. His name plate was already removed from the board table. Adams said the board won't comment further on the controversy and is moving forward as if "he is no longer a board member."

Board member Reverend David Murray called the allegations "a terrible thing" but said he doesn't believe the 55-year-old Mathis should quit.

"It happens to a lot of young men. They engage in behavior they feel is harmless and it's offensive to certain people," Murray said. "... It could be deemed offensive, but some women are more sensitive to those types of things than others."

"I feel bad for him because he probably felt that it was something she would probably like or she got humor out of it."

Gueyser's letter describes in detail an incident during a meeting about her employment agreement. Her contract is to be reviewed tonight.

"President Mathis continued to fondle his genital area for approximately 20 minutes, or the entire time I was talking," Gueyser wrote. "At one point, I lifted some papers from my binder above my eyes to separate my peripheral view in order to avoid watching his activity."[101]

To abandon Detroit is to abandon Black America[102], but middle class Black residents are beginning to leave the city in droves[103] leaving a city populated and run by alleged perverts as *The Wall Street Journal* reports:

---

[101]   http://detnews.com/article/20100618/METRO/6180414/Detroit-schools-president-accused-of-lewd-acts-at-work#ixzz0rLYKaEIC

[102]   http://atlantapost.com/2010/06/02/opinion-abandon-detroit-abandon-black-america/

[103]   http://www.businessinsider.com/the-crisis-in-detroit-is-worse-than-a-recession-2010-6#ixzz0rLZSuLoe

This shrinking city needs to hang on to people like Johnette Barham: taxpaying, middle-class professionals who invest in local real estate, work and play downtown, and make their home here.

Ms. Barham just left. And she's not coming back.

In seven years as a homeowner in Detroit, she endured more than 10 burglaries and break-ins at her house and a nearby rental property she owned. Still, she defied friends' pleas to leave as she fortified her home with locks, bars, alarms and a dog.

Then, a week before Christmas, someone torched the house and destroyed almost everything she owned.

In March, police arrested a suspect in connection with the case, someone who turned out to be remarkably easy to find. For Ms. Barham, the arrest came one crime too late. "I was constantly being targeted in a way I couldn't predict, in a way that couldn't be controlled by the police," she says. "I couldn't take it anymore."

Ms. Barham's journey from diehard to defector illustrates the precarious state of Detroit today. The city—which has shed roughly 1 million residents since the 1950s—is now losing the African-American professionals who had stayed steadfastly, almost defiantly, loyal.

Through decades of white flight and economic distress, these diehards have sustained the city's cultural institutions and allowed prime neighborhoods such as Indian Village and Palmer Woods to stave off the blight that infects large swaths of Detroit.

Today, frustrated by plummeting property values and high crime, many diehards have hit their breaking point. Their exodus is consigning borderline neighborhoods to full-blown blight and putting prime residential areas at risk. By some estimates, this year's Census will show a population drop of 150,000 people from the 951,000 people who lived within city limits in 2000. That would be roughly double the population loss in the 1990s, when black, middle-class flight began replacing white flight as the prevailing dynamic.

There are other signs the middle class is throwing in the towel. From 1999 to 2008, median household income in Detroit dropped nearly 25% to $28,730, after growing 17% in the 1990s, according to Data Driven Detroit, a nonprofit that analyzes Census data for the city. Over that period, the proportion of owner-occupied homes fell to 39% from 49%, while the proportion of vacant homes nearly tripled to 28%.[104]

You always hear white people say they move to Whitopia's for the 'good schools' that their children will attend, forever fearful of admitting why those schools are so good. A cursory glance at Detroit, where Mr. Otis Mathis finds 'choking the chicken' a more suitable action at a Board of Education meeting than fixing the city's near 50 percent illiteracy rate provides an incredible glance into part of the problem.

Of course, Mr. Mathis is also the same individual who confessed to being incapable of putting together a cogent sentence, despite his apparent dexterity in 'rubbing one out':

As if Detroit doesn't have enough problems these days, the president of the city's school board offered the shocking admission that he can't pen a coherent sentence.

Otis Mathis, who oversees the academic future of 90,000 public school students, told the Detroit News that he's a "horrible writer" after reports surfaced that he sent a Feb. 29 e-mail to the financial manager of Detroit Public Schools that was rife with spelling, punctuation and usage errors.

"If you saw Sunday's Free Press that shown Robert Bobb the emergency financial manager for Detroit Public Schools, move Mark Twain to Boynton which have three times the number seats then students and was one of the reason's he gave for closing school to many empty seats," the e-mail read, according to the paper.

Mathis, 56, of Detroit, has had difficulties with language as early as fourth grade, when he was placed in special

104

http://online.wsj.com/article/SB100014240527487042920045752305322487 15858.html?mod=WSJ_WSJ_US_News_3

education classes. His college degree was also held up for more than a decade due to repeatedly failing English proficiency exams required for graduation from Wayne State University, the paper reported.

Some parents are now questioning whether Mathis is fit for his role. "It's kind of scary to even talk about," Patrick Martin, 49, a Detroit contractor whose 12-year-old son is a student at Noble Middle School, told the paper. "If this is the leader, what does it say about the followers? It explains a lot about why there's so much confusion and infighting with the board and Robert Bobb."

Mathis has also worked as a substitute teacher in Detroit schools, which are ranked among the lowest-achieving metropolitan public school districts in the country. But he told the paper his story is about someone who has managed his limitations.

"Instead of telling them that they can't write and won't be anything, I show that cannot stop you," Mathis told the paper. "If Detroit Public Schools can allow kids to dream, with whatever weakness they have, that's something. ... It's not about what you don't have. It's what you *can* do."[105]

---

[105]   http://www.foxnews.com/us/2010/03/05/detroit-school-leader-sends-wrong-message-parents-say/

The Detroit News reports the school system in Detroit is the worst in the nation.[106] A school system is only as proficient as the students who sit in the classrooms, regardless of the amount of Crusading White Pedagogues attempting to Teach for America and enlighten the minds of the hopelessly erudite-less masses.[107]

Of course, President Otis Mathis - who resigned his post as president of the school system only to ask for it back (apparently he…misfired?) - can't be blamed for all the problems plaguing Detroit, the nations most violent city.[108]

The glory of earning that ignominious title falls squarely on the shoulders of the cities Black residents.

However, being inclined to participate in chronic masturbation - even to the point of fondling oneself in the workplace - well... that seems to be a skill that Mr. Mathis can add to his resume.

There's something about Otis Mathis besides his self-acknowledged inability to formulate a rational sentence, and in case you ever have the chance to shake his hand, that isn't gel in his hand.

Otis Mathis joins Alvin Greene in the Pantheon of *Stuff Black People Don't Like* Heroes.

We don't like poking fun at Detroit here at SBPDL, it's just sometimes that city blows an impressive load that we can't help but comment on. Wasting raccoons is one thing; Otis Mathis pulling a Judge Reinhold from *Fast Times at Ridgemont High* is a horse of a different color.

Relax by Frankie Goes to Hollywood has been confirmed as Otis Mathis' favorite song.

---

[106] http://www.detnews.com/article/20100304/OPINION03/3040437/

[107] http://detnews.com/article/20100520/SCHOOLS/5200459/Detroit-students-at-bottom-of-national-reading-test-scores

[108] http://www.clickondetroit.com/video/23956233/index.html

171. Wasting Raccoon's in Detroit

Black people love Detroit. Comprising nearly 92 percent of the inhabitants of the 11th most populated city in the United States, Black people can take umbrage at any other city in America trying to classify themselves as the ultimate Black - or Chocolate city.

Detroit has a very colorful city council to represent the citizenry - even though many of those elected to protect the public interests are themselves currently under indictment for fraud, bribery and misuse of public funds - as they try and fight off massive job loss, rising crime rates(one of the most dangerous city in America), failing schools (Forty Schools closing) and the potential bulldozing of large sections of the city.[109]

CNN reports that you can buy a house for $100 down in Detroit:

> "Dragging down the average are homes that are long abandoned or foreclosed on that are selling for pennies on the dollar. Detroit already had the lowest market value houses in Michigan before the latest rounds of job losses at GM and other huge employers, market analysts say."[110]

Suffice it to say, Detroit is a thriving Black metropolis, a beacon and a veritable citadel for Black people's crowning achievement in America and an example of what Black people can bring to other major cities throughout the nation.

Black people love Detroit, for it is their city and the epitome of change and hope that all cities can look forward to undergoing during the Kafkaesque transformation of America.

Detroit no longer has a major grocery chain within city limits:

---

[109] http://www.freep.com/article/20090617/NEWS01/906170313

[110] http://www.cnn.com/2009/US/06/17/detroit.artists.homes/

"No national grocery chain operates a store here. A lack of outlets that sell fresh produce and meat has led the United Food and Commercial Workers union and a community group to think about building a grocery store of its own."[111] This void has left the fine citizens of Detroit with the major problem of how to acquire food. Thankfully, raccoon is filling that vacuum.

What Black people do not like though, is wasting good raccoon in the catacombs of the decaying, crumbling city that is Detroit. Raccoon is considered a delicacy in Detroit, a rare treat that is vital to nourishing Black people and enabling them to continue the cities meteoric rise to the top of the Green Revolution in America. White people might like LEED certification; Black people just like nature baby.[112]

And in nature, anytime a raccoon passes away, the true urban hunter Glemie Dean Beasley - a 69-year-old retired truck driver - swoops in to cook it. [113]

Travels with Charlie, reports:

"While economic times are tough across Michigan as its people slog through a difficult and protracted deindustrialization, Beasley remains upbeat.

Where one man sees a vacant lot, Beasley sees a buffet.

"Starvation is cheap," he says as he prepares an afternoon lunch of barbecue coon and red pop at his west side home."[114]

---

[111] http://finance.yahoo.com/family-home/article/107206/retailers-head-for-exits-in-detroit.html?mod=family-autos

[112] http://www.detroitblog.org/?p=287

[113] http://www.detnews.com/article/20090402/METRO08/904020395/1439/METRO08/To-urban-hunter--next-meal-is-scampering-by

[114] http://www.detnews.com/article/20090402/METRO08/904020395/1439/METRO08/To-urban-hunter--next-meal-is-scampering-by

The Raccoon raconteur continues:

> "Coon or rabbit. God put them there to eat," Beasley said....Hunting is prohibited within Detroit city limits and Beasley insists he does not do so. Still, he says that life in the city has gone so retrograde that he could easily feed himself with the wildlife in his backyard, which abuts an old cement factory."
>
> "This city is going back to the wild," he says. "That's bad for people but that's good for me. I can catch wild rabbit and pheasant and coon in my backyard."[115]

The saga of Detroit is encapsulated in the saga of Beasley. Knowing over 100 ways to cook Raccoon, Beasley is a thriving entrepreneur who sells his wares to the cities inhabitants. The city might not resemble the optimistic future imagined in the film Robocop, but Black people don't like wasting raccoon in any environment.

Stuff Black People Don't Like does not include Detroit, which is the ultimate Black people's city, but it does including wasting Raccoon there, for any meal that can be found is a fine one indeed.

---

[115] Ibid

What do most of the 30 Brokest Cities in America have in Common?

Remember that town in Alabama that couldn't pay retired city employees their pensions anymore? We do. It was Prichard, Alabama, a once thriving white community that was overwhelmed by the Black Undertow.[116]

116

http://www.detnews.com/article/20090402/METRO08/904020395/1439/METRO08/To-urban-hunter--next-meal-is-scampering-by

As Black people became the majority of the town's population, businesses shuttered and the tax base dried up; thus, no new revenue to pay the pension of retired white city employees who worked their entire lives to help build a city, only to see the Black Undertow Effect undermine it all.

The phenomenon of the Black Undertow Effect is readily observable in the ruins of Detroit and Birmingham, two formerly world-class cities now both teetering on the verge of complete financial ruin. Odd that the suburbs of both dying metropolises (Detroit's suburbs are 82 percent white, compared to the core of the city being only 8 percent white) are some of the most desirable in all the country.

CNBC did a hilarious story on *20 Cities You Don't Want to Live in... Yet*, which included both Detroit and Birmingham. Presumably when the Black Undertow is forcibly moved into the white suburbs via Section 8 Housing[117] and removed from prime real estate in the core of these cities, then and only then will *you want to live in these cities.*[118]

All across the country, Black people - who have been a significant population of failing major cities - are moving to the white suburbs.[119] White people are moving into the cities.[120]

The dream of owning your own home - and the relaxed lending standards introduced to help facilitate this for primarily non-white buyers - has ravaged formerly prosperous counties, especially in the Metro Atlanta area. Clayton County, once one of the top places to live in Atlanta - almost all of the founder of Chick-fil-A's entire family still lives there - is now the prime example of what happens when

---

[117]   http://floydreports.com/obama-wants-to-move-the-hood-into-your-neighborhood/

[118]http://www.cnbc.com/id/42135402/20_Cities_You_Don_t_Want_to_Live_In_Yet

[119]http://gawker.com/5784380/black-people-moving-to-suburbs-as-white-people-move-to-cities

[120]
http://blog.al.com/spotnews/2011/03/birmingham_changes_as_blacks_m.html

---

the Black Undertow takes over.[121]

Though Atlanta has the highest income inequality in the nation (yes, this is largely a Black-white issue)[122], it does not rank as one of *America's 30 Top Brokest Cities*. According to The Daily Beast[123], four other Georgia cities rank in that dubious list:

> To find the most struggling cities in the country, we used three data points weighted equally: the most recently available unemployment rate (August 2011), median household income, and average debt. Data is from a recent report by Experian and the Bureau of Labor Statistics. The average credit score for each city is included in the gallery, though not taken into account to determine the final ranking. If this data is any indication, the cities struggling the most right now—the ones that may take the longest to recover— are clustered in the South and along the Pacific Coast.[124]

And only here at SBPDL, will you learn that those four cities (and the majority of the 30 Brokest Cities) are overwhelmed in the Black Undertow, with many boasting some of the largest percentages of overall Black population in the nation.

Savannah, Macon, Augusta, and, the No. 1 brokest city in America, Columbus, Georgia comprise four spots on that illustrious list. And with Georgia adding the most Black people to its overall population then any other state over the past 10 years, how long until Atlanta nudges onto that list?:

---

[121]   http://news.investors.com/Article/589858/201110310805/Housing-Crisis-Obama-Clinton-Subprime.htm

[122]http://www.ajc.com/news/atlanta/atlanta-had-greatest-income-1211646.html

[123]   http://www.thedailybeast.com/galleries/2011/10/31/america-s-30-brokest-cities-photos.html

[124] http://blogs.ajc.com/business-beat/2011/11/01/four-georgia-cities-make-list-of-brokest-in-america-can-you-guess-them/

The state added 1.5 million people over the past decade for a total of 9,687,653, according to new Census data. Georgia's black population growth — 579,335 — was greater than either the Hispanic (418,462) or white (285,259) population growth, says William Frey, demographer at the **Brookings Institution**. "Georgia is just a major magnet for African Americans, both high-skilled and low-skilled," he says. "For cultural reasons and for economic reasons, the black migration to the state is significant."[125]

Let's see: Savannah is 55 percent Black; Augusta 54 percent Black; Macon 62 percent Black; and Columbus is 44 percent Black. Gosh, what does each of these cities have in common?

What about the other 26 brokest cities in America? It reads like a who's who of the cities with the greatest percentage of Black people in America:

Beaumont is 45 percent Black; Greenville, NC is 32 percent Black; Mobile is 50 percent Black; Tampa is 26 percent Black; Toledo is 24 percent Black; Waco is 23 percent Black; Greensboro is 40 percent Black; Wilmington is 26 percent Black; Detroit is 83 percent Black; Montgomery is 56 percent Black;Tyler is 25 percent Black; Charleston is 26 percent Black; Birmingham is 73 percent Black; Fort Myers is 34 percent Black; Flint is 57 percent Black; Jacksonville is 30 percent Black; Miami is 19 percent Black; and Orlando is 28 percent Black. [126]

125

126

http://en.wikipedia.org/wiki/List_of_U.S._cities_with_large_African_American_populations

These cities also have extreme levels of segregation, with predominately Black areas completely distressed and reliant on federal funds (welfare, EBT/SNAP, free lunches at school, Section 8/Public Housing) to subsist. Just like Silicon Valley, there aren't many Black entrepreneurs in these cities either. Businesses can't stay open in the majority Black portions of these cities, because your average Black person has no purchasing power.

Know this: Savannah, Miami, Augusta, Orlando and the other cities listed have very nice areas where people can live, work, and play. But they also have incredibly scary areas, with one common denominator that you'll soon learn the answer.

Notice that a good portion of the brokest cities are in the south, where 54 percent of Black people in America reside; other cities include those dying Rust Belt cities (Detroit, Flint, Toledo) where Black people went to escape the "discrimination" of the Jim Crow South, only to leave these towns in horrible condition, with low property values, crumbling infrastructure, high crime rates and low Trick-or-Treating rates.

That is the lasting Black footprint on America (the same goes for Cincinnati, Cleveland, Dayton, New Orleans, Jackson, Memphis, Philadelphia, Hartford, Harrisburg, Kansas City, Newark, Camden, etc.) and one that must be addressed moving forward.

Consult this list of the whitest big cities (Portland, Seattle Pittsburgh, Indianapolis, Boston, etc.) and realize that the old "Republican vs. Democrat" debate has no merit in what makes a great city. It isn't liberal politics; it isn't conservative politics. It has everything to do with the type of community - the kind Robert Putnam discussed - that can be created.[127]

Those brokest cities? No social trust, because white families are constantly having to move from one suburb to the next to avoid the encroaching Black Undertow. And as we have learned, the Blacker the city, the lower the social trust and the greater the inability for complete community breakdown.

---

[127]

http://www.oregonlive.com/news/index.ssf/2009/01/in_a_changing_world_ portland_r.html

Just look at Detroit and Birmingham.

And such is life in the dying days of Black-Run America (BRA), when two Black men are seriously being considered to represent the Republican and Democrat parties in a bid for the POTUS in 2012.

So what do most of the *30 Brokest Cities in America* have in common? If your answer was the Black Undertow makes owning and operating a business (plus remains a huge burden on tax revenue, with a small percentage collected from Black people and a much greater percentage going to policing and protecting citizens from them), then you are today's winner.

Moving forward, remember this: anytime you see a list that purports to delineate the worst cities in America for (crime, property value, standard of living, schools, raising a family, living, staying in shape) instinctively know it will be a run-down of those places hit hardest by the Black Undertow.

The worst cities in America might be dominated by Democrats (because Black people vote that way), but some of the best cities in America are as well. What's the difference?

#891. The Demise of the Pontiac Silverdome

Black people love sports. Years of watching sports have helped people from across the United States develop favorable images of Black people, through vast consumption of sports, which is explained with the process of "Mainstreaming":

> "A corollary of cultivation theory, the concept of "mainstreaming" implies that heavy television viewing contributes to an erosion of differences in people's perspectives that stem from other factors and influences.
>
> It is based on the argument that television serves as the primary common storyteller for an otherwise heterogeneous population. As the source of the most broadly shared images and messages in history, television represents the mainstream of the common symbolic environment into which children are born and in which we all live out our lives."[128]

---

[128]http://www.communicationencyclopedia.com/public/tocnode?id=g97814 05131995_chunk_g978140513199518_ss4-1

We have documented the amount of time people spend watching the National Football League (NFL), college football and other professional sports, and with this repeated viewing of 13 percent of the population dominating the airwaves on Saturday and Sunday, the concept of 'mainstreaming' has created a false dichotomy of the world.

Fall Saturday's and Sunday's both serve as Holy Days in America and the worshiping of the new Gods from Olympus occurs. The only sacrifice made in 21st America comes from the pocketbooks of taxpayers, for they must fit the bill for erecting these massive structures that will play host to the religious gatherings, as the book *Field of Schemes* outlines:

> *"Field of Schemes* is a play-by-play account of how the drive for new sports stadiums and arenas drains $2 billion a year from public treasuries for the sake of private profit. While the millionaires who own sports franchises have seen the value of their assets soar under this scheme, taxpayers, urban residents, and sports fans have all come out losers, forced to pay both higher taxes and higher ticket prices for seats that, thanks to the layers of luxury seating that typify new stadiums, usually offer a worse view of the action."[129]

A fantastic blog detailing this pervasive technique that rivals Scientology in its excesses can be found here, as the authors of the book work prodigiously to document continued abuses of stadium erection at the tax payer expense.

It is in these Holy sites that occupy hundreds of acres in every major city that Black people have temporarily utilized the power of 'mainstreaming' to garner a hypnotic effect over the entire country, for their exploits are fodder for ESPN junkies and account for countless hours of wasted productivity from these citizens.

Perhaps this is why the sudden demise of the Silverdome is such a shocking blow to the continued 'mainstreaming' of a new social order:

---

[129] http://www.nebraskapress.unl.edu/product/Field-of-Schemes,673388.aspx

"The town of Pontiac, Michigan, a suburb of Detroit, sold the 80,300-seat Silverdome on Monday, along with 127 acres of nearby land. The massive stadium complex, which once hosted the Detroit Lions, the Detroit Pistons, and the Michigan Panthers, cost more than $55 million to build in 1975.

Its selling price in 2009? $583,000.

Of course, Detroit's decay extends beyond its residential areas. As upsetting as it is to see once-beloved Victorian homes and beautiful apartment buildings sinking into disrepair, the loss of industrial space is even more significant. The hulking ruins of auto buildings like Fisher Body 21, the Packard Plant and the Piquette Plant (where Ford's (F) Model T was first built) seem to suggest not only a local loss of population but a larger loss of purpose."[130]

Yes, the Detroit Silverdome was sold for a mere $583,000, less than 1 percent of what it was built for in 1975:

"It cost more than $55 million to build the Silverdome football stadium in Pontiac, Michigan. Yesterday, it sold for the price of a one-bedroom apartment in Manhattan.

The former home of the U.S. National Football League's Detroit Lions sold at auction for $583,000, or about $7.25 per seat, as the debt-ridden city of Pontiac sought to raise cash.

The area's unemployment rate is 35 percent and emergency financial manager Fred Leeb was hired in March as Pontiac faced a $6.5 million deficit on a $100 million general fund budget, plus $103 million in bond debt, Leeb said."[131]

Let's take a quick look at the census of Pontiac, Michigan's population:

---

[130] www.dailyfinance.com

[131]

http://www.bloomberg.com/apps/news?pid=20601079&sid=adFUGa0HXuZ o

"As of the census 2000, there were 66,337 people, 24,234 households, and 15,267 families residing in the city. The population density was 3,318.2 per square mile (1,281.3/km²). There were 26,336 housing units at an average density of 1,317.3/sq mi (508.7/km²). The racial makeup of the city was 39.09% White, 47.92% African American, 0.58% Native American, 2.40% Asian, 0.04% Pacific Islander, 6.47% from other races, and 3.50% from two or more races. Hispanic or Latino of any race were 12.76% of the population."[132]

SBPDL has friends with houses worth 4 or 5 times the amount of what the Pontiac Silverdome went for, and is shocked that the stadium even fetched $500,000.

In a town where raccoons are now seen as a delicacy, Detroit can be proud to know the stadium that once hosted the Lions is now worth less than a studio apartment in Manhattan.[133]

The Silverdome played host to Superbowl's, Wrestlemania's, major concerts and even an episode of Home Improvement in the 1990s. Now, the ghost of these events haunt the empty building and the 20 acres the massive structure sits upon.[134]

Detroit has seen better days. The fall of the Pontiac Silverdome has a distinct correlation with the collapse of that city and what it portends for the rest of America, as Pre-Obama America is eradicated throughout the land:

---

[132] http://en.wikipedia.org/wiki/Pontiac,_Michigan

[133]
http://www.fieldofschemes.com/news/archives/2009/11/3922_silverdome_s old.html

[134] http://football.ballparks.com/NFL/DetroitLions/index.htm

---

"By any quantifiable standard, the city is on life support. Detroit's treasury is $300 million short of the funds needed to provide the barest municipal services. The school system, which six years ago was compelled by the teachers' union to reject a philanthropist's offer of $200 million to build 15 small, independent charter high schools, is in receivership. The murder rate is soaring, and 7 out of 10 remain unsolved. Three years after Katrina devastated New Orleans, unemployment in that city hit a peak of 11%. In Detroit, the unemployment rate is 28.9%. That's worth spelling out: twenty-eight point nine percent.

That's because the story of Detroit is not simply one of a great city's collapse. It's also about the erosion of the industries that helped build the country we know today. The ultimate fate of Detroit will reveal much about the character of America in the 21st century. If what was once the most prosperous manufacturing city in the nation has been brought to its knees, what does that say about our recent past? And if it can't find a way to get up, what does that say about our future?"[135]

Black people see the writing on the wall in Detroit. A city that is run by Black people (indeed, Detroit is one of the Blackest big cities in America)[136] is in complete and utter chaos. Some people have envisioned razing Detroit and turning it into farmland.[137]

And through it all, the Pontiac Silverdome will stand as a sorry example of social engineering run afoul and worse, what happens when government attempts at creating a sports utopia backfire:

---

[135] http://www.time.com/time/nation/article/0,8599,1925796,00.html

[136] http://www.theroot.com/views/detroit-too-black-fail

[137]   http://ideas.blogs.nytimes.com/2009/11/09/plowing-detroit-into-farmland/

"The Silverdome opened in 1975 and cost taxpayers $55.7 million to build and $1.5 million a year to maintain, Leeb said. By contrast, the New York Giants and the New York Jets will play next year in a new stadium estimated to cost $1.6 billion."[138]

This could happen in your town. In fact, chances are, it will.

Stuff Black People Don't Like must include the demise of the Pontiac Silverdome, for the less than $600,000 sale of a building that would cost $220,000,000 million to build today is just a perfect example of what happens when you live in a Black world.

Not even Hulk Hogan slamming Andre the Giant could save Detroit now.

#368. Enterprise Zones

The late Jack Kemp was a defender of free markets and fanatically believed that were "enterprise zones" adopted in majority Black countries - like Haiti - or failed Black Undertow cities like Detroit, Birmingham, or Newark, that in only a few years capitalism would flourish in these currently desperate places and be the envy of the world.

He also stated - "bragged" is the correct word - that his admiration for civil rights, equality of opportunity, liberation, love of affirmative action (basically fundamental and foundational beliefs of Black-Run America) were based upon his experiences showering with his Black NFL teammates:

138

http://www.bloomberg.com/apps/news?pid=20601079&sid=adFUGa0HXuZo

He connected his concern for minorities with his respect for his black teammates, especially the linemen who had protected him from pass rushers.

Vin Weber, a former congressman from Minnesota and a close friend, said Mr. Kemp would often say, "I can't help but care about the rights of the people I used to shower with."[139]

Basing ones political philosophy and outlook on life - regarding choices that will greatly impact fellow citizens through legislation they work to pass - on "encounters in the shower" is not a recipe for sound government or economic decisions or policies.[140]

So what is an "enterprise zone" exactly? Here's one definition:

In the United States, Urban Enterprise Zones (UEZs), also known as Enterprise Zones, are intended to encourage development in blighted neighborhoods through tax and regulatory relief to entrepreneurs and investors who launch businesses in the area. UEZs are areas where companies can locate free of certain local, state, and federal taxes and restrictions. In other countries, a region that offers this type of special economic incentive is often referred to as a Special Economic Zone.[141]

---

[139] http://www.nytimes.com/2009/05/03/us/03kemp.html?pagewanted=all

[140] http://articles.latimes.com/1992-08-14/news/mn-5373_1_gulf-war

[141] http://en.wikipedia.org/wiki/Urban_Enterprise_Zone

Sounds simple enough, but doesn't a signficant portion of the population of "blighted" (a synonym for Black Undertow) communities already subsist of entrepreneurial activities, such as drug dealing and the re-selling of goods and merchandise procured via thievery? And, of course, a large percentage of their other income is provided by the taxpayer. [142]

Even if a company were to relocate to Detroit, Birmingham, or Haiti (or other "bad" - read Black Undertow - areas) for the purpose of paying minimal to no taxes as part of the EZ scheme, this entity would inevitably have to import new citizens to the city to serve as the bulk of the workforce, meaning that gentrification would take place in an effort to curb the negative effects of *Climate Change*.

Then again, *Inc Magazine* (like *Fast Company*, a radically Disingenuous White Liberal publication) recently found that it's easier to open business in Rwanda than the United States. [143] Knowing all the EEOC requirements a company must pass, and the constant fear of employees claiming "discrimination" and filing a lawsuit, what's the point? Not to mention majority-minority owned firms now getting preferential treatment when it comes to government (no-bid) contracts, you begin to see that perhaps a state (or city) is in need of declaring a BRA-Free Zone to stimulate economic activity. [144]

Imagine how many people would move there if this were done... Juxtapose that with how many people would move to "depressed" (Black Undertow... there's those clever words again to hide the truth) cities that were declared Enterprise Zones, that which was championed by Jack Kemp - a man whose philosophy was guided by his close proximity to Black males in the shower - and fiscal conservatives everywhere.

Do we hear crickets?

---

[142]   http://newsone.com/nation/newsonestaff4/government-aid-cut-poverty-rate-nearly-in-half/

[143] http://www.inc.com/ss/9-best-countries-start-business-right-now#0

[144]   http://mangans.blogspot.com/2011/04/ikea-workers-complain-of-discrimination.html

---

We already know that Jefferson County recently declared bankruptcy and Detroit isn't far behind. The reasons for both cities failure is 100 percent racial, though Koch and other adherents to strict free market/capitalism principles will assert it so combination of socialism and evil leftist policies (though Norway is doing just fine Dr. Sowell).

No, it's just that this system of economics never factored in how the invisible hand guiding capitalism would be covered up by the highly discernible hand of the Black Undertow. "If it fits, you can't acquit!"

Back to Detroit:

Here's what Mayor Dave Bing and Detroit City Council members didn't want anyone to know when they met behind closed doors in late October to discuss a still unreleased $1.7 million report from Ernst & Young on the city's finances: They're a lot worse than we thought.

Detroit is fast running out of cash. Already, roughly half the city's vendors aren't being paid each month, City Hall sources say, and some are waiting 18 months for their checks.

By late December, the acute cash flow problem may mean Detroit won't be able to fully cover payroll. And by April, it will be out of cash.

Gov. Rick Snyder hasn't accepted the deficit reduction plan the Bing administration submitted last summer because the numbers don't add up. Without approval, the city can't sell bonds to finance much-needed water department projects, or to get the Woodward light rail project started.
The budget gap pegged at $155 million last spring may now be twice that.

So what are the mayor and council doing with the cold, hard facts presented at that October meeting? Squabbling.

Icy relations between the 11th and 13th floors of City Hall are again standing in the way of swift and decisive action to avert a financial catastrophe.

Bing had been meeting with certain council members for weeks on a plan to cut spending, but those members felt sand-bagged when he announced he'd be open to having Gov. Rick Snyder appoint him as emergency manager.

Snyder isn't going to do that. And it's not necessary at the moment anyway.

The mayor and council ought to be able to resolve this themselves. Some on the council have been pushing the mayor to immediately lay off 1,500 city workers, including 500 cops and 300 firefighters. It is a painful choice, and one Bing is resisting out of public safety concerns, but it is likely to be unavoidable.[145]

Make every majority Black city a Enterprise zone; make every majority Black county an Enterprise Zone; double taxes on every Whitopia and majority white major city and divert those funds immediately to Detroit and other failed Black Undertow areas and build a statue to Jack Kemp (naturally, where he is in the shower) while you're at it... and you still make a dent in the problem.

For this reason, *Stuff Black People Don't Like* includes Enterprise Zones. Black Undertow areas already have plenty of street enterprise going on, and to create an EZ would inevitably lead to gentrification and the methodical displacement of such street enterprise activity.

Then, they'd have to get a job, where their labor won't bring in the type of profit margins as pushing illegal narcotics. No offense, but the top degrees with **lowest unemployment rate** aren't exactly those awarded by **barber school**. [146]

"America I AM": What is the real "Black Imprint" in America?

Do you live far away from a major urban area – such as one of these cities - and commute to work?[147]

---

[145]http://detnews.com/article/20111113/OPINION03/111130305/Column--Detroit-nearing-a-cash-crisis#ixzz1doAVBi2n

[146] http://news.yahoo.com/blogs/lookout/10-college-majors-lowest-unemployment-rates-163049193.html

[147] _cities_with_large_African_American_populations

Do you watch your local nightly newscast and shake your head at the stories of human misery, crime, corruption, murder, and mayhem?

Do you watch the local nightly newscast from the living room of your home in a comfortable, safe neighborhood? Chances are, that neighborhood is in a Whitopia.

The collapse of major cities (population of more than 100,000) such as Atlanta, Washington D.C., Birmingham, Memphis, Detroit, Baltimore, Columbia (South Carolina), St. Louis, Richmond, Cleveland, Cincinnati, Philadelphia, Harrisburg (Pennsylvania), New Orleans, Newark and others on this list, warranted the creation of Whitopia's surrounding these abandoned metropolitan areas (consult this link on Thomas Sowell vs. Norway to learn more).

It is with this in mind that we now consider the following exhibit:

> Tavis Smiley presents "America I Am" The African American Imprint at the National Geographic Museum in Washington D.C. Presented by Walmart, Microsoft, Northern Trust and the Boys & Girls Club of America.[148]

What is the Black imprint in America? An online exhibit tour of the "America I Am" gallery is available here.

---

[148] http://www.americaiam.org/Pages/home.aspx

The real Black imprint (you've heard of a "Carbon footprint" so perhaps it should be the "Black footprint") is not the pictures you will see in the Tavis Smiley exhibit.

To understand what the real Black imprint in America is one only need to look at Detroit. Or any of the other cities mentioned above.[149]

Exclude two of those cities however, as both Atlanta and Washington D.C. are undergoing rapid gentrification, which threatens to destroy the firmly ensconced Black political class in those cities. Black leaders in Atlanta wrote a memo about their constituents dispossession by free market forces (white people buying up cheap property) and what their reaction should be in the face of losing power in the city.

---

[149]   http://newsfeed.time.com/2011/03/24/vanishing-city-the-story-behind-detroit%E2%80%99s-shocking-population-decline/

The same thing will happen soon in Washington D.C., where *The Washington Post* is already lamenting the displacement of Black people by the gentrifying white population. That crime rates are falling as whites move into the city and crime rates are rising in the surrounding suburbs that Black people end up (most notably Prince Georges County) is not a connection the *Post* will report on... ever.[150]

One can only guess the percentage of city employees in both Atlanta and Washington D.C. (consider MARTA and The METRO rail transportation systems in those cities) that are Black. We would wager in both cities it is more than 90 percent.

One could also spend all day trying to quantify the opportunity costs lost by whites living in suburban of both cities who were forced to commute two hours each day so they could live in a peaceful city.

As gentrification raises the white percentage of the population in each city, when will city employees reflect those changes?[151]

Worse, people in these cities will slowly learn that public schools and public transportation can work, if you remove one variable from the equation. Just **look at Portland**, where Disingenuous White Liberals (DWL) there bemoan the fact that things actually work and look forward to the day they don't.

This, Tavis Smiley, is the real Black Imprint in America. That Detroit is the butt of jokes across the world is why one Black writer in Atlanta wrote this:

---

[150] http://www.washingtonpost.com/local/pondering-meaning-of-changing-dc-demographics/2011/03/30/AF02nCHD_story.html

[151] http://www.washingtoncitypaper.com/articles/40614/will-white-identity-politics-come-to-post-post-racial-dc/

Detroit is a microcosm of Black America. I believe if you cannot love Detroit, you cannot fully love Black people. The Detroit Metropolitan area represents the best and the worst that Black folks in this country have to offer. The Black middle class was solidified in and around Detroit with steady unionized blue collar labor in the auto industry.

The middle class expanded as more Black folks with college educations occupied managerial positions. Detroiters experienced and vigilantly fought the racisms of housing redlining, riots, as well as White and Black flight. Detroit has benefited and suffered at the hands of White and Black leadership. If there is a city that tells us about the promise and perils of Blackness, it's Detroit. I'm so interested in what happens in Detroit because if we can turn it around, we can turn around the rest of our cities.[152]

---

[152] http://atlantapost.com/2010/06/02/opinion-abandon-detroit-abandon-black-america/

Detroit is being abandoned by Black people who have the means to leave. Areas of the city are being abandoned by the Black city government and turned over to nature.[153]

Sadly, Detroit is not the only collapsing American city. Birmingham, Cleveland, Cincinnati, Memphis, and, well every city on this list, are failing for exactly the same reason: the Black Imprint.[154]

Atlanta and Washington D.C. are thriving (or on the verge of thriving) for reasons that aren't too hard to explain.

Chances are, if you go to the "America I Am" exhibit, any pictures of Detroit under Black governance will be censored (just go here to see them).[155]

Far too much focus is put on Detroit though, as many of the cities **listed here** have property available for purchase that rival Detroit's famed prices.[156]

The Black Imprint can be felt in those cities listed above and will no doubt be left out of the discussion at Tavis Smiley's exhibit.

Funny though, when the Black Imprint is removed through gentrification -- as in D.C. and Atlanta -- everyone seems to complain.

Why don't these nice Disingenuous White Liberals who write for *The Post* or live in Portland just move into these areas they care so much about?

---

[153]http://online.wsj.com/article/SB100014240527487042920045752305322 48715858.html

[154]http://en.wikipedia.org/wiki/List_of_U.S._cities_with_large_African_Amer ican_populations

[155]http://www.time.com/time/photogallery/0,29307,1864272_1810098,00.ht ml

[156]   http://www.guardian.co.uk/business/2010/mar/02/detroit-homes-mortgage-foreclosures-80

#519. Home Improvement

When attempting to ascertain the ultimate Pre-Obama America television show of the past thirty years, a number of contenders leap to the front immediately.

The saccharine FULL HOUSE was a show set in San Francisco that implanted a highly positive image of that Stuff White People Like (SWPL) city in the viewers mind, who would be blissfully unaware of what life was actually like on the bay.

In actuality, virtually every sitcom that has aired on ABC, CBS, NBC and Fox in the past 30 years could be considered blissfully unaware of the sweeping societal changes that are transpiring in the real world.

Sure some shows have an agenda, but most exist in a vacuum as if the United States had never undergone such massive demographic changes. Pressure groups have long bemoaned the lack of diversity on network television and in sitcoms, but drastic demographic changes must be pushed slowly so the populace will hardly notice (see MODERN FAMILY and GLEE). With the cancellation of M.A.N.T.I.S, Black people faced a traumatic setback in the goal of landing another THE COSBY SHOW style hit, a blow they have yet to recover from fully.

This study, Prime Time Now 2001-2002, is a diversity study that documents the gross absence of Black people in sitcoms. It's now 2011 and the latest network television shows continue to be bathed in a sea of whiteness, an occasionally life boat thrown out to Black actors to ensure such studies won't be commissioned again.[157]

One television show in the past 30 years can be labeled as the ultimate Pre-Obama America sitcom and it was set in the outskirts of The Motor City, ostensibly in an alternate reality where Black people rarely interact with white people (of course, this is considered the real world).

That show? HOME IMPROVEMENT. Tim Allen's show about a bumbling tool-man, loving husband and father to three sons is set in a lily-white Detroit suburb and rarely does the harsh reality of life in that Black-run city interfere with his families existence.

---

[157] http://www.childrennow.org/uploads/documents/fall_colors_2001.pdf

A show that also ran on ABC, THE DREW CAREY SHOW, was set in Cleveland and many people found the whitewashing of that majority Black city unsettling. STUFF BLACK PEOPLE DON'T LIKE can locate no articles that point out the lack of Black characters in the strange universe HOME IMPROVEMENT was set in, perhaps because anyone from the real Detroit greatly desired living in that fictional world.[158]

Consider the uproar a new ABC show entitled Detroit 1-8-7 is causing, casting that crumbling city in a more realistic, gritty role it serves on a daily basis:

> Growing up near Detroit in the '70s and '80s, I was jealous of other cities that had their own TV shows. New York City, L.A., Boston, Chicago — even Milwaukee had both Happy Days and Laverne and Shirley. (Milwaukee!) Eventually, Detroit got a few sitcoms (Martin, Home Improvement), but no series ever really explored the dramatic possibilities of this sprawling Rust Belt city.
>
> Cut to the first scene of Detroit 1-8-7, which makes its debut on ABC Sept. 21. A policewoman shows us the homicide-division whiteboard, too small to accommodate the growing list of murders. "We may be the last assembly line left in Detroit," she says. Later, a homicide cop is searching for a spent bullet on a roadside and finds it — after sorting through a slew of other bullets.

---

[158]http://www.cleveland.com/homegrown/index.ssf?/tv/more/drew/herodrew.html

It's not exactly a tourism brochure. Some locals say Hollywood is giving the city a Gucci-shod kick while it's down: 24% unemployment, a hobbled auto industry and now this? ABC didn't help matters by shooting the pilot in Atlanta or by making a promo that erroneously gave Detroit the highest murder rate in the U.S. (It comes in fourth.) City councilman Kwame Kenyatta sponsored a resolution asking ABC to change the show's title, which he says equates the city with murder. (187 is police code and slang for homicide.) The resolution failed. But the question remains: Does a show set in a troubled city have a responsibility beyond the ratings?[159]

The only 1-8-7 in HOME IMPROVEMENT was the running gag of Tim Taylor (played by Tim Allen) constantly hurting himself on the show he hosted within show, TOOL TIME. It's hard to conjure up a more family-friendly show then HOME IMPROVEMENT, with jokes mature enough to fool young people watching but entertain parents at the same time.

Still aired in syndication today, the show holds up remarkably well as opposed to other 1990s (and even 2000-era) comedies.

Watching the show and growing up with the Taylor family (HOME IMPROVEMENT was one of the few shows that maintained a high level of continuity and would constantly allude to prior episodes in other seasons) one was tragically unaware of the dire situation unfolding in the real-world of Detroit.

A brief synopsis of the show:

---

[159] http://www.time.com/time/magazine/article/0,9171,2013831,00.html

The series centered on the Taylor family, which consists of father Tim (Tim Allen), his spouse Jill (Patricia Richardson) and their three children: the oldest, Brad (Zachery Ty Bryan), the middle child Randy (Jonathan Taylor Thomas) and youngest, Mark (Taran Noah Smith). The Taylors live in suburban Detroit, Michigan and have a neighbor named Wilson (Earl Hindman) who is often the go-to guy for solving Tim and Jill's problems.

Tim is a stereotypical American male, who loves power tools, cars and sports (especially the local Detroit teams). He is a former salesman for the fictional Binford Tool company, and is very much a cocky, accident-prone know-it-all. Witty but flippant, Tim jokes around a lot, even at inopportune times. Family life was boisterous, with the two oldest children, Brad and Randy, tormenting the much younger, Mark, while continually testing and pestering each other. This rough by-play happened especially throughout the first four seasons, and was revisited occasionally until Jonathan Taylor Thomas left at the beginning of the eighth season.

Brad, popular and athletic, was often the moving factor, who engaged before thinking, a tendency which regularly landed him in trouble. Randy, a year younger, was the comedian of the pack; known for his quick-thinking, wisecracks, and smart mouth. He had more common sense than Brad but was not immune to trouble. Mark was somewhat of a mama's boy, though later in the series (in the seventh season) he grew into a teenage outcast who dressed in black clothing (a goth). Meanwhile, Brad became interested in cars like his father and took up soccer. Randy joined the school drama club, and later the school newspaper; in the eighth season, he left for Costa Rica.[160]

---

[160] http://en.wikipedia.org/wiki/Home_Improvement_%28TV_series%29

A ratings titan, Home Improvement showed us a world inhabited by the Taylor family (Tim, Jill, Brad, Randy and Mark), Tim's affable assistant on Tool Time Al Borland, the vivacious Heidi and the lovable, erudite neighbor Wilson Wilson Jr.

It was a show that was a testament to Robert Putnam's study on how diversity breeds distrust in a community, for the world of HOME IMPROVEMENT seemed to be a thriving, tightly nit group of white Americans that would congregate at the local hardware to swap stories of life, family, cars and the dreams, aspirations and hopes for the future.

Putnam's study shows a much different for the real United States:

> IT HAS BECOME increasingly popular to speak of racial and ethnic diversity as a civic strength. From multicultural festivals to pronouncements from political leaders, the message is the same: our differences make us stronger.
>
> But a massive new study, based on detailed interviews of nearly 30,000 people across America, has concluded just the opposite. Harvard political scientist Robert Putnam -- famous for "Bowling Alone," his 2000 book on declining civic engagement -- has found that the greater the diversity in a community, the fewer people vote and the less they volunteer, the less they give to charity and work on community projects. In the most diverse communities, neighbors trust one another about half as much as they do in the most homogenous settings. The study, the largest ever on civic engagement in America, found that virtually all measures of civic health are lower in more diverse settings.
>
> "The extent of the effect is shocking," says Scott Page, a University of Michigan political scientist.[161]

161

http://www.boston.com/news/globe/ideas/articles/2007/08/05/the_downside_of_diversity/

HOME IMPROVEMENT is the ultimate sitcom that glorifies Pre-Obama America, and though it was made in the 1990s, the show reminds of all that was once good in this nation. Sadly the show completely excuses any mention of Black Detroit from polite conversation, a city that recently sent out 60,000 incorrect tax bills.[162]

Detroit, a city that may have to close half of its schools (only 50 percent graduate anyways, so some would say they are already closed) after initially closing 40 schools earlier in 2010. [163]

The world of HOME IMPROVEMENT is a thriving one, a white one and a peaceful one. Detroit 1-8-7 seems light years away from the world the Taylor's inhabit, though it should be right around the corner from their fictional home in the Detroit suburbs.

We have talked about Detroit before here at SBPDL, though we have never brought up the sore subject of the happy fictional Taylor clan and HOME IMPROVEMENT.

Stuff Black People Don't Like includes HOME IMPROVEMENT, a sitcom that shows normal suburban life in a Whitopia. Juxtaposed with the reality of Detroit, a city destroyed not by regulation, unions, socialism or natural disaster, but by white flight and a majority Black-run government, HOME IMPROVEMENT shows us all what Pre-Obama America was really like.

---

[162]   http://www.dailymail.co.uk/news/article-1347711/60-000-Detroit-homeowners-left-incorrect-tax-bills-sent-city.html

[163] http://www.theblaze.com/stories/detroit-may-close-half-of-its-schools-to-pay-for-union-benefits/

Black Privilege articulated in One Article: Grand Rapids Public Schools punished for punishing Black Students Disproportionately

Remember that in Black Run America (BRA), Black people are never at fault for their actions. Black (mis)behavior can only be explained by rampant racism inherent in a corrupt system that demands that they abide by the same rules as everyone else.

Only when you consider how BRA influences governing decisions in America will this story make sense. The Grand Rapid Public School System in Michigan must divert money from education to address the disproportionate suspensions of Black students:

> The state has cited Grand Rapids Public Schools for suspending a "significantly disproportionate" number of black and special education students -- a move that has forced the district to shift $1 million in federal funds to address the problem.

> The district is reexamining policies and creating early intervention strategies, but it has not stopped suspending students for serious offenses, Superintendent Bernard Taylor said this week, seeking to dispel misconceptions.
> "It is a misnomer that anyone has been told not to suspend students," he said.

"Every concerted effort is being made to address issues around safety," Taylor said. "We have built a support structure around students that is designed to keep them in school -- but not at all costs. We are not talking about weapons violations, bomb threats or fights."

He said the district is under sanction by the state Education Department requiring it to redirect $1 million in special education funds into general education "to deal with the over suspension of special education students and African American males."

The state monitored Grand Rapids for rates of suspension and expulsion greater than 10 days for black students with disabilities, and for all students with disabilities.

"They were selected for monitoring because the data reported by GRPS indicated a significant discrepancy in the rate of suspensions for all students with disabilities as well as African American students with disabilities," the state reported.

GRPS was directed to develop a plan and be in compliance within a year.

The state's findings came in the spring of 2010, but they were disclosed by Taylor this week because of growing public questions about suspension policies. The report, which reviewed 2008-09 data, revealed that out of 268 special education suspensions/expulsions, 186 were black, 34 Hispanic, 29 white, 18 multi-ethnic and 1 Asian. Ottawa Hills had the most of the high schools with 22, all black students.
The building principal ultimately makes the decision whether someone warrants suspension, administrators said.

The state said GRPS was required to reserve 15 percent of its federal IDEA (Individuals with Disability Education Act) funds for early intervention services. The state says this is not a financial sanction, but a requirement that more special education funds be used for programs to prevent high rates of suspension and expulsion.

"We began last March doing some pretty comprehensive planning involving principals and departments such as student services, to figure out how we could not suspend as much and also come up with some alternative interventions," said Veronica Lake, the district's executive director for accountability and compliance.

For example, she said, intervention rooms were implemented this school year.

Taylor said what gets students suspended often is that catch-all category, disruptive behavior.

"'I think direction from the board is going to have to be obtained in order for us to seriously deal with this issue about over-representation of student groups that comprise the highest number of suspensions," Taylor told his board Monday.

The district has nearly 19,000 students and blacks represent more than 40 percent of the population. Taylor said the issue of minority suspension rates has come up in previous decades.
"It is clearly something that is not a recent phenomenon."[164]

---

[164] http://www.mlive.com/news/grand-rapids/index.ssf/2011/03/state_says_grand_rapids_school.html

We no longer direct money towards advancing the best and brightest in America, but instead allocate money to uplift the obtuse and the miscreants who cause trouble in classes. Worse: schools are punished for punishing those who act out in class, if those punished happen to be overwhelmingly Black.

It should be noted that those who don't get into trouble in Grand Rapids require bribes from a community initiative called *I Believe, I Become* where they get free laptops for completing the program, because the graduation rates in this school system that disproportionately suspends Black students is abysmal:

> Success stories of high school heroes such as Campbell are being shared by a community coalition launching a grassroots initiative called I Believe, I Become, with the goal of improving high school graduation rates and eliminating the achievement gap between white and minority students.
>
> The campaign -- reportedly backed by the Doug and Maria DeVos Foundation and 50 community partners -- had a soft launch this summer with billboards showing the smiling faces of local students. I Believe, I Become also is rewarding 250 middle school students who complete an extended-day summer school with an $800 laptop computer and 200 high school students who recover credits in summer school with a paid work experience.
>
> The first of four five-week community development meetings kicks off Thursday evening with a forum for residents of central neighborhoods.
>
> Similar series will be scheduled in 2011 in western, eastern and southern neighborhoods, which are home to about 15,000 children, many of them economically disadvantaged and Hispanic or black.

To entice community participation, the organizers are providing dinner, child care, raffle prizes and $25 gift certificates to the first 250 adults, just for attending. "To use the wisdom of the residents, we've got to respect what will bring them to the table," said Jeremy DeRoo, executive director of Lighthouse Communities, a Grand Rapids nonprofit community development organization.

While the community development planning will be compressed into a few weeks, the commitment to work the plan likely will extend a decade or more, said Joe Jones, of the communications group E.E. Milestone.

"Grand Rapids Public Schools can do a lot, but it can't be expected to do it all," said Jones, noting that only about 25 percent of a child's time is spent in school. "What we're talking about here is everything it takes to teach a child."

The school district is launching several secondary reforms in the coming year with the hope of improving graduation rates, even though the state is imposing tough new graduation requirements for the Class of 2011.

Four-year graduation rates from 2009 at the district's alternative schools is dismal -- as low as 8 percent at Southeast Career Pathways.

Graduation rates also are low at the district's comprehensive high schools: Ottawa Hills, 65 percent; Central, 71 percent; Creston, 72 percent; Union, 74 percent.

Graduation rates are 93 percent at City High School and Grand Rapids Montessori High School.[165]

Even worse than the poor graduation rates are the academic records of those who do graduate:

> GRPS loses a third of its freshman before graduation. In some schools, over half of freshman have cumulative grade point averages less than 2.0 on a 4.0 scale, she said.[166]

That school systems are now punished for punishing Black students that act out in class because they can't follow the same rules that white and Asians students have no problem following is a cause for federal involvement.

[165] http://www.mlive.com/news/grand-rapids/index.ssf/2010/08/campaign_to_improve_grand_rapi.html

[166] http://www.mlive.com/news/grand-rapids/index.ssf/2010/04/grand_rapids_public_schools_ho_1.html

Never mind that in such diverse geographic areas as Charlotte, Seattle, Chicago, and Delaware that the one constant variable in school discipline is a propensity for Black students to be overly represented in those suspended.[167]

This could never explain why the proficiency of Black male students was found to be much lower than anticipated, right?[168]

The federal government will soon require every school system to be cognizant of Black student's proclivities for not abiding by the rules governing proper behavior. Their rebellion will be a state-sanctioned form of self-expression.

Money dedicated to teaching and educating will now be diverted for discipline and being tolerant of those who are intolerant of the behavioral guidelines in class.

In Black Run America (BRA) the worst behavior by Black people is protected and ultimately excused by those in power. Black people can never be shown in a negative light and for Grand Rapids School Public Schools to dare defy this decree is grounds for immediate action.

It seems the federal government is demanding a cessation of rule enforcement in schools, because those who disobey and are reprimanded for scholastic infractions have the misfortune of being overwhelmingly Black.

To the tune of $1 million, Grand Rapids Public Schools must now shift money that they don't have to address the problem of Black students misbehaving.

---

[167] http://www.seattlepi.com/disciplinegap/61940_newdiscipline12.shtml

[168] http://www.nytimes.com/2010/11/09/education/09gap.html

Thomas Sowell vs. Norway: Why Failed Liberal Policies in the United States work in Scandinavia

Reading a recent Thomas Sowell column[169] bemoaning liberalism, the nanny-state mentality, and the welfare-state in the United States for some reason jogged our memory of a piece published in *Inc.* magazine. That latter article discussed how socialism works in the Scandinavian nation of Norway, a country that has some of the highest rates of entrepreneurship in the world. Sowell's article discussed how Black people are now fleeing cities and states that their ancestors once fled to during "the great migration" of the early 20th century.[170]

Sowell wrote this:

169

http://townhall.com/columnists/thomassowell/2011/03/29/voting_with_their _feet/page/2

170　http://www.inc.com/magazine/20110201/in-norway-start-ups-say-ja-to-socialism.html

---

140

The latest published data from the 2010 census show how people are moving from place to place within the United States. In general, people are voting with their feet against places where the liberal, welfare-state policies favored by the intelligentsia are most deeply entrenched.

When you break it down by race and ethnicity, it is all too painfully clear what is happening. Both whites and blacks are leaving California, the poster state for the liberal, welfare-state and nanny-state philosophy.

Whites are also fleeing the big northeastern liberal, welfare states like Massachusetts, New York, New Jersey and Pennsylvania, as well as the same kinds of states in the midwest, such as Michigan, Ohio and Illinois.

In more recent decades, blacks have been moving back to the South, however. While the overall black population of the northeastern and midwestern states has not declined in the past ten years, except in Michigan and Illinois, the net increase of the black population nationwide has increasingly been in the South. About half of the national growth of the black population took place in the South in the 1970s, two-thirds in the 1990s and three-quarters in the past 10 years.

While the mass migrations of blacks out of the South in the early 20th century was to places where there were already established black communities, such as New York, Chicago and Philadelphia, much of the current movement of blacks is away from existing concentrations of black populations.

Blacks are moving to suburbs, and even to cities like Minneapolis. Overall, the racial residential segregation patterns are declining in the great majority of the largest major metropolitan areas.[171]

171

http://townhall.com/columnists/thomassowell/2011/03/29/voting_with_their_feet/page/2

Are we the only people who caught that slippage of truth? White people with the monetary means are fleeing cities and states that have created vast nanny-states and welfare-states to take care of Black populations that fled the South. Those policies -- enacted by liberals -- are forcing whites to leave, because the costs associated with taking care of a Black population disproportionately reliant on the state have become too great to defend.

Sowell then went on to lament the fate of Detroit:

> Detroit is perhaps the most striking example of a once thriving city ruined by years of liberal social policies. Before the ghetto riot of 1967, Detroit's black population had the highest rate of home-ownership of any black urban population in the country, and their unemployment rate was just 3.4 percent.

> It was not despair that fueled the riot. It was the riot which marked the beginning of the decline of Detroit to its current state of despair. Detroit's population today is only half of what it once was, and its most productive people have been the ones who fled.

> Treating businesses and affluent people as prey, rather than assets, often pays off politically in the short run-- and elections are held in the short run. Killing the goose that lays the golden egg is a viable political strategy.

> As whites were the first to start leaving Detroit, its then mayor Coleman Young saw this only as an exodus of people who were likely to vote against him, enhancing his re-election prospects.

> But what was good for Mayor Young was disastrous for Detroit.

> There is a lesson here somewhere, but it is very doubtful if either the intelligentsia or the politicians will learn it.

Detroit didn't collapse because of liberal policies. Vermont (with a Black population of .5 percent)[172] is an incredibly liberal state with a generous welfare and nanny-state, and unlike Detroit, it isn't on the verge of completely failure (this *New York Times* article on how the city of Detroit is abandoning blighted neighborhoods is incredible). Detroit collapsed because white flight transferred ownership of the city (meaning control of the government, city council, school board, police, etc.) over to Black people.[173]

If liberal policies, as Sowell contests, are the reasons behind the monumental collapse of Detroit, then what is the reason for Norway's success. Why do entrepreneurs there have an easier time starting up businesses in a land with much higher taxation then in the United States? The liberal policies enacted in Norway benefit that homogeneous population, whereas the liberal policies passed in Detroit (and in Oakland, which was recently profiled in *Townhall* magazine -- April 2011 issue, page 42 -- as yet another city where liberal ideas doomed that city and not its majority population) seem to bring about only ruin.

Why is that? The *Inc.* article reports:

> Norway, population five million, is a very small, very rich country. It is a cold country and, for half the year, a dark country. (The sun sets in late November in Mo i Rana. It doesn't rise again until the end of January.) This is a place where entire cities smell of drying fish—an odor not unlike the smell of rotting fish—and where, in the most remote parts, one must be careful to avoid polar bears. The food isn't great.

---

[172] http://www.ipoaa.com/us_black_population.htm

[173] http://www.nytimes.com/2011/04/06/us/06detroit.html?_r=1&hp

---

Bear strikes, darkness, and whale meat notwithstanding, Norway is also an exceedingly pleasant place to make a home. It ranked third in Gallup's latest global happiness survey. The unemployment rate, just 3.5 percent, is the lowest in Europe and one of the lowest in the world. Thanks to a generous social welfare system, poverty is almost nonexistent.

Norway is also full of entrepreneurs like Wiggo Dalmo. Rates of start-up creation here are among the highest in the developed world, and Norway has more entrepreneurs per capita than the United States, according to the latest report by the Global Entrepreneurship Monitor, a Boston-based research consortium. A 2010 study released by the U.S. Small Business Administration reported a similar result: Although America remains near the top of the world in terms of entrepreneurial aspirations -- that is, the percentage of people who want to start new things—in terms of actual start-up activity, our country has fallen behind not just Norway but also Canada, Denmark, and Switzerland.[174]

---

[174] http://www.inc.com/magazine/20110201/in-norway-start-ups-say-ja-to-socialism.html

Yes, people do start companies in the United States and comparing a diverse nation of 312 (not counting illegal immigrants) million people to a tiny, all-white nation of 5 million people isn't exactly fair. But it is intriguing to juxtapose the two articles, and realize the truths that are so obviously inescapable.

A good friend told us over dinner recently that a nation can have a Black population or it can have a space program. The costs of both, however, no honest accountant can sign off on.

The United States is scrapping its space program for a reason; it does have something to do with the fact that NASA can't find a Black engineer, but more to do with the rising costs of caring for a population of 36 million that disproportionately receive Federal aid to exist and subsist.

Prince George's County in Maryland is considered to be the greatest place for upper-class Black people in the nation. Largely a creation of the out-of-control Federal government growth in Washington D.C., that county boasts an artificially-created Black middle-class. It is also home to Black people who are being displaced from Washington D.C. in that cities conversion to a white majority, which is having the unintended consequence of exploding the crime rate there.[175]
Starting a small business in the United States is still a great idea, but eventually you must adhere to an incredible gauntlet of labor laws and be compliant with the EEOC. That is a problem the Norwegians no longer face. The costs of doing business in a diverse United States city (such as Detroit) are exponentially higher then in Norway's worst city. (

Sowell also pointed out that the Black population is exploding in Minneapolis. Situated in a state renowned for its liberal policies and generous welfare, one particular group of people took advantage of this benevolence without any shame:

---

[175]   http://washingtonexaminer.com/local/dc/2011/04/slayings-across-region-2011

Minnesota long has waved a welcome mat for war refugees -- first Koreans, then Hmong, Vietnamese and Ethiopians. Minneapolis provided subsidized housing and generous benefits. The newcomers found low-wage jobs at chicken-processing factories where English was not required.

The first wave of Somalis arrived here after 1991, when the country descended into a fierce clan-based civil war that still rages. More Somalis came each year, and family members soon followed, as was mandated under U.S. law. Others moved here from other U.S. cities.

Many in the community started families, opened businesses and achieved financial stability. They wired money to relatives back home, followed Somali news in ethnic papers and websites, and in some cases invested in Somali businesses even as their children became American doctors and lawyers.

Others became mired in brutal poverty. Many of the women were illiterate, and old men who had herded goats struggled in the rugged winters. Unemployment and school dropout rates soared. So did incidents of intolerance.

"We're an obvious minority here, and have a different religion and culture," said Abdiaziz Warsame, 37, an interpreter and youth counselor who has worked with local gangs such as the Somali Hard Boys and RPG's. "So people feel a high level of racism."

A 2007 tally counted 35,000 Somalis in Minnesota, the vast majority of whom live in Little Mogadishu, the gritty Minneapolis zone between two highways and the Mississippi River.[176]

---

[176] http://articles.latimes.com/2009/nov/25/nation/la-na-little-mogadishu25-2009nov25/2

A city; a state; a nation is but a reflection of its citizens. Detroit once thrived when it was a majority white city. Under majority Black-rule it is the laughing-stock of the world. Liberal policies seem to be working fine in Vermont; strangely they fail -- and conservatives point this out with glee -- when Black people are in charge, as this is an easy way to blame Black failure on liberalism.

Strange that Norway can succeed and prosper under the same conditions. Vermont too. But a sizable Black population that relies on that same nanny-state and welfare system is a lethal combination.

A nation can have a space program or a Black population, but it can't have both. The costs to the state requires far too much capital, so one must go. The United States axed the former.

A better metaphor for 21st century America cannot be found. Sowell can blame liberal policies for wrecking Northeastern states and cities, but he shows in his column that "the great migration" by Blacks from the South to these places might have put too much stress on the nanny-state and welfare-state in these areas.

Norway, meanwhile, has high rates of taxation, high rates of employment and high rates of success.

This article is not an endorsement of socialism by any means. However, it is an endorsement of this question: Would you rather live in socialist Norway or Black-run Detroit (a city that Black people run away from and proud Black families still try and defend)?[177]

---

[177]   http://www.theatlantic.com/national/archive/2011/03/detroit-was-like-cheers-everyone-knew-your-name/72226/

The Visible Black Hand of Economics

The world is nothing more than all the tiny things you left behind.

- Gran Torino

In reading the powerful essay on Highland Park, Michigan (*Return to a Darker Age*) that HW put together, the whole concept of the Visible Black Hand governing economics came to me in a moment of clarity rivalling the epiphany the esteemed Dr. Emmett Brown had when he visualized the flux capacitor. [178]

By a strange twist of fate, the Clint Eastwood directed film *Gran Torino* was set in Highland Park. Odd, the population of actual city is 93 percent Black; watching Eastwood's insipid movie, you'd have never known this fact. [179]

If you've been a regular reader of *Stuff Black People Don't Like*, then you are aware that some key terms for understanding life in Black-Run America (BRA) originated here: Climate Change; the Black Undertow; Man-Made Climate Change; Disingenuous White Liberals (DWLs); Black Fictional Heroes; and now, we give you the reality of Visible Black Hand governing economics.

While reading about the nearly all-Black inhabitants of Highland Park and their inability to create, innovate and even

---

[178] http://www.occidentaldissent.com/2012/01/10/return-to-a-darker-age

[179] http://www.wsws.org/articles/2008/dec2008/high-d06.shtml

maintain an economy (with the discriminatory remains of a long-gone civilization providing them shelter, signs of structural inequality), my mind drifted to the city envisioned by Henry Ford once his Highland Park Ford Plant was built and thriving roughly one hundred years ago.[180]

Is 2012 Highland Park, where the Highland Park Schools recently failed an Emergency Manager Review, the vision Ford had as he looked upon plant back in 1912?[181]

Between 1910 - 1920, Highland Park would expand more than an order of magnitude in its population (from 4,000 to 46,000). Now, the population of Highland Park is around 11,000 and the last inhabitant to leave won't have to be reminded to turn the lights off: just as 42,000 home owners in Wayne County[182] could soon lose their homes because they can't pay the taxes, Highland Park recently turned off 66 percent of its streetlights:

> Highland Park, Michigan, a city in the greater Detroit area, is the latest town to implement dramatic austerity measures, according to the Associated Press.
>
> With $58 million in municipal debt and a $60,000 monthly electric bill that it can't pay, Highland Park has elected to remove 1,000 of its 1,500 streetlights -- not just turning the power off, but tearing the poles themselves out of the ground.
>
> It's a strategy that's unlikely to fix most of Highland Park's economic woes. The town's unemployment rate

[180] http://en.wikipedia.org/wiki/Highland_Park,_Michigan#Demographics

[181]   http://www.huffingtonpost.com/2012/01/05/highland-park-schools-emergency-manager_n_1184623.html

[182]   http://www.freep.com/article/20120108/NEWS05/201080511/Unpaid-taxes-put-thousands-of-metro-homeowners-at-risk-of-foreclosure?odyssey=tab%7Ctopnews%7Ctext%7CFRONTPAGE

is 22 percent -- more than twice the national rate -- and 42 percent of residents live below the poverty line.[183]

How many millions of people worked in Detroit, punched their card, endured long-shifts at the factory, all the while hoping that their children would one day live in a better city than they did? How many thousands of people raised families in Highland Park, walking their children down the same sidewalks that are now bathed in the silent darkness where laughter once preceded it?

White people left Highland Park - well, they abandoned it really - to the current Black inhabitants of the city. Just like thousands of other cities across the nation, the fate was of the Highland Park was sealed by this gesture. No formal surrender took place nor was a ceremony commemorating the transfer of power necessary.

Adam Smith's concept of the invisible hand goes something like this:

> In economics, invisible hand or invisible hand of the market is the term economists use to describe the self-regulating nature of the marketplace... individual ambition benefits society, even if the ambitious have no benevolent intentions.[184]

In Black-Run America, the ultimate aim of the government, church, media/entertainment industry, academic sector, and private sector is the enhancement of the quality of life for Black people, at the expense of everyone else.

Worse, on the dime of everyone else through a redistribution of tax-revenue to Black people via TANF/Welfare, EBT/Food

---

[183]   http://www.huffingtonpost.com/2011/11/07/highland-park-sreetlights_n_1079909.html?

[184] http://en.wikipedia.org/wiki/Invisible_hand

Stamps, Section 8 Housing, and the prison industry (police/incarceration/probation/court costs) that disproportionately go toward the Black Undertow.

It has been official government policy for some time that the collective needs of Black people outweigh individual ambitions in America, negating the entire concept of Smith's invisible hand. DWLs understand, hence their desire to live in Whitopia's like Portland, San Francisco, Boulder, Washington D.C., and Silicon Valley where the nullifying presence of visible Black Hand governing economics has been minimized (in the case of D.C., priced out and pushed to Prince George's County)

Consider Frédéric Bastiat parable of the broken window:

> [It] illustrate[s] why destruction, and the money spent to recover from destruction, is actually not a net-benefit to society. The parable, also known as the broken window fallacy or glazier's fallacy, demonstrates how opportunity costs, as well as the law of unintended consequences, affect economic activity in ways that are "unseen" or ignored. [185]

The Climate Change in major metropolitan areas like Detroit, Atlanta, Birmingham, Memphis, Cleveland, St. Louis, Philadelphia and Milwaukee is a form of destruction. Knowing that the Black people who inherit the city will face structural inequality, because they lack the ability to collectively sustain an economy - whether its a major city like Detroit or a small one like Highland Park - the destruction of the that city's key sources of tax-revenue is guaranteed. [186]

You can see the visible Black Hand of economics at work when you drive into areas of city where commerce was once prevalent. Be it a mall, shopping center, restaurant, strip mall, or autonomous car dealership, a noticeable indicator you have

---

[185] http://en.wikipedia.org/wiki/Parable_of_the_broken_window

[186] http://reason.com/archives/2010/09/08/the-confrontation/singlepage

---

152

drifted into a Black Undertow city is the sign that civilization once flourished there but has since been replaced with hair accessory stores, liquor stores, pawn shops, and title stores.

There is no reason to rebuild these cities, unless you plan on removing the population that was instrumental in its decline (since the population that was instrumental in its ascent left because of the influx of the Black Undertow). Thus, the money spent to try and bring recovery to Detroit or Birmingham is of no net-benefit to society. The visible Black Hand of economics is at work in these cities; so is Bastiat's parable.

Black people had nothing to do with building Detroit into a world-class city; they had everything to do with its removal from that select list of world-class destinations though. The same goes with Highland Park, a city that *Dirty Harry* himself couldn't save now.

Aren't convinced of the awesome power that the visible Black Hand of economics has over our lives? Let's take a look at a city that experienced an unhealthy dosage of Climate Change in a span of just 20 years. Spanish Lake (outside St. Louis) was 99 percent white in 1970; now, it's 77 percent Black. It's a safe bet that when it was an all-white city, the police primarily preyed upon teenagers. Now, they are forced to deal with the Black Undertow which **preys upon everyone**:

> County police have responded so many times to calls from Countryside Townhomes that they are now posting officers at the 787-unit apartment complex that has become synonymous with trouble in the Spanish Lake area.
>
> Of the 6,525 calls for police help logged by the 1st Precinct since the start of 2009, more than 3,600 were from that area — for a murder, robberies, assaults, burglaries and other crimes, officials said.
>
> Beginning Sept. 1, officers have been pushing back with foot patrols aimed at protecting the good residents

and visitors — and routing out the bad. They made 18 arrests on just the first day.

Commanders said if they don't act aggressively and swiftly, the problems at the complex, along Rosado Drive off Bellefontaine Road, will just spill into the surrounding neighborhoods. The effort includes code enforcement and sobriety checkpoints.

Capt. Troy Doyle, the precinct commander, said he expects the tactics to continue as long as necessary. "Hopefully, until the problems get rectified," he said.[187]

The Visible Black Hand of Economics on display. Phillip Andrew Morton, who grew up in Spanish Lake when it was that quintessential American city Norman Rockwell once celebrated, decided to make a movie about the **changes there**:

Phillip Andrew Morton has made two trips since 2007 to the house at 1238 Maple Street where he grew up.

On both occasions, he was shocked at the profound changes the little frame house had undergone in a matter of a few years.

Morton, 32, is now an independent filmmaker based in Los Angeles. The rapid transformation of the north St. Louis County community he calls his hometown, though it has never been incorporated, forms the basis of his documentary, "Spanish Lake."

The movie combines the warm feelings that Morton has for the area with a case-study of what many feel was governmental action — or inaction — that changed its bucolic nature into one that, in some sections, is more befitting of an urban ghetto.

---

[187] http://www.stltoday.com/news/local/metro/article_45bf0fb2-9644-5212-9176-43995f202fcc.html#ixzz1j6Je8B3j

---

"I really wanted to research all the dynamics that went into the phenomenon of white flight in Spanish Lake," Morton said in a recent telephone interview from Los Angeles. "I came away convinced that this is not an issue of race but of class and opportunities.

As recently as 1970, Spanish Lake was 99 percent white and 1 percent black.

But the 1970s also marked the beginning of a mass migration of African-Americans from the city of St. Louis. Many left failed housing complexes such as Pruitt-Igoe to settle in government-subsidized Section 8 housing in North County.

The city of Black Jack, which abuts Spanish Lake, feared that the poverty and crime that plagued the St. Louis complexes could recur in apartment complexes planned for their city. To thwart that possibility, Black Jack officials enacted zoning ordinances that prohibited multi-family housing.

In 1975, the 8th Circuit Court of Appeals struck down Black Jack's zoning ordinance, ruling that it violated the Civil Rights Act of 1968, commonly known as the Fair Housing Act.

The construction of apartment complexes in North County proliferated during that period. Many were upscale, designed to attract well-heeled singles.

But as they lost their luster, they were transformed into Section 8 housing.

RISE IN BLACK POPULATION

By 1990, 17 percent of Spanish Lake's residents were African-American. By 2010, with the population at 19,650, the percentage of blacks had soared to 77 percent, with many living in Section 8 apartments.

Among the biggest of these Section 8 complexes is the Countryside Townhomes in Spanish Lake, built in 1971. In recent years, it has become a hotbed of crime.[188]

Section 8 = Man-made Climate Change. Just like Highland Park, Spanish Lake has been destroyed; knowing your Basitat, any money spent trying to restore it is folly, because those responsible for the economic ruin of the city still reside there.

It's the economy! It's all about class! It's about the de-industrialization of the country!

No.

Pittsburgh never experienced Climate Change, so the visible Black Hand governing economics never destroyed that city. Instead, the invisible hand of economics flourished there, with primarily white citizens trying to find new ways to a make a living as the steel industry collapsed. Through innovation and via the free market, Pittsburgh is now even attracting DWLs from Portland.

Halftime for America?

Much will be made about the Clint Eastwood's "Halftime in America" commercial during the Super Bowl. Few will point out that the city in which his 2008 movie *Gran Torino* -

---

[188] http://www.stltoday.com/news/local/metro/article_45bf0fb2-9644-5212-9176-43995f202fcc.html - ixzz1j6Je8B3j

---

Highland Park - was set in has already had the lights turned out in it:

> Highland Park, home of Henry Ford's first moving assembly line, was once a well-off enclave of 50,000 residents. Ford left long ago, and Chrysler's corporate headquarters moved away in the 1990s. Now it has fewer than 12,000 residents — half the size it was just 20 years ago.

> So for this city, a shrunken tax base and financial crisis have been long in the making, and the recent national downturn has only made matters worse. More than 42 percent of Highland Park's residents live in poverty, unemployment is high and the median income here is nearly $30,000 below that of the state.

> "To understand our street lighting situation is to understand the wealth that Highland Park once had; it was a situation where we had the best of almost everything and an abundance of lights," said Rodney Patrick, whose father insisted on moving his family to Highland Park in the early 1950s because of its advantages — its status, in his words, as the shining city on the hill. "But we don't have the residents to have the luxuries we had when we were a city of 50,000."[189]

Highland Park is 93 percent Black, mind you. It was this city where Eastwood tried to rekindle some of the fire that made him such a formidable defender of the law in the *Dirty Harry* films. Watching the Chrysler commercial with Eastwood, well, it was sad:

> One of the biggest surprises of the Super Bowl was Clint Eastwood surfacing at halftime in an ad for Chrysler, although he never had to utter the car maker's name.

---

[189]   http://www.nytimes.com/2011/12/30/us/cities-cost-cuttings-leave-residents-in-the-dark.html?pagewanted=all

It was the the Clint Eastwood of his movie "Gran Torino," in which he played a Motor City retired Ford factory worker, not the Clint from "Every Which Way but Loose," in which he played a truck driver with a pet orangutan named Clyde.

In the Chrysler ad, Eastwood offers a message in his "Dirty Harry," "Unforgiven," "Gran Torino," "Million Dollar Baby" gruff voice about the gritty, tough America, embodied in Detroit's car comeback, an industry that "finds a way through tough time."

In 2008, Chrysler was bailed out with $12.5 billion from the U.S. government, and following bankruptcy restructuring is majority owned by Fiat SpA. In 2011, Chrysler earned $183 million, compared with a loss of $652 million in 2010.

Eastwood seems to also be sending a political message in the ad, saying the "fog, division, discord and blame make it hard to see what lies ahead," but America (and presumably Chrysler with the help of the U.S. government) "knows how to come from behind to win."

"This country can't be knocked out with one punch. We get right back up again, and when we do the world is going to hear the roar of our engines. Ya, it's halftime in America, and our second half is about to begin," Eastwood says as he drifts off camera and the Chyrsler, Jeep, Dodge and Ram logos appear.[190]

Detroit isn't coming back. Though Pittsburgh lost its steel industry, its citizens found ways to diversify the economy there and turned *The Steel City* into perhaps the best place to live in America. After the Black Riots of 1967, white people fled

---

[190]   http://www.cbsnews.com/8301-31751_162-57371716-10391697/clint-eastwoods-super-bowl-halftime-for-america/

Detroit. By default, Detroit became the Black capital of America.

And by becoming the Black capital of America, Detroit was socked with a punch that will keep it forever on the ground from and incapable of meeting the referees 10-count.

But why must we look at Detroit was being the microcosm for the future health of America? The white people who fled from Detroit have flourished in the suburbs, basically rebuilding the city in the numerous suburbs surrounding the decaying metropolis where *Ruin Porn* is the primary export.

In Ze'ev Chafets *Devil's Night and Other True Tales of Detroit*, we learn that "Detroit is one of the few places in the country where blacks can live in a sympathetic, black-oriented milieu."

That this milieu is the subject of numerous photo essays discussing the complete degeneration of the city back into nature is not a tolerable subject for conversation.

Black people have destroyed Detroit. The History Channel show *Life After People* didn't need CGI to show what will happen when people no longer populate Detroit. It has already happened:

> The History Channel will be re-airing its "Life After People" series that premiered in April, and anyone who missed it the first time around might want to check it out. Just be ready to see Detroit in a very unflattering light.
>
> The ten-part series, a spin-off of the channel's 2008 documentary by the same name, looks at what will happen to earth after humans are gone.
>
> The ninth episode, "The Road to Nowhere," is the one that features Detroit. The narrator first talks us through what would happen to the Renaissance Center after 25 years without people. Then, the show takes us to another part of Detroit, which it uses as an example of an area already in the throes of abandonment.

What will Detroit look like 40 years after people?" the announcer asks. "We already know...it's already happened."

There's also an extended scene on history.com that shows how lack of human attention already has worn down one abandoned factory.[191]

Wait a second... why isn't Pittsburgh used for real-life video for *Life After People*? Well, that's because Pittsburgh is one of the biggest cities in America with the whitest population. In fact, Stuff White People Like (SWPL) whites consider the next Portland:

Out: Portland

In: Pittsburgh.

This year's List has spoken, and writers Dan Zak and Monica Hesse have laid their anointed hands upon my hometown for 2012. Pittsburgh, Pa., is cool now. Sorry, Portland hipsters!

Pittsburgh is poised to offer a new type of lifestyle. And the Steel City has its own bike routes, microbreweries, organic food markets, art and lush scenery. Pittsburgh was named one of the world's 20 must-see destinations by National Geographic Traveler in 2011 (Only one other place in the United States, Sonoma, Calif., made the list). And with its dramatic merging of two rivers, it has one of the best skylines in America. And don't forget that it has one of the country's weirdest and most delicious sandwiches.[192]

---

[191] http://www.mlive.com/entertainment/detroit/index.ssf/2009/06/history_channels_life_after_pe.html

[192] http://www.washingtonpost.com/blogs/arts-post/post/portlandia-your-15-minutes-are-up-long-live-pittsburgh/2012/01/03/gIQAMUISYP_blog.html

---

Portland (Metro area: 78 percent white/Core city: 74 percent white/Suburbs: 80 percent white) and Pittsburgh (Metro area: 88 percent white/Core city: 67 percent white/Suburbs: 91 percent white) represent the polar opposite of Detroit (Core city: 82 percent Black). It's not coming back. White people are flocking to the two former cities, while even Black people are fleeing Detroit as the primary industry for growth seems to be in providing compelling real footage for *Life After People*.

American can make a comeback, but only if we admit why Detroit failed, and why Pittsburgh flourishes.

Detroit is a Black city; Pittsburgh is a white city.

It's a quote from Chafets book that warns us what happens to any city that goes majority Black. Writing about yet another re-election for Detroit Mayor Coleman Young (1989), Chafets states:

> A few days after the election, [Detroit] News columnist Chauncey Bailey, a thoughtful man who Coleman Young once branded an Uncle Tom, explained why.
>
> "Observes miss the point when they suggest that Young is less of a historical figure because he does not come across as "moderate" as do other African-American leaders now making inroad in less black cities, and is therefore out of step with a "new generation" of leadership.
>
> Only New York City and Chicago have more African-American residents than Detroit. new York is 25 percent African-American and has just elected its "first Black" mayor. Chicago is 40 percent African-American but lost power when African-Americans showed disunity. Due to their racial makeups, leaders in those cities must be more moderate to win. But Detroit is where more big cities will be in the coming decades. Young's legend will be the model, not a myth, that many will turn to."

Bailey's prediction reminded me of something I had heard more than a year earlier from Father William Cunningham, a very savvy white priest who has worked in the inner city for twenty years. "Detroit is the center of an American revolution," he had told me. "We're twenty years ahead of Chicago, forty years ahead of New York City. God knows where we are in comparison to San Diego. In terms of civil rights, this is Broadway. There's no place else where black power has spoken like it has in this city. And what happens here will eventually happen in the rest of the country.[193]

This was written in 1989. In 2012, Detroit is on the verge of being taken over by a form of financial martial law. In 2012 Detroit is used as the basis for real-life footage for *Life After People*. In 2012, Detroit is the Mecca for those seeking photographs for Ruin Porn coffee table books. There is no place in America where Black power has spoken like it has in Detroit, a profound reminder that the concept of "Black power" is an anathema to the building, maintaining, or survival of civilization.

Halftime in America? Sorry Clint Eastwood, just like the city where *Gran Torino* was based, the game is over for Detroit. The lights are going out.

This revolution spoken about in Chafets book must not be allowed to destroy another American city. The lights are dim all around Detroit, because "Black Power" lacks any ability to keep actual electricity going. It's a reminder of what happens in *Life After White People*.

We can't allow the fate of Detroit to befall another American city. So Clint Eastwood is wrong: it isn't halftime in America, but sudden death. We can see the reason Detroit is on the verge of complete collapse and juxtapose it with why Pittsburgh has become one of the most liveable cities in

---

[193] Chafets, Ze'ev. *Devil's night: and other true tales of Detroit*. New York: Random House, 1990. 231-232

America, or we can watch that revolution (what we call Actual Black Run America- ABRA) of "Black power" spoken so fondly of in *Devil's Night* swallow more and more of America.

It all starts with one simple statement: Black people are responsible for the decline of Detroit. Once white people, who founded, built, sustained Detroit were forced to flee for their safety after the Black Riot of 1967, those same Black agent provocateurs were incapable of running The Motor City or creating new industry or economic activity (drug dealing doesn't count) in the wake of the decline of the auto industry.

White people in Pittsburgh? Well, its one of the best places to live in America, 20 years after the ruination of the steel industry. Why? Whites created a new economy.

So it's sudden death America. Can you admit Detroit failed because it represents a post-colonial African society in America, where Black people lacked the ability to run a functioning government, sustain infrastructure, or create new industries or businesses that promoted growth (save Ruin Porn)?

If not, then America is finished. Black Power did speak in Detroit. What we have heard is available in Season One of *Life After People*.

"Detropia" as the future for all America: Why 'drifter colonies' must come to an end

The other day, I happened to watch *Titan A.E.* Strange as this may sound; it came out when I was in high school. It's not a good movie by any stretch of the imagination, but the general thrust of the story intrigued me enough to watch bits and pieces of it while I finished reading a book called *Detroit Divided*.

First off, it's a cartoon set between 3028 – 3043 A.D. The world has been destroyed (as in the planet has been blown up by an alien life-form made of pure energy) and only a few pockets of humanity escaped of earth.

Wikipedia describes beautifully what comes next:

> Titan A.E. primarily deals with the idea of human existence after the destruction of Earth. The movie opens with the destruction of Earth and primarily takes place 15 years after this event. Since that time, humans' numbers have dwindled and there is a general prejudice against them from other species. Many humans, even ones who once fought to save humanity, have given up on the species and concluded that extinction is only a matter of time. Cale is initially cynical in this way but begins to believe in saving his species more after spending time on a "drifter colony" full of humans and relics from Earth.[194]

It was while watching the apathy of the Cale character (voiced by Matt Damon) toward fighting to save humanity, that I realized the movie was a perfect metaphor for our time. Sometimes, I wonder how many people have given up on defending the historic majority population of not only America, but of Europe and the civilizations her people gave birth too.

There's a reason the entire non-European world wishes to live in the European-created world; they'd rather live in a world created and sustained by what Disingenuous White Liberals (DWLs) call 'white privilege' then their native land. The only 'white privilege' that white people have left in Europe, America, Australia, New Zealand, and South Africa is the privilege of watching their nations become submerged by people who have no vested interest in maintaining the culture (an extension of race) that created it.

---

[194] http://en.wikipedia.org/wiki/Titan_A.E.

People dissent on what they are allowed to dissent on (in our strange world, we'd call these people "libertarians") and the rest go about their pointless lives, hoping to get through the work week so they can spend a few hours in ecstasy watching a collegiate or professional sporting contest.

They remain comfortably numb to anything outside the micro-paradigms they've created for themselves, while a macro-paradigm shift has occurred which governs all of our lives.

Hard to believe, but 100 years ago white people made up roughly 33 percent of the world's population; today, less than 8 percent of the population is white.

In many ways, we live in a world like that in *Titan A.E.* Europe is quickly becoming Eurabia; South Africa and ~~Rhodesia~~ Zimbabwe are done; Australia and New Zealand will be swallowed by the demographic tidal wave; and the United States of America is governed by Black-Run America (BRA), where the slightest dissent means complete ostracism from respectable society.

For four generations now, white Americans have participated in the abandonment of major city after major city. The consequences of this pulling up tent and running away from major cities that become untenable to raise a family in (always due to the same reason: high rates of Black crime that drive down property value, force the closing of businesses, and worse, bring ruin to the schools) have been disastrous.

The collapse of Detroit into barbarism is the perfect reminder of why we live in a world much like that of *Titan A.E.* Detroit's collapse is 100 percent racial; the original Detroit, like earth in *Titan A.E.*, has been destroyed irrevocably.

Detroit had a Black riot in 1967 that convinced white people of the need to flee for the suburbs if they were to survive and flourish. Multiple Coleman Young mayoral terms in Detroit convinced those few remaining white people to completely give up on the city.

Civilization is, for all intents and purposes, dead in Detroit. Though few will state it – remember, Detroit is 84 percent Black now – the collapse of The Motor City is 100 percent a reminder that Black people lack the capacity to even sustain a city they are given through the attrition of white people.

Heidi Ewing and Rachel Grady, two filmmakers, have captured what happens when white people leave a towering metropolis that their ancestors created behind. Called *Detropia*, their documentary shows a glimpse of the future for all cities or counties that the Black Undertow submerges:

> Detroit lost 25 percent of its population between 2000 and 2010, and now, broke, finds itself on the verge of a possible state takeover. Yet visual reminders of a better time both haunt and anoint the residents here. The past is achingly present in Detroit, and the way its citizens interact with the hulking, physical remnants of yesterday is striking.
>
> A few years ago, there was a rash of power outages in Detroit, caused by people illegally cutting down live telephone wires to get to the valuable copper coils inside. The Detroit police created a copper theft task force to deter the so-called "scrappers," young men who case old buildings for valuable metals, troll cemeteries to steal copper grave plates and risk their lives to squeeze any last dollar out of the industrial detritus.
>
> One freezing evening we happened upon the young men in this film, who were illegally dismantling a former Cadillac repair shop. They worked recklessly to tear down the steel beams and copper fasteners. They were in a hurry to make it to the scrap yard before it closed at 10 p.m., sell their spoils and head to the bar.
>
> Surprisingly, these guys, who all lacked high school diplomas, seemed to have a better understanding of their place in the global food chain than many educated American 20-somethings. The young men regularly checked the fluctuating price of metals before they determined their next scrap hunt, and they had a clear view of where these resources were going and why. They were the cleanup crew in a shaky empire.

Somebody's got to do it.[195]

Will *Detropia* admit the racial aspect of Detroit's collapse? Will it even broach the racial aspect of the collapse? Doubtful.

But those hated white people, who will continue to face increasing prejudices as their numbers decrease (and yet still be given the bill to pay for entitlements to subsidize the high growth rates of minority populations) will forever search for new homes to raise families free of crime, with safe streets, and with a flourishing school system.

They'll search for "drifter colonies" – as in *Titan A.E.* – where the relics of an almost all-white society from the past is kept alive, if only fleetingly. To paraphrase one of my favorite lines from a movie, kids who get to grow up in a Whitopia – isn't that all a "drifter colony" is in BRA? – get to see what all of America was once like, just a glimpse that will eventually be lost, like tears in the rain.

. Those people who yearn for the "good ole days" of America actually yearn for a world that has been dismantled, and can never be restored. The Detroit of yesterday is but the scrap metal of today.

How many other cities will eventually see a similar fate? Milwaukee, Cleveland, Baltimore, and Birmingham all are at the top of a growing list.

Surrounding these dying cities reside flourishing "drifter colonies" that will eventually be abandoned to the expanding Black Undertow, fleeing the very major city they couldn't sustain.

The Detroit Free Press profiled *Detropia*, publishing these words:

> The city's struggles have had no lack of attention recently. There have been other documentaries, as well as national TV reports, photo books, art exhibits and references in pop songs.

---

[195] http://www.nytimes.com/2012/01/19/opinion/dismantling-detroit.html

But "Detropia" seems different, for a couple of reasons. One, it's made by Oscar-nominated documentary filmmakers Heidi Ewing, who grew up in Farmington Hills, and Rachel Grady. They are best known for the controversial 2006 documentary "Jesus Camp," which focused on an evangelical Christian summer camp. Two, it frames the story from the perspective of the decline and collapse of America's manufacturing base, with Detroit being at the epicenter.

"Our intention is not that somebody point the finger and say, 'Man, Detroit's really got problems.' If that's what happens, then we've failed at our job," Ewing said this week.

"We want people to say, 'Man, that's happening in my city, too. How did we let it go this far? What is our American identity when we've allowed a city to come to this point? And what are our priorities?'

"Really, we want the story of Detroit to boomerang back to the viewer and reflect upon what's going on around them and their part of the country."

With evocative music and hauntingly lovely cinematography, "Detropia" conveys some of the emptiness and beauty of the city while delving deeply into the economic battering it has taken.

The villain of the piece could be the shift of manufacturing power from the U.S., where making things fueled the rise of the middle class, to countries such as Mexico and China, where the costs of producing goods can be much cheaper. The movie, which took two years to plan and complete, doesn't shrink from harsh realities. There are familiar scenes of an abandoned house being torn down, people scavenging for scrap metal amid ruined buildings and community meetings filled with pain and resentment.[196]

---

196   http://www.freep.com/article/20120120/ENT01/201200411/-Detropia-documentary-Sundance-Film-Festival-shows-different-view-Detroit

Pain and resentment. In how many hearts, in how many minds, in how bodies of those searching for the next ~~Whitopia~~ "drifter colony" to try and raise a healthy family in, do these two words register?

Just as in *Titan A.E.*, a high number have privately realized what is happening, but the majority of them have accepted that extinction of their way of life is all but finalized.

Why stand in the way of history, when it would only prevent you from cheering on your alma mater or favorite professional team to victory?

Steve Lasser recently wrote an op-ed for *The New York Times*, claiming optimism is the only way forward for Detroit. Knowing that the city is being scavenged by scalpers seeking a quick profit, while simultaneously deserted by the very people who precipitated its demise, one can only conclude that Lasser is mentally unstable.[197]

But is one mentally unstable for hoping that the day comes when those congregating in "drifter colonies" amid the outskirts of once mighty cities all across this nation (Chicago, Detroit, Atlanta, Memphis, Birmingham, St. Louis, Cleveland, Los Angeles, Milwaukee, Richmond, and others come to mind) realize that for the sake of the future generations of the unborn, an end to the system of BRA must end?

Detroit is the future for America if nothing changes, if the system of BRA remains in place.

If it does not, well, just like at the end of *Titan A.E.* we'll get to create our own world, how ever we see fit.

The other day, I happened to watch *Titan A.E.* As the credits rolled, it dawned on me: the days of hoping to find the next *US News and World Report* or *CNN/Money* "Best Place to Raise a Family" ~~Whitopia~~ "Drifter Colony" must end. Once, all of America looked like this dwindling-in-cities; now, the Federal government plots to put refugees or Section 8 housing in their midst's.

---

[197]http://www.nytimes.com/2012/01/19/opinion/in-detroit-a-fresh-wave-of-hope.html?_r=2&ref=opinion

Looking at the pictures of the old Detroit - the beautiful edifices of majestic buildings-you start to understand that they represent relics of a lost country, one that is still worth defending to the end.

Those residing in "Drifter Colonies" still seek out some semblance of that lost America, even if they won't admit why they move from one Whitopia experiencing *Climate Climate* to one unmolested by this real phenomenon. A temporary 'drifter colony' for safe harboring.

Cynicism that the end of BRA will come must end. What comes when it does end, well, that's the real question.

"Wanted" Comes to Life in Detroit: The Black Insurrection of 1967 about to end by its own hand

If you've ever seen the movie *Wanted* with Angelina Jolie, you need to check out the source material by Mark Millar. It's a graphic novel that bares little resemblance to its big screen spawn. The story centers around a war waged by all the world's super-villains - who joined together - against the few superheroes, and how this ingenious plan eventually overwhelmed the good guys. This "Fraternity" of villains took over the world - dividing the nations among themselves - and used advanced technology to erase every inhabitant of the earth's memory that the heroes or villains ever existed.

Only faint, cloudy memories remain of the heroes who were trounced by evil.

The main character of the story, Wesley Gibson, is told of this by The Professor (who devised the plan of villains teaming up to defeat the heroes), and is incredulous as to how the real history of the world could be distorted:

> Wesley: "I don't understand. How come this isn't in the history? Even there'd been one superhero, would that have been all over the news and stuff?
>
> The Professor: "Ah, but it wasn't enough just to beat them, Wesley. We had to strip them of their memories and make sure that even their greatest fans didn't remember them.
>
> "Such science might seem comical in this new world that we molded for you, but believe me when I say that reality itself can be rewritten if we desire it, boy." (*Wanted*, Millar, trade paperback, p. 47)[198]

Reality itself can rewritten.

The story of *Wanted* is just a graphic novel. A comic book. But in our world, history can be rewritten. Actual events can be forgotten. No story verifies this fact more than what has happened in Detroit since 1967. We are on the verge of the state of Michigan assuming control of Black-run Detroit (82 percent now; roughly 35 percent Black at the time of the riots; less than 2 percent Black in 1912), a city that is now completely out of money:

> The law that threatens Detroit with direct state rule may be repealed through a petition drive powered by unions and residents opposed to white control of a city that's 82 percent black.
>
> "It's nothing but a takeover bill," said Brandon Jessup, chairman of the Stand Up for Democracy coalition seeking 161,300 signatures to place the measure on the November ballot. "This is definitely a race issue. It's affecting people of color not only in this generation but future generations."

---

[198] Millar, Mark, and J. G. Jones. *Wanted*. Los Angeles, CA: Top Cow Productions ;, 2007.

Detroit needs to be run by Detroiters," Mayor Dave Bing, a black Democrat, said last week at a press conference the day before Snyder called for the review.

Councilwoman JoAnn Watson compared the city's resistance to Rosa Parks' refusal to move to the back of a bus, an act that began the Montgomery boycott in 1955 and a civil-rights watershed.

Councilman Kwame Kenyatta said an emergency manager would be "a master, as someone to control the plantation," according to the Detroit Free Press.

Forgotten is that Rosa Parks was once assaulted by a Black man in Detroit, long after her exploits in Montgomery made her a household name. This occurred in 1994 (when Detroit was more than 75 percent Black) and is a fitting reminder of the true legacy of the Civil Rights Movement.[199]

Black-Run Detroit has failed. Liberalism didn't fail the city; the Black leadership, elected from the electorate, failed. Black people left to their own devices when white people fled into the suburbs (and created thriving cities, some of the top school districts in the nation, and bustling economies) failed.

The racial dynamics of Detroit - when it was considered the "Paris of the West" - was more than 70 percent white. In less than six years after Black people rioted in 1967, the city was majority Black and Coleman Young was the mayor.

Just like in *Wanted*, we forget the battle that took place in Detroit in 1967. High rates of Black crime (in 1960, Black people were only 24 percent of the population of Detroit, but they accounted for 65 percent of the violent crime) were already forcing white people to flee to the suburbs. It was the Black insurrection - and the white capitulation that followed - that occurred in 1967 which has been completely forgotten about.

---

[199]   http://www.nytimes.com/1994/08/31/us/rosa-parks-robbed-and-beaten.html

---

Recently, I acquired the *Life* magazine from August 4, 1967. Just like the world of *Wanted,* what I read doesn't seem real in a nation governed by the principles of Black-Run America (BRA). The cover of this magazine shows the ominous outline of two National Guardsman - guns drawn - with a fire blazing in the background. With the main caption reading "Negro Revolt: The Flames Spread," this issue of *Life* seems like a glimpse into another world.

A World where the insanity of BRA was just bubbling to the surface, before its tentacles would ensnare every public and private institution in America.

It was in this issue that you can read the article "City at the blazing heart of a nation in disorder." It is these words that read like something out of the world of *Wanted,* where the villains won and the mere existence of heroes is but a shadowy memory:

> With exploding heat and violence, the flames of Negro revolt crack led across the nation, bringing federal troops into riot duty for the first time in a quarter of a century. The disorder was country-wide, but at is blazing heart was Detroit, where the racial rioting ranked as the worst in U.S history. like Newark a few days earlier, the Detroit insurrection was touched off by a minor police incident - this time a raid on a Negro speakeasy.
>
> But it quickly flared into an even more destructive and persistent pattern of looting, arson and sniping. Whole city blocks went up in smoke, setting streets shimmering in waves of heat, and bullets whined and ricocheted unpredictably through the ruins. Unable to control the chaos with police and 8,000 national guardsmen, Mayor Jerome Cavanagh and Michigan Governor George Romney finally prevailed upon President Johnson to take the extraordinary step of supplying federal troops. Paratroopers from the 82nd and 101st Airborne Divisions - many of them veterans of Vietnam - rolled into the continuing fray. Not since 1943, and then, too in Detroit, had U.S. forced been so employed.
>
> Even so, death and destruction mounted. By midweek, at least 38 persons lay dead, including a policemen and a

fireman. Looters and snipers died, as well as many innocent people caught in the often random cross-fire.[200]

This was the Negro Revolt of 1967, an event that helped bring about Black-rule in Detroit. Under Black rule - in the past year - we have seen what Life After White People looks like. With the city on the verge of being taken over by the state of Michigan, we can only ask how did it come to this? It's simple: the Negro Revolt that *Life* magazine spoke so openly about in 1967 has been forgotten, replaced with the progressive idea that Black people would be able to sustain a civilization - and city - they had no part in building, but had every part in destroying.

A world where affirmative action destroyed the police, leaving the city in the hands of vigilantes in 2012. A city where the National Tuskegee Airmen Museum rests, a reminder of, something that really has nothing to do with Black people in 2012. Detroit is truly too Black for civilization, and *Life* magazine hinted at this back in 1967. It's the city where Freedom Failed, and where the game has already ended (sorry Clint Eastwood).

But we can't even acknowledge any of the role Black people had in destroying Detroit, but must blame liberalism as the true culprit. Strange, liberalism flourishes in Pittsburgh, but that city survived the horrible decline of its steel industry.

But Detroit can't survive its Blackness. It chokes on this Blackness, but because we live in a world where we can't acknowledge racial differences (because of that strange victory - like the one of the villains in *Wanted* - in 1967), the people of Detroit must drown in a sea of Black violence. Two stories from this past week illustrate the despondent reality of what Black-rule in Detroit means. One, the 43 murder of 2012[201], represents something truly sinister (*Fight at Shower cited in slaying of 9-month-old baby,* by George Hunter, Detroit News, February 25, 2012):

---

[200] Life,"City at the blazing heart of a nation in disorder," 19. August 4, 1967

[201]
http://www.detroitnews.com/article/20120221/METRO01/202210373/1409/
metro/Detroit-baby-43rd-homicide-victim-bloody-start-year

A fight over a seat at a baby shower triggered the killing of a 9-month-old boy, according to the victim's grandmother.

Delric Miller IV died Monday as he slept on the couch in his home on the 8400 block of Greenview Avenue. Police said someone fired at the house with an AK-47-type assault rifle about 4:30 a.m., leaving behind 37 shells. One of the rounds hit the baby, who was pronounced dead at Sinai-Grace Hospital.

Delric Miller IV died Monday as he slept on the couch in his home on the 8400 block of Greenview Avenue. Police said someone fired at the house with an AK-47-type assault rifle about 4:30 a.m., leaving behind 37 shells. One of the rounds hit the baby, who was pronounced dead at Sinai-Grace Hospital.

Delric's grandmother, Cynthia Wilkins, said she believes the shooting was retaliation for a skirmish Sunday at a baby shower at Club Celebrity on Plymouth Rd. in Detroit."The shower was overbooked, and there was an argument because there weren't enough seats," said Wilkins. Her daughter, Diamond Salter, attended the shower, which was thrown by a friend, Wilkins said.

"A woman got mad because she couldn't find a seat, so she started knocking tables down, and it escalated from there," Wilkins said. "My daughter and her friends left the club, but (a group of men and women) followed them to a gas station, and there was a fight with one of the guys who was at the shower with my daughter. Then, they followed them to the house.
"I think they came back the next day and shot up the house," said Wilkins, who sobbed as she recounted the events.
"They went to the shower to celebrate life; instead, a life was destroyed."

The shooting has outraged both police and residents, and prompted Detroit 300, a group of community activists fed up with crime, to go door-to-door asking questions, in hopes of finding the killer or killers.
A task force consisting of the FBI, the Bureau of Alcohol Tobacco Firearms and Explosives and the Wayne County

Sheriff's Office is investigating the case."Life is not valued in Detroit. It's a war zone here," Wilkins said. "We need some ground troops patrolling these streets; they send them all overseas, but they need to be here."

The death was the 43rd homicide in the city this year, up from 35 in the period last year. It's also the second killing of a youngster in Detroit in the past month."Again, adult behavior has brought another child in Detroit to an end," said Police Chief Ralph Godbee.[202]

No, adult behaviour didn't bring about the end of another child's life in Detroit. Black behaviour did. Interesting that calls for ground troops to patrol the city of Detroit - just like New Orleans, where Black violence might bring about a call for ground troops as well - are needed in the last days of Black-rule, just like the beginning of Black-rule in those dark days of Negro Rebellion back in 1967.

Those days that we have forgotten about.

Life is balance. Never forget that. In the Alpha and Omega of Black-rule of Detroit, federal troops will occupy the city.

If not, more stories like the one of an 86-year-old Black guy being assaulted by a young Black punk will persist (With Video, Passers-by ignore injured car-jacked victim, 86, crawling at Detroit gas station, by Tammy Battaglia, *Detroit Free Press*, February 24, 2012):

> The 86-year-old World War II Air Corps veteran, knocked to the ground during a carjacking on Detroit's west side, crawled across the gas station parking lot as people walked by.
>
> No one stopped to help, he says. Aaron Brantley, who worked for 31 years as a welder at a Chrysler plant in Hamtramck, recalled the ordeal Friday, two days after he was robbed outside the BP gas station on West McNichols at Fairfield, just east of the University of Detroit

---

202

http://www.detroitnews.com/article/20120225/METRO01/202250346/Fight-shower-cited-slaying-9-month-old-boy?odyssey=tab%7Ctopnews%7Ctext%7CFRONTPAGE

Mercy campus.[Brantley estimates that at least four customers walked past him as he struggled for help, unable to walk because his leg was broken. "I never bothered anybody, and I always try to help somebody else when I could," he said Friday from home, his leg in a soft cast to his hip and not a tinge of bitterness in his voice.

Brantley was on his way home from Bible study at Corinthians Baptist Church in Hamtramck, where he's a trustee, when someone hit him from behind and grabbed his keys at 10:40 a.m. Wednesday. The thief drove off in Brantley's 2010 Chrysler 200 -- bought to replace another car recently stolen."I noticed when I was crawling to the gas station, people were walking past by me like I wasn't there," he said. "I said, 'Lord, have mercy.' I said, 'Lord, some of them didn't even look around, just going to get their gas.' "

Once Brantley got inside the gas station, the shocked attendant, Haissam Jaber, 37, and other customers called for help.
"I've seen everything in here, but I couldn't believe it happened at 10 o'clock in the morning," said Jaber, who has worked at the station for 10 years. "And he actually pushed him down. It was a bad scene. He must be on drugs or something -- to push an old guy like this is sad. They do anything these days."

It took so long for an ambulance to arrive, Brantley said, that he offered cash to a stranger to take him home. The Good Samaritan refused the money and drove him anyway. The ambulance met Brantley at home and transported him to Sinai-Grace Hospital.
"I thought they ran over my leg," he said. "I didn't know what happened -- I didn't see him. When he had hit me and knocked me down on the ground, I went to get up and couldn't get up. So I crawled into that filling station there."

A few hours after the carjacking, a man found Brantley's name and phone number in his Bible, still on the car's front seat, and called him. The car had been abandoned on the city's east side, the wheels and radio missing.

Detroit police spokeswoman Sgt. Eren Stephens said no one has been arrested, and the case is under investigation.

"Whenever a member of our community -- but especially a senior citizen -- becomes a victim of crime, it is very upsetting and disturbing," she said, requesting anyone with information to call police or Crime Stoppers.

This is the legacy of the Negro Revolt that *Life* magazine documented in 1967. White people fled Black crime - just as they do in every major metropolis in America - but because of the high concentration of Black people from the Great Migration (the most disastrous migratory movement in America, the complete reverse of Manifest Destiny), it quickly became the Black capital of America.

Now, with its school system perhaps the worst in the Western world (and already taken over by the state of Michigan); the lowest property value imaginable in America; and crumbling; the most unsafe streets in America, with violence and crime not even seen in war-torn areas; neglected buildings built by white people and burnt down by Black people during "Devil's Night" each year, Detroit is truly the best representation of what happens when Black people take control.

It is in that same *Life* issue from seemingly another world that an article, "On guard, spectre of backlash" is printed on p. 24:

> Of all the cities engulfed by negro violence, Detroit seemed one of the least likely candidates.
> Federal officials considered Detroit's anti-poverty program a model: up to last week it has poured more than $250 million into urban renewal and projects for the poor. Negroes had also attained a share of the political power. Detroit is the only city in the U.S. that has two Negro congressmen, and its young, progressive mayor, Jerry Cavanagh, had been popular with the Negroes. Unlike Newark and Watts, Detroit had no single ghetto (*PK NOTE: no all of Detroit is a ghetto*).

But beneath the surface, the city simmered. Few of the statistics meant much to the Negroes who inhabited the eight-block area of 12th Street where the rioting erupted. The unemployment rate there was still 11%, and even higher among Negro youth. The area was the most densely populated in the city. Only 17% of the residents owned their own homes- compared with 60% in the entire city. A recent survey indicated that 91% feared being robbed and 93% wanted to move out. Even though economic conditions had improved, it served simply to raise Negro expectation - and the inevitable frustration when those hopes were not quickly satisfied. In the carnival-like revel of looting, Negroes took the luxuries they felt had been denied them - expensive liquor, color TV sets and hi-fi phonographs. "It looked like a singing commercial for all the things they had seen on television, says a Detroit sociologist.

The rioting demonstrated the power of the discontented to disrupt and paralyze any city and the difficulty of reimposing law and order. It also raised the menacing prospect of white backlash. Whites already have started a run on gun shops and there was a danger that any community confronted by racial violence might be split into armed camps, white vs. Negro. If this occurs, an important lesson of the violence will be obscured. That lesson, says a Detroit psychologist, is "Learn, whitey, learn."

There was no white backlash. Whites left Detroit; Black people took over. Now, Detroit is one of the most unsafe cities in the world, because of the Black population present there.

We saw violence explode across the nation - Black violence - in the summer of 2011. The lessons that should be learned come directly from the Negro Revolt that *Life* magazine discussed openly in its August 4th, 1967 issue.

Just like in *Wanted,* the bad guys have won and remade the world in their image. We have forgotten the lessons of the past, and for this reason, we can't confront the reason that life is held in such low esteem in Detroit.

We can't even remember what the past looked like, because the world of BRA has clouded it in a shroud of white racism, bigotry, discrimination, and ultimately, white supremacy.

Looking at what happened in Detroit in the summer of 1967, there's a reason all of those things existed.

Detroit's collapse is near. The city is forced to sell of assets to make payroll. We must remember that it was a Negro Revolt - as *Life* told us - that made this all possible.[203]

It wasn't a white privilege that killed the 9-month-old in Detroit; it wasn't white privilege that refused to help an 86-year-old carjacked Black man in Detroit; it was a city where Black privilege has reached its startling conclusion.

The biggest news story in America right now is the impending collapse of Detroit, perhaps the biggest Black metropolis in the entire world. Under Black-rule, Detroit has become the poster-child for corruption in America[204], and as custodians of a city whose famous landmarks and buildings were all erected by white people, have watched them become the subjects capable of fueling the addiction of "ruin porn" aficionados from around the world.[205]

Once a symbol of economic might, the majestic Packard Plant ruins are a reminder of what *Life after White People* looks like. Neither Black developer nor outside investor ever converted these abandoned buildings into lofts, one of the hallmarks of a city seeking urban renewal by attracting bohemian white people there from the boring, lily white suburbs. Now the Packard Plant shall be demolished.[206]

[203] http://www.detroitnews.com/article/20120213/METRO01/202130329

204

http://www.detroitnews.com/article/20120301/METRO/203010423/1409/FBI-unveils-public-corruption-task-force-Metro-Detroit

[205] http://www.freep.com/article/20090929/BLOG36/90928073

206

http://www.freep.com/article/20120303/BUSINESS04/203030406/Dilapidated-Packard-Plant-reminder-of-Detroit-s-industrial-fall?odyssey=tab%7Ctopnews%7Ctext%7CFRONTPAGE

Why couldn't Black entrepreneurs in Detroit convert these old buildings into something useful, as have their white counterparts in Pittsburgh (and many other cities where America's former manufacturing might is now the playground for Stuff White People Like - SWPL - whites)? Where once buildings produced the steel used by companies all around the world, now these buildings are lofts and residential space for the citizens of Pittsburgh, considered one of the best places to live in America.

In the 1960s, Disingenuous White Liberals (DWL) like Detroit Mayor Jerry Cavanagh thought that massive spending programs - redistribution of wealth - could maintain a steady peace between the white and Black populations of the city. These dreams would spectacularly end in late July 1967 when Black people rioted, but the rest of the nation still clings to the belief that the government can redistribute money to the Black community to maintain the peace.

The August 4, 1967 issue of *Time* magazine produced this nugget of information for us to ponder. On p. 13:

> Fully 40 percent of the city's Negro family heads own their homes. No city has waged a more massive and comprehensive war on poverty. Under Mayor Jerry Cavanagh, an imaginative liberal with a knack for landing Government grants, the city has grabbed off $42 million in federal funds for its poverty programs, budgeted $30 million for them this year alone. Because many of the city's 520,000 Negroes (out of a population of 1,600,000) are unequipped to qualify for other than manual labor, some $10 million will go toward special training and placement programs for the unskilled and the illiterate. A $4,000,000 medical program furnishes family planning advice, outpatient clinics and the like. To cool an potential riot fever, the city had allotted an additional $3,000,000 for this summer's Head Start and recreation programs. so well did the city seem to be handling its problems that Congress of Racial Equality Director Floyd McKissick excluded Detroit last winter when he drew up a list of twelve cities where racial trouble was likely to flare.

All of this wasn't enough to keep Black people from burning down 1300 buildings and sacking 2700 businesses in late July of 1967 during the worst racial riot in American history.

Just like in the summer of 2011, when Black people engaged in riots all across the nation causing Newark, Chicago, Atlanta, Baltimore, Columbia, Philadelphia, Milwaukee, Peoria, and New Orleans to pass emergency curfews, Black people across the nation were rioting in 1967. The same types of activities used now to stop the violence were used then. From that same *Time* article (p. 14):

> Ironically, New York, - like Detroit - has launched a major summer entertainment program designed to cool the ghettos by keeping the kids off the streets. "We have done everything in this city to make sure we have a stable summer," said Mayor John Lindsay. But after one of these stabilizing events, a Central Park rock-'n' roll concert featuring Smokey Robinson and the Miracles, a boisterous band of some 150 Negroes wandered down toward midtown Manhattan, heaved trash baskets through the windows of three Fifth Avenue clothing stores and helped themselves. The looters' favorite was a $56 Austrian alpaca sweater, which is a status symbol in Harlem. Among the 23 who police were able to catch; four Harlem summer antipoverty workers who earn up to $90 a week from the city.

The more things change, the more they stay the same.

It was after the Black insurrection of 1967 that white people surrendered the city of Detroit over to Black rule. In B.J. Widick's 1972 book *Detroit: City of Race and Class Violence*, we learn quickly that the Visible Black Hand of Economics was already proudly on display during the transitioning of power from white rule to Black rule. On p. 195:

> The limitations of black capitalism were especially visible in the city of Detroit, where in 1966, 65 percent of the inner-city population was black, but only 38 percent of the businesses were owned by blacks. Of these - mostly small retail and service operations - 60 percent had an annual net income of less than $8,000.

The concluding chapter of Widick's book is titled *Black Metropolis of the Future*. The Motor City indeed did become a Black Metropolis, a direct representation of what the Black inheritors (perhaps conquerors is the apt word?) were capable of producing, maintaining, and building. The "Ruin Porn" that is now one of the cities primary exports (no less than five books have been produced detailing the ruins of the white city under Black rule). Widdick points out in the early days of Black rule seeping into Detroit, businesses fled the city (p. 210):

> For every new business moving into the city, two more move out. There are over 7,000 vacant store fronts. Thousands of other small stores look like tiny military posts under siege because of their wire or steel fronts and closed doors. Symbolic of the city's new look is the *Detroit News* building downtown, with its surrounding brick wall reminiscent of a medieval fortress.

This was before Coleman Young was elected the city's first Black mayor. Libertarians always make the claim that people will innovate when businesses leave, because "free markets" dictate it, or some other nonsense.

Why have the descendants of those who conquered Detroit been incapable of creating new businesses and industry in the city? The white people of Pittsburgh - whose steel industry collapse in the 1980s took with it more than 100,000 jobs - have survived, and built a city considered the "most liveable" in America.

Black people in Detroit? The honor bestowed upon the city under their custodianship is "most dangerous."

As Black-run Detroit limps to its death, *Inc.* magazine has dubbed the former Motor City a "Start-up City for Business." In the dying days of Black-run Detroit, the cost-of-living and starting a business in the city is so low, that entrepreneurs are flocking to the city.[207]

A city, mind you, whose death was sealed because Black people lacked the ability to innovate on their own. They lacked the ability to even sustain the city. Were it not for Coleman Young International Airport, one wonders where many of the Black people who actually work (and don't live off the government) would find employment?

At the Inc.com sub-site "Innovation Hotspots: Detroit" we learn about those hip, SWPL white people who will build the next Detroit:

---

[207] http://www.freep.com/apps/pbcs.dll/article?AID=2012120302025

For the most recent Startup Weekend in Detroit in mid-February, organizer Brandon Chesnutt cap attendance at 120, and still had people banging down his door.

"We literally just ran out of space," Chesnutt says. "I can't go an hour without getting e-mail from somebody wanting to attend."

The most popular Startup Weekend in the city's history took place inside the M@dison building, a modern five-story start-up Mecca that—as home to several VC firms and many of their portfolio companies—is part of the groundwork for a tech-centered rebirth of Detroit. The building is the brainchild of Dan Gilbert of Quicken Loans, who has been making it his crusade to reignite Detroit's downtown by buying property, seeding ventures, and moving thousands of Quicken employees into the area.

The M@dison is located on a stretch of Woodward Avenue that is poised to become Detroit's own Silicon Alley: Gilbert has dubbed it "Webward Avenue" for its burgeoning concentration of tech businesses and incubators. And with the neighborhood's surge in restaurants, bars, and entertainment options, Webward just might become the movement that is key to transforming Detroit back into a great American city.[208]

The seeds are being planted for the rebuilding of Detroit. Black-run Detroit is coming to an end, yet Black people nationwide will resist this usurpation of power by the state of Michigan. But even to the end, the only contributions of Black people will be more violence and more corruption from the elected officials. It will be up to white people to pull Detroit from the doldrums of Black-rule, the real lesson of the *Inc.* magazine expose on innovation in the city.

Once you've hit bottom, there's only one place to go: up. The only hope for Detroit is for white people to flock to the city and utilize the existing infrastructure (repositioning it in the process) to rebuild and create a thriving metropolis that can eventually attract outside

---

[208] http://www.inc.com/hot-spots-detroit/tim-donnelly/how-detroit-got-its-groove-back.html

capital for renovation projects such as the Grand Central Station, a dilapidated building whose past opulence is lost on Black people.[209]

If this does not work, Detroit must be evacuated entirely and left to stand as a monument to DWL folly, a reminder of what the power of Black-Run America (BRA) did to *The Paris of the West*.

This is the lesson to draw from the "ruin porn" that people capture through photos and video of a decaying city whose current majority population can't sustain. And yes, downtown Detroit is more than 90 percent Black (the city is 82 percent Black).

The *Black Metropolis of the Future*... fitting that the city looks less like *The Jetsons* and more like a Black version of *The Flintstones*.

Start Game: New York Times, Mother Jones, and The Nation all Lament the Death of Black-Run Detroit

The cats out of the bag. *The New York Times, Mother Jones* and *The Nation* are all beginning to understand the implications of what happens to cities in America that represent Actual Black-Run America (ABRA), with each news organization publishing editorials and lengthy articles lamenting (and condemning) the emergency management takeover of cities like Benton Harbor (89 percent Black)[210];

---

209   http://www.inc.com/hot-spots-detroit/nicole-carter/detroit-start-up-education.html

210

http://www.nytimes.com/2011/04/27/us/27michigan.html?pagewanted=all

Inkster (73 percent Black); and Pontiac (52 percent Black); Michael Moore's hometown of Flint, (53 percent Black); and, inevitably, Detroit (which *The Nation* claims it is 89 percent Black). [211]

The end of democracy for Black-ruled cities is coming to Michigan, a state where 60 percent of the people on TANF/Welfare are Black. Only 14 percent of the overall population is Black.[212]

The Republican Governor Rick Snyder signed into law sweeping welfare changes last year, that instantly removed 6,500 families in Detroit from the ranks of those receiving government assistance. Knowing who receives the bulk of the welfare in Michigan, it's obvious that Black people were impacted the most by these austerity measures.[213]

The New York Times editorial notes that the "Auto Industry received a bailout, but Detroit was left behind." Wrong. The majority of the citizens of Detroit subsist on handouts and EBT cards, as the taxpayer has been bailing out Black Detroit for decades. Every child now eats for free in school, another gift of the taxpayer.

There is no discernible return on investment for this act of benevolence, save for the government assisting higher rates of criminality by providing sustenance for the city's inhabitants.

Remember this: when the steel industry collapsed in Pittsburgh, that industry wasn't bailed out. The citizens of The Steel City rebuilt their economy into one that is attracting people from all over America. Consequently, it's one of the whitest big cities in America.

---

[211]   http://www.thenation.com/article/166297/scandal-michigans-emergency-managers

[212] http://www.acf.hhs.gov/programs/ofa/character/fy2009/tab08.htm

[213] http://www.wsws.org/articles/2011/sep2011/mich-s16.shtml

---

Detroit? The only people the city attracts are those hoping to get-off to "Ruin Porn," as the Black people who inherited the city were incapable of innovation and restructuring the economy there. Strange that white people who fled to the suburbs of Detroit didn't have that problem.[214]

Let this be said: Detroit was 75 percent white in 1960, and Black people at that time were roughly 24 percent of the population and were responsible for 66 percent of the violent crime. This is the reason white people flocked to outlying areas of the city, establishing economically thriving suburbs (and some of the top schools in all of Michigan) that were peaceful, while Detroit succumbed to world where the Black Undertow assumed power.

Though the city has almost half of the population it had when Black people engaged in the insurrection of 1967 (causing billions in damage, in today's inflated currency), the crime rates, when adjusted for this decrease, haven't changed dramatically.

In a STRESS-free Detroit, the police have even announced they are going to stop responding to emergency calls.[215]

Every lie told about equality and race dies with Detroit. *The Nation, Mother Jones,* and *The New York Times* writers understand this fact, with the belief in "race being a social construct" only believed by those with lying eyes at this point.

To look upon the ruins of Detroit and not understand this fact should be grounds for having your sanity checked. To understand that the other cities losing their autonomy to emergency managers are almost all-Black as well... you begin

---

214

http://www.detroitnews.com/article/20120305/BIZ/203050424/Photographers-other-artists-flock-Packard-site?odyssey=tab%7Ctopnews%7Ctext%7CFRONTPAGE

215 http://www.myfoxdetroit.com/dpp/news/local/detroit-police-roll-out-new-911-policy-20120305-ms

to understand why this Disingenuous White Liberal (DWL) publications are foaming at the mouth, rabid to misdirect the blame to the anyone but the Black people who run the cities and are responsible for creating and maintaining the local economies.

Here's the NYT on the story:

> No one, least of all the state, wants that to happen. In Michigan, emergency managers can break union contracts, fire city officials and sell off city assets. That has already begun in four other cities, all of them largely black, that the state has taken over in the last few years. Black officials and union leaders have charged that Gov. Rick Snyder, a Republican elected in 2010, has an ideological and racial agenda, and taking over Detroit, which is 83 percent black, would only magnify the tension.

> Chrysler's gleaming Jefferson North plant on the east side of town does churn out Jeep Cherokees and Dodge Durangos, and President Obama noted in a speech last week that it has been adding new shifts. But it is not enough. Just blocks from the plant is some of America's worst urban devastation, acre upon acre of vacant land, abandoned houses, burned-out stores. A city that held nearly two million people in the 1950s is now down to 714,000, more than a third of whom live in poverty.

> There are glimmers of hope on the city's southwest side, where newcomers from Mexico and other countries have revived several avenues with restaurants, groceries and other stores. "More diversity, more immigrants — that's the key for the future," said Jordi Carbonell, born in Barcelona, who runs Café con Leche, a coffeehouse crowded with young patrons and laptops.

But rebuilding the city with coffee cups will take too long, and Detroit is running out of time. Crime is going up, buses are breaking and left unrepaired, and the exodus continues. Even if City Hall can stave off a takeover with union givebacks, layoffs and pension cuts, it will only be for a short time.

The solution may be in the suburbs that have siphoned off Detroit's money and jobs and talent for decades. A true emergency manager, as many people here have suggested, would have the power to begin merging the tax base of the city with that of suburban counties in hopes of saving the region. Bailouts can come in many different forms.[216]

Here's The Nation:

The implications went beyond Benton Harbor. "Since the beginning of your administration, communities facing or under emergency management have doubled," Michigan Forward and the NAACP wrote to the governor, citing a "failure of transparency and accountability" in the process of determining which jurisdictions need an emergency manager. The financial review team assigned to Detroit, for instance, had recently met in Lansing, nearly 100 miles away—"a clear example of exclusion and voter disenfranchisement," according to the authors. On February 6 an Ingham County circuit judge ruled that the Detroit team's meetings must be held in public.

Of Detroit's 713,777 residents, 89 percent are African-American. The city of Inkster (population 25,369), which recently got an EM, has a black population of 73 percent. Having EMs in both cities would mean that more than half the state's black population would fall into the hands of unelected officials.

---

[216]   http://www.nytimes.com/2012/03/05/opinion/a-government-bailout-saved-the-auto-industry-but-detroit-was-left-behind.html?_r=2&ref=opinion

* * *

Everyone agrees that something must be done to "fix" Michigan's struggling urban centers and school districts, although news of a $457 million surplus in early February prompted the state budget director to declare, "Things have turned." But at what cost? In 2011 Governor Snyder stripped roughly $1 billion from statewide K-12 school funding and drastically reduced revenue sharing to municipalities. Combined with poor and sometimes corrupt leadership and frequently dysfunctional governments, these elements have brought Michigan cities to the brink of bankruptcy. Residents of the hardest-hit places have fled if they are able.

The state's first emergency managers—previously known as emergency financial managers—were appointed between 2000 and 2002 by Republican Governor John Engler in the cities of Hamtramck, Flint and Highland Park to prevent them from declaring bankruptcy. Although all eventually left when their job was done—the last in 2009—all three cities are back in the red. In January the Highland Park School District was assigned an EM. (That city—population 11,776—is 93.5 percent African-American.) Others followed, in Ecorse, Benton Harbor and Pontiac, as well as Detroit public schools.[217]

And finally, here's Mother Jones:

"We haven't seen anything this severe anywhere else in the country," says Charles Monaco, a spokesman for the Progressive States Network, a New York-based advocacy group. "There's been nothing in other states where a budget measure overturns the democratic vote." Williams says emergency managers are able to

---

[217]   http://www.thenation.com/article/166297/scandal-michigans-emergency-managers

enact draconian policies that would cost most city officials their jobs: "They couldn't get elected if they tried."

Benton Harbor, Ecorse, and Flint are also currently under emergency management. In Flint, the emergency manager has promised to restructure collective bargaining agreements with the city's police and firefighters unions. Benton Harbor's emergency manager banned elected officials from appearing at city meetings without his consent. Detroit, which is facing a more than $150 million budget shortfall, could be next:

Mayor Dave Bing has proposed laying off 1,000 city workers and wrung concessions from public-sector unions in hopes of preventing Gov. Snyder from appointing an emergency manager.[218]

The iconoclastic Occidental Dissent broke down the reliance that Black people in Michigan have on the EBT card (using outdated 2009 data), showcasing that a growing majority of them have their grocery bills bailed out each month.[219]

There's a reason that Detroit has become a primary subject matter here at SBPDL and that it will continue to be discussed: the curtain falling on ABRA in not only Detroit, but in Black-run cities throughout Michigan reveals once again that nature can only be tossed out for so long. Ignoring her and collectively shutting our eyes to her fury and might doesn't mean you can't feel nature's presence.

She'll return with a vengeance.

---

[218] http://motherjones.com/politics/2012/02/michigan-emergency-manager-pontiac-detroit

[219] http://www.occidentaldissent.com/2011/05/10/black-apocalypse-ebt-card-food-stamp-usage-michigan/

In a hilarious review of *Robocop 2* from a People magazine dated July 2, 1990, Ralph Novak laments the racial undertones of the movie:

> The movie is also a vile insult to Detroit. The character of the city's black mayor, played by Willard Pugh, borders on racist: He's so inarticulate, panicky and given to running away that you half expect him to say, "Feets, do yo' stuff."[220]

Knowing that nearly 50 percent of the city of Detroit is illiterate, and that the Black mayor of Southfield Brenda Lawrence touts something called Revolution Read as the key to that cities future prosperity, the character of Willard Pugh is perhaps the most honest casting of Black person in the history of cinema.[221]

Though if you read the *"You're Gonna Be a Bad Motherfucker": Robocop's Racial Subtexts* essay from "The Souls of Cyberfolk: Posthumanism as Vernacular Theory" by Thomas Foster, you'll get a better understanding of the white privilege endemic in the *Robocop* films.

The hour draws near. The End of History is only the beginning.

Sadly, conservatives will scream that liberalism ruined Detroit stating that Democrats or Unions are to blame for the similar fiasco's in the other cites of Michigan that emergency managers now run. All the while, the lily-white suburbs of Detroit flourish.

It's time to open your eyes, people. Stop lying to yourself.

---

[220] http://www.people.com/people/archive/article/0,,20118085,00.html

[221]

http://www.detroitnews.com/article/20120305/METRO02/203050409/Mayor-Southfield-becoming-stronger-city-?odyssey=tab%7Ctopnews%7Ctext%7CFRONTPAGE

Join the ranks of Those Who Can See. *The New York Times, The Nation, and Mother Jones* understand what this moment is all about.

It's time we all do as well.

The end of ABRA in Detroit is the ultimate chance to roll back Black-Run America (BRA) everywhere.

The words of Frank Owen from the article "Detroit, Death City," found in the August 2004 issue of *Playboy* (they really do have great articles) is apt to close this piece:

> If Detroit were a character in a novel, it wouldn't be believable. What madness could possess a civilization to construct such a grand and magnificent place and then, within half a century, to obliterate so thoroughly what it had created? What talking about the state of Detroit, one is tempted to compare it to a natural disaster - some earthquake that laid waste to the landscape. Except there's nothing natural about what has happened to Detroit in the past 30-plus years. Humans built this city, and humans - an unholy and unconscious alliance of fat-cat businessmen and street-corner criminals - destroyed it. (p. 61-62)

Mr. Owen, it was white people who built Detroit. It was Black people who killed it. Same goes for Birmingham, Alabama, and Memphis, Tennessee. Richmond, Virginia too.

Same goes for Milwaukee and Baltimore. Same goes for Philadelphia.

Detroit is believable when you understand that the lessons of the city's demise are being played out all across America.

Once you go Black, you never go back. Well, unless you live in Michigan, where the concept of democracy ends when financial martial law is declared.

History is about to begin again.

Start game.

"Escape from Detroit: The Collapse of America's Black Metropolis"

In the small book "The Quotations of Mayor Coleman Young" a particular interesting quote is found on p. 20. The first Black mayor of Detroit, when asked of his place in history, said:

> "If I don't write it, or a friend of mine doesn't write it, I'm in bad shape."

Coming April 1, 2012, just in time for the state of Michigan declaring financial martial law over Detroit, SBPDL is proud to announce that "Escape from Detroit: The Collapse of America's Black Metropolis" will be released.

To the memory of Mayor Coleman Young, it won't be kind. The truth will be told.

When John Carpenter directed *Escape from New York*, that city appeared to be knocking on death's door. Same with *Escape from Los Angeles,* a movie written only a few years after the LA Riots.

It's Detroit though that should have been the city used as a penal colony for one of Carpenter's films, where Snake Plissken (played by the reclusive Kurt Russell) could have saved the day as only he can. Read the latest news from Detroit's Fox Affiliate, courtesy of Charlie LeDuff (Detroit Police Roll Out New 911 Policy, March 5, 2012) and begin to understand that the world of Detroit is far worse than that of Carpenter's fictional films:

An old man beaten down by a carjacker last month. People stepping around him like he's garbage. Ignoring his calls for help.

But what if somebody had the heart to call the police? There's a distinct possibility they wouldn't have come. Not with the new 911 policy. Unknown to most people, the Detroit police last week quietly rolled out its latest plan to save money: Virtual 911.

This is how it works. If you've been held up and the gunman is long gone, or you've been assaulted but not too badly, or your home has been broken into, that's not 911 anymore. They'll transfer you or you can call the Telephone Crime Reporting Unit yourself at 313-267-4600.
Since officers couldn't get to a majority of the 850,000 calls to 911 last year, most of the time you'll talk to an operator, not a cop.

Nobody in the police department wanted to explain this on camera, but I'm told by a spokesperson if your call is life-threatening, you'll get an officer. Nobody we spoke to, however, thought this was a good idea.

"It's giving criminals the wrong idea," said Tony Wright, a retired Detroit homicide detective. "If you want to do something, do it in Detroit. The police won't show up." Former FBI agent Hank Glaspie feels the same way. "I'm not going to move into any area with my family where I don't think the law enforcement safety standards are up to the level where they should be," said Glaspie.

And 86-year-old Aaron Brantley, the man who was beaten at that gas station last month, he definitely doesn't agree with the new policy. "People called the police and the ambulance. It was so long, I had to get somebody else to bring me home."[222]

So many cities are on the verge of being *Detroit-ed* (when the Black Undertow becomes a numerical majority and assumes control of the city's government). In Michigan, you can add Flint, Saginaw, and Pontiac to the list of *Detroit-ed* cities. All are majority Black cities, with Black people being the root cause for the crime found there:

> Gov. Rick Snyder wants add 180 state troopers, hire 20 forensic scientists and expand drug and mental health courts throughout Michigan.
>
> The public safety plan unveiled by Snyder in Flint on Tuesday includes strategies to fight truancy, joblessless and other root causes of crime in Michigan's four most violent cities.
>
> The governor focused many aspects of the plan on the delivery of what he called "smart justice" in Detroit, Flint, Saginaw and Pontiac. He was joined in the presentation by top law enforcement officials, judges and state officials, including Michigan State Police Director Col. Kriste Kibbey Etue and Maura Corrigan, director of the state Department of Human Services.[223]

---

[222] http://www.myfoxdetroit.com/dpp/news/local/detroit-police-roll-out-new-911-policy-20120305-ms

[223]

http://www.detroitnews.com/article/20120307/POLITICS02/203070402/Snyder-crime-fighting-plan-includes-180-troopers-smart-justice-cities?odyssey=tab%7Ctopnews%7Ctext%7CFRONTPAGE

Truancy, joblessness? The root cause of crime in Michigan is its Black population and the fact that so many cities have been *Detroit-ed*. There is one way to keep peace in a city with a large Black population, and that is through the erection of a mini-police state. Prior to Mayor Coleman Young being elected as mayor of Detroit in 1973, the police force there had an undercover force called STRESS.

It was one of the first things to go under Young's new regime, because it dared target Black people (because, like now, it was Black people in Black neighborhoods that were committing the crime).

Not even Omni Consumer Products (OCP) could save Detroit now.

The truth of Detroit's demise will be told. Not by an admirer, Mr. Young, but by someone with a warning to other cities and counties across America that they must not be *Detroit-ed*.

Guns Don't Kill People; Dangerous Minorities Do -- The Detroit Edition

It gets tiring reading reports on how "liberals," "Progressives," and "unions" destroyed Detroit. The state of Vermont is one of the most liberal, progressive place on earth, with plenty of unions. As one of the whitest states, crime is virtually non-existent. Well, save for the contributions of the small Black population of Vermont, who prison population is 20 times that of the civilian population.[224] *The Burlington Free Press* laments the fact that Black people commit a disproportionate amount of crime.[225]

It just proves what we already know: "Guns don't kill people, dangerous minorities do."[226]

The cities that are used by our own government to train Army, Air Force, and Navy medics preparing for war-zone environments overseas are places, not coincidentally, that are almost 70 percent or higher Black.

Someone named Bill Zettler penned these words, before stating how crime is due to hyper-liberalism and a toleration of unions; an anti-business bias; and, worst of all, an acquiescence to the proliferation of rap/hip-hop:

---

[224] http://www.wcax.com/Global/story.asp?S=6828591&nav=4QcS

[225]

http://www.burlingtonfreepress.com/article/20120227/NEWS03/120227002/Vermont-race-crime-prison-data-troubling?odyssey=tab%7Ctopnews%7Ctext%7CFRONTPAGE

[226]   http://www.vdare.com/articles/libertarian-steve-chapman-thinks-mississippi-has-more-crime-than-vermont-because-of-excessi

---

Washington, D.C. and Chicago have some of the strongest gun control laws in the country.
Obviously, the criminals who committed these crimes were ignoring those laws. In fact, according to Chicago Police statistics from January 1st through April 30th, 96% of murderers had criminal records, as did 72% of the victims.

So what we have are criminals, who should not have guns under current gun control laws, killing mostly other known criminals. Of course, about 30% of victims (and maybe more) were innocent bystanders or victims of robbery and home invasion.

The question is why are these violent criminals on the street? Isn't that a "crime control" problem rather than a "gun control" problem? And who is in charge in these high crime areas? By and large, liberal Democrats control American cities.

For example, in Illinois, if you eliminate Chicago murders, the state's murder rate is about the same as Finland's, while Chicago's rate would be greater than Mexico's, whose murder rate is the sixth highest in the world. Mexico, by the way, has more restrictive gun laws than the U.S., but a murder rate three times that of the U.S. And, no, restrictions on gun sales do not help. Mexico has only one gun store (in Mexico City) and it takes 30 days for a citizen to be approved to purchase a very restricted list of guns. This pretty well disproves Chicago Mayor Daley's contention that tighter government control of gun store sales would minimize gun crime. Another very liberal Democratic city is Detroit--where no Republicans hold an elected citywide office. Disproving Rev. Jeremiah Wright's contention that it is the white power structure responsible for the African-American dilemma, the mayor, the district attorney and eight of the nine city council members are black.

No white guys to blame in this city, just liberal Democrats. Again, when we separate Detroit from the rest of Michigan we find the gun crime problem concentrated in the Democratic areas with Detroit's 8% of the state's population perpetrating 59% of the murders. That puts Detroit's murder rate above Jamaica's, which is the third highest in the world.

And Jamaica's gun laws may be the most restrictive in the world. Possession of a single bullet, with or without a gun, is punishable by life in prison.[227]

---

[227]http://rffm.typepad.com/republicans_for_fair_medi/2008/06/is-baghdad-safer-than-chicago-or-detroit-liberal-politicians-blame-guns-not-the-gunners.html

Wait a second. This guy appears to get it (though he doesn't mention the racial dynamic of those contributing to the lawlessness and violence in D.C. and Chicago -- hint, it's Black people) when he mentions Detroit's racial group as providing the evidence needed to showcase who it is committing the crimes.

But again, he continues to live by the rules, criminal = Democrat. Without operating under this equation, all illusions of crime for these hopelessly I HAD people (I Have a Dream people, since only white people tried - and still try - to live by the decree issued by St. Martin in 1963) collapse to the ground.

It is this propensity for criminal behavior by "The Blacks" that drove white people - 76 percent of Detroit's population in 1960 - into the suburbs. They weren't escaping unions, an anti-business bias (okay, judging by the lack of businesses in majority Black city's and county's, one can conclude that high numbers of Black people are undeniably bad for the maintaining of a business and thus, anathema to sustaining a local economy) or hip-hop/rap; they were retreating from the expanding Black Undertow, which the US Supreme Court declaring restrictive covenant as unconstitutional makes forever impossible to escape.

Those suburbs flourish - however fleeting that might be until those white residents are forced to retreat farther away from the No Man's Land of Detroit due to the expanding Black Undertow - with virtually no crime. Meanwhile, in Detroit, the feds continue to pursue a color-blind policy of enforcement:

> Gun crimes in a section of Detroit's east side will get extra attention from federal officials under a program announced Thursday that is part of a crackdown on violence across the city.

The effort, called "Project 48205" after the area's zip code, was announced by U.S. Attorney Barbara McQuade.

In August, McQuade said her office added more attorneys to its violent crime unit and would pursue more convictions for gun crimes in Detroit.

A federal agent is looking at gun-related crimes that could be prosecuted in federal courts. Using stolen guns or weapons that have scratched off serial numbers is a federal crime. McQuade's office also will look at cases in which convicted felons are caught with guns during crimes, McQuade said.

Federal charges typically carry harsher prison sentences than charges in state courts, she added.

"We want criminals to know that there are very serious consequences to possessing firearms in Detroit," McQuade said Thursday.

The 48205 zip code partly covers one of the more blighted, crime-ridden parts of the city.

"We're letting criminals know their day is done," Mayor Dave Bing said.[228]

---

[228] http://www.mlive.com/news/detroit/index.ssf/2011/09/feds_focusing_on_gun_crimes_in.html

Tell that to the majority of the - yes, they are virtually all Black people - government officials (elected or appointed) in Detroit, where "criminality" has been the word of the day since Coleman Young took power in 1973.[229]

Ten years ago, the state of Michigan made it much easier for the law-abiding citizen to procure a concealed weapon license. Not surprisingly, in a state where the Black crime found in Detroit has spread to Pontiac, Flint, etc., the law-abiding of Michigan have good reason to get their concealed permit:

> Ten years after Michigan made it much easier for its citizens to get a license to carry a concealed gun, predictions of widespread lawless behavior and bloodshed have failed to materialize.
>
> Today, nearly 276,000 -- or about four out of every 100 eligible adult Michiganders -- are licensed.[230]

Unsurprisingly, crime has dropped and those law-abiding citizens with a CWP haven't gone on killing sprees (even in Wayne County, home to Detroit):

---

[229]

http://www.detroitnews.com/article/20120307/METRO01/203070333/Audit-Part-11M-grant-Detroit-job-seekers-only-aided-2?odyssey=tab%7Ctopnews%7Ctext%7CFRONTPAGE

[230] http://www.freep.com/article/20110731/NEWS06/107310482/10-years-after-concealed-weapons-law-unclear-why-many-state-were-gun-shy

During the debate, opponents of the change warned of gun-toting, trigger-happy citizens loose on the streets. But violent crimes have been rare among carrying a concealed weapon license holders. Only 2% of license holders have been sanctioned for any kind of misbehavior, State Police records show.

Wayne County Sheriff Benny Napoleon said he had been opposed to the law and was concerned about flooding the streets with guns. But, he said, "it has turned out not as bad as I suspected that it would."

Napoleon said he would like to see expanded training for people seeking concealed weapons permits.[231]

Every sane person in America hoping to keep their family and person safe should acquire a concealed weapons permit. It should also be noted the progressive, liberal state of Vermont has some of the most gun-friendly laws in the nations.

It should also be noted Black people fill that states jail cells at rates that alarm the good Disingenuous White Liberals (DWLs) of Vermont.

---

[231] Ibid

To his credit, Mayor Coleman Young opposed gun-control laws, but for odd reasons. Remember, when you outlaw guns, only the criminals have them. In "The Quotations of Mayor Coleman A. Young" we find on p. 29 this hilarious quote, On why he refuses to support local anti-gun laws:

> "I'll be damned if I'm going to let them collect guns in the city of Detroit while we're surrounded by hostile suburbs and the whole rest of the state who have guns, and where you have vigilantes practicing Ku Klux Klan in the wilderness with automatic weapons."

Oh that loquacious Coleman Young, never laconic when it comes to expressing his hatred of whitey. Those white people in the "hostile" suburbs have guns precisely because of what happened in late-July 1967, when Black people engaged in what Young labeled an "insurrection" (the worst riot in American history) and burnt significant portions of the city to the ground:

> After the 1967 Detroit riot, for example, gun sales skyrocketed: Detroit issued four times as many handgun permits in 1968 as it did in 1965, and a nearby, predominately white suburb issued five times as many permits.[232]

The Tri-City Herald reported this on April 14, 1968:

---

[232] http://www.saf.org/LawReviews/Riley1.htm

> Gun sales have soared in predominately white suburbs
> of Washington, Baltimore, and Kansas City since
> looting and violence erupted in the Negro
> neighborhoods of those cities this month. Rioting that
> followed the murder of Dr. Martin Luther King Jr. on
> April 4 marked the first major racial disorders in any of
> the three cities in recent years.[233]

And why must Black people always believe that a white-sheet wearing bogeyman awaits them around every corner, under every bed, and in every closet? Last we checked, it was Black people who were responsible for 90 percent of the interracial crime between whites and Blacks in America.

And it is Black people killing fellow Black people in cities all across the nation, especially in Detroit, where vigilante killings are rising because the overwhelmingly Black police force is perhaps the most inept in all of America at doing its job. It wouldn't be a stretch to say that Detroit's police force operates year-around, as the New Orleans police force did in the days after Katrina.

---

[233]http://news.google.com/newspapers?nid=1951&dat=19680414&id=8mQ
hAAAAIBAJ&sjid=JIcFAAAAIBAJ&pg=841,3465441

White people in America just want safety. They want peace of mind. Perhaps this is why gun sales are through the roof right now? Some have said President Mein Obama is the greatest guns salesman of all time, and they'd be wrong. The threat of wide-scale Black violence or the random Black thug trying to mug you always has been (at least since the Indian threat was neutralized).

If you remove the Black contribution to criminality in America (be it home invasion, rape, murder, assault, sexual assault, theft, trespassing, etc.), pretty soon you have an entire nation looking like Vermont when it comes to a peaceful place to live. Of course, you'd have to remove the grossly overrepresented Black prison population - who represent one half of one percent of the Vermont general population - from the equation. Then, then you'd have the kind of America where no one locks their doors.

Doesn't sound like too progressive a place. Sounds like America...

Black America Fists Detroit: That Joe Louis Statue

Whenever a Black individual triumphs over a white individual, this event is seen as a repudiation of white racism, a blow to white supremacy, and a lesson administered to white society. It is a milestone that all Black people believe is somehow representative of their combined might, an indication that Black people collectively have achieved some shining victory, the rectification of some previous wrong. It must be celebrated.

Conversely, this is not the case for white individuals. For white people to take pride in an achievement of one of their own is the ultimate manifestation of racism.

Joe Louis – an individual Black dude – knocking out a German in 1938 in a boxing ring somehow nullified the belief in "Aryan Supremacy." This moment was a watershed for all Black people, just like every Black "First" – i.e., first Black person to balance a checkbook, etc. – which, strangely enough, the commemoration comes long after the actual discovery or achievement has been recorded by a white individual (or member of another race.

That it was largely the contributions of German scientists working with white American engineers that hurled the Apollo astronauts to the moon on July 20, 1969 – sadly, the only Black contribution to this mission was the janitor who cleaned up after NASA's scientists and engineers were done for the day – isn't worthy of discussing.

The Detroit that Black people inherited after the Black Riot of 1967 – the same Detroit that white people fled from only to rebuild in the suburbs – was a veritable symphony, the magnificent collective glory of white individuals working together to build what was deemed "The Paris of the West."

With the election of Coleman Young as the first Black mayor of post-riot Detroit, the symphony that white individuals collectively composed has become a noisome cacophony, as individual Black people have collectively defaced all there that was once good and grand.

And then they stole the orchestral instruments.[234]

Black people were handed a completed opus with Detroit, a concerto of unprecedented beauty and grandeur, all meticulously composed and arranged by white people. Well, it wasn't a complete work of art. One can't forget that Black people had already rioted in 1967 and burnt down large segments of the city, never bothering to clean up the mess or rebuild what they never built in the first place.

You see, it was Black individuals engaging in a chorus of disharmony that brought the symphony that was Detroit to a screeching halt. The melancholy state of Detroit in 2012 is only the expression of the citizens who live there, the combined result of hundreds of thousands individual Black people in America's most homogenous – and Blackest – big city.

234

http://www.reddit.com/r/politics/comments/lhexc/detroit_struggles_to_keep _lights_on_copper/

Where once the white citizens of Detroit built resplendent monuments inspired by the architecture evidenced in the ruins of Ancient Greece and Rome – reminders that though time and neglect are forces that can't be stopped, beauty and lore can linger even in stones cut thousands of years ago – Detroit's new Black rulers elected to build a fitting monument to the era of Black-Run America (BRA): a giant Black fist in honor of Joe Louis.[235]

Sports Illustrated commissioned this sculpture by putting up $350,000 dollars for its erection, and it has come to symbolize "Black power" in a city where the truest display of this phrase has come to fruition in all its absolute finality.[236]

The Los Angeles Times reported this in 1986 about "the fist":

> "I know money is tight, but you would think the city could have afforded a whole statue," says a bewildered Barbara Johnson.
> "It's terrible. I don't see the symbolism in it at all," echoes Renee Leblanc.
>
> Complaints like those are already pouring in here over a stark, abstract memorial to Joe Louis, the late heavyweight champion, which is to be officially unveiled today.
>
> Already dubbed the "fist" by disgruntled downtown office workers, it is just that--a 24-foot, 8,000-pound clenched black fist and forearm, horizontally suspended in midair beneath a pyramidical steel A-frame in the middle of downtown Detroit's busiest intersection. Exudes Brutal Force.

---

[235] http://apps.detnews.com/apps/history/index.php?id=165

[236] http://www.huffingtonpost.com/2012/02/16/monument-to-joe-louis-fist-sculpture-25-years_n_1275709.html

Produced by acclaimed sculptor Robert Graham, who stirred up Los Angeles in 1984 with his sculptures of headless torsos for the Olympics, it seems to jut through the cityscape with the same kind of brutal force Louis used to knock out Max Schmeling.

In a city that conjures up images of vacant buildings, unemployment lines and gray skies, the fist also seems to accentuate the toughness of Detroit's past and present.

But for many in Detroit, it isn't enough. Joe Louis, who grew up here and held the heavyweight boxing crown longer than anyone in history, was perhaps Detroit's greatest hero; the city's largest and most modern civic arena already bears his name.

Both before and after his death in 1981, black Americans have lionized Louis for being among the first major black figures to smash through racial barriers in the pre-World War II era.

Local Reaction Swift

So some here were surprised and a little disappointed that the city wasn't getting a more traditional Louis monument. And even though the bronze sculpture, just installed last week, was visible for only one day before it was covered with a tent in preparation for its official unveiling, local reaction has been swift and generally negative.

"I can't say anything negative about Joe Louis, but I think most of us would rather have a whole statue," says one city employee.

Other downtown workers say they think that the work looked too much like a symbol for militant black power and worried about the impact that kind of symbolism might have in a city still deeply divided along racial lines.

"It is billed as a tribute to Joe Louis, but it looks like a black power fist," notes one. "If it is a monument to Joe Louis, why isn't there a boxing glove on it?"[237]

A giant Black fist, built as a monument in a city where the concept of "Black power" erupted into a conflagration that ultimately convinced white people to abandon the metropolis… you can't get more poetic than this.[238]

In 2004, *USA Today* reported that the statue was vandalized, publishing this revealing quote in the process:

> The fist was erected in 1986 as a gift from Sports Illustrated to celebrate the centennial of the Detroit Institute of Arts. At the time, it evoked a variety of reactions.
>
> "It almost obviously says black power," said Richard Marback, an associate professor of English at Wayne State University who has written about the fist. "People said that is the appropriate way to honor Joe Louis. Here is a black man fighting against racial oppression: He knocked out Max Schmeling, the Nazi boxer." [239]

Wait, the statue representing "Black power" was vandalized? What happened? What could possibly have transpired for people to be so malicious?:

> Two suburban Detroit men pleaded guilty Thursday to defacing a downtown monument honoring boxing great Joe Louis.

---

[237] http://articles.latimes.com/1986-10-16/news/mn-5641_1_joe-louis

[238] http://www.huffingtonpost.com/2012/02/16/monument-to-joe-louis-fist-sculpture-25-years_n_1275709.html

[239] http://www.usatoday.com/sports/boxing/2004-02-23-louis-statue_x.htm

---

Brett Cashman, 45, and John T. Price, 27, could face up to five years in prison at a sentencing hearing scheduled for May 14.

But the Wayne County Prosecutor's Office expected Circuit Judge James Chylinski to approve its recommendation that the men serve 30 days in jail and the remainder of their sentence on probation, and also pay $1,000 in restitution before sentencing, spokeswoman Maria Miller said.

Cashman and Price were charged with malicious destruction of property after using mops to swab white paint on the 8,000-pound sculpture depicting the arm and fist of Louis, who grew up in Detroit.

With credit for three days spent in jail after their Feb. 23 arrest and 21 days served on house arrest, the two residents of Washtenaw County's Superior Township actually will spend just six days behind bars, said Cashman's attorney, Marc Beginin of Birmingham. "He's satisfied with (the sentence) — otherwise he wouldn't have agreed to it," Beginin said of Cashman. "They did what they did, and they're willing to take responsibility for it."

Price's attorney, David Rosenberg, did not return a telephone message left Thursday afternoon at his Southfield office.

The monument is a tribute to Louis and considered by many a symbol of black power and triumph over injustice. But Cashman said earlier that he and Price targeted the fist because of its "violent imagery" and because it was an inappropriate symbol of a city bedeviled by crime, guns and drugs.

Police found photos at the base of the statue of two white police officers shot to death during a Feb. 16 traffic stop. Their suspected killer is black.

"This regrettable event could be used to divide the community," Prosecutor Kym Worthy said in a statement. "We should learn from this incident and use it as another step that will bring the community together."

Cashman and Price have insisted that their action was not racially motivated.

Louis, who lived from 1914 to 1981, moved to Detroit with his family when he was a boy and is a hero in the city. The Red Wings play in a downtown arena named for him, and the sculpture, called Monument to Joe Louis but known to residents as simply "the fist," enjoys a prominent location along Jefferson Avenue.[240]

Defacing the statue? What about the crime of what happened to the infrastructure of the city once Black people took over? The buildings and monuments erected by a different people – those whites who sought refuge in the suburbs – have been defaced and neglected by Black people, who look upon the "Black fist" as the true embodiment of the city's new image:

Detroit's Brown Bomber shattered the myth of racial supremacy with one decisive fight. After suffering a humiliating loss to the German fighter Max Schmeling in 1936, Louis trained tirelessly for a rematch two years later, and defeated the Nazi poster boy in just two minutes and four seconds.

The sculpture that honors him is a 24-foot-long, defiant right-handed punch, suspended above Jefferson Avenue.

---

[240]   http://www.usatoday.com/sports/boxing/2004-03-25-louis-monument_x.htm

Former Detroit Mayor Coleman Young once said that Joe Louis stood for everything that was good about Detroit. I can't help but agree. Joe Louis is the symbol of all that I love about this city.

Lots of people hate this sculpture, saying it glorifies violence. The statue was installed in the late 1980s, back when Detroit was known as the nation's murder capital, and the damage from the '67 riots still felt fresh.[241]

If one fight can shatter the myth of "racial superiority" (whatever that means), what do you call the combined Black individual contributions that were the primary factors in the downfall of Detroit?

Black-rule was abysmal for Detroit. It was a total failure.

Realistically, the only thing to show after nearly 40 years of Black people running Detroit – after Coleman Young was elected in 1973 – it this statue of a Black fist.

It is a reminder that Black people fisted the Detroit that white people left behind. To employ a musical metaphor, Detroit represents a symphony that Black people couldn't perform once they picked up the instruments and tried to play.

No one will ever dare suggest that the Black residents of Detroit are at fault for the city's condition. And no one will openly imply that it was Black individuals who collectively defaced an entire metropolis handed to them once white people were forced out.

---

[241] http://www.npr.org/templates/story/story.php?storyId=103412267

If Joe Louis knocking out some Nazi pugilist helps destroy the belief in racial superiority, can we agree that the abysmal failure of Black-rule in Detroit abolishes the belief in equality? After all, it was individual white people working as a community that raised Detroit; and it was individual Black people working as a community that razed Detroit.

The Joe Louis "Black fist" statue in Detroit is the finest expression of BRA in all the land. The entire city of Detroit has been spoiled by the feckless hands of Black-rule (remember, Detroit is 89 percent Black), and yet this statue stands resolute, a silent, stoic reminder that Black people can never be blamed for their failings whether collectively or individually.

That is the essence of "Black power" in BRA, which ensures more cities will share similar fates and inevitably be Detroit-ed.

Harrisburg, Pennsylvania anyone?

The GM Renaissance Center: A Monument to Black-Run America

Reading Steve Rattner's Overhaul: An Insider's Account of the Obama Administration's Emergency Rescue of the Auto Industry brought about a politically explosive revelation.

GM, the company that was bailed out with your tax-dollars through the Troubled Asset Relief Program (TARP), is headquartered in the GM Renaissance Center (RenCen), which at 73 stories is the tallest building in Detroit.[242]

Built in 1977 as part of the effort to revitalize the downtown area amid growing urban decay after the disastrous Black Riots of 1967 led to the abandonment of the city by white people (white flight had rebuilt Detroit in the suburbs, with the remaining Black population under Mayor Coleman Young busy bringing ruination to what was left behind), the Renaissance Center complex never lived up to its name.[243]

Built for $350 million, but sold for a mere $76 million to GM in 1996 – *The New York Times* reported there were absolutely no takers at $125 million - was an abysmal failure from the start.[244]

The Mackinac Center reports:

> Indeed, the $350 million (in 1970s dollars) "Renaissance" Center was supposed to anchor Detroit's revival. According to The Detroit News, on unveiling a plaque dedicated to the building's private financiers, Henry Ford II (who conceived the Center) said, "Detroit has reached the bottom and is on its way back up."

---

[242] http://en.wikipedia.org/wiki/Renaissance_Center#cite_note-makeover-9

[243]

http://www.jstor.org/discover/10.2307/25652152?uid=3739256&uid=2129&uid=2&uid=70&uid=4&sid=55874691073

[244]   http://www.nytimes.com/1996/05/17/us/gm-buys-a-landmark-of-detroit-for-its-home.html

In 1996, the Center was sold to General Motors for just $76 million, a fraction of what it cost to build. It is difficult to overcome the message such a return on investment sends to entrepreneurs and other investors. The failure of the Renaissance Center to generate an actual renaissance in the Motor City should have undermined municipal leaders' faith in the power of big symbols.[245]

Before GM was bailed out by the government – well, by you, the tax payer – there was talk of a possible merger between Chrysler and GM, which Maura Webber Sadovi reported on in the October 29, 2008 issue of The Wall Street Journal:

> When the hulking complex now known as the GM Renaissance Center was conceived in the wake of Detroit's 1967 riots, civic and business leaders hoped its construction along the Detroit River would help revive the city's downtown. These days it's the battered General Motors Corp. that is looking at the cluster of towers as a potential financial lifeline. The cash-strapped auto maker wants to unlock its equity in the five Renaissance Center towers it owns, which boast millions of square feet of office space, GM's headquarters, movie theaters and a hotel, says Dan Flores, a GM spokesman. GM this month asked a city pension fund to refinance the property and is alternatively considering finding an interested investor to buy it from whom GM would then lease space, Mr. Flores says. The board of the Police and Fire Retirement System of the City of Detroit has no plans to pursue GM's refinancing proposal, says Walter Stampor, executive secretary of the Retirement Systems of the City of Detroit. GM earlier this year spent about $626 million to pay off its debt on the property, according to Mr. Flores.

---

[245] http://www.mackinac.org/8340

The potential sale of one of Detroit's most prominent properties comes as area building owners have taken cold comfort in knowing they already have been tested by high vacancy rates and falling rents, challenges that are new to many of their counterparts in healthier U.S. markets just now facing slowing demand.

Recently that equanimity has begun to evaporate as the increasingly tenuous state of the U.S. car makers that drive demand for the Motor City's property is emerging. Even a potential merger of GM and Chrysler LLC -- while viewed by some as a better scenario for the ailing Detroit-area economy -- would likely result in a flood of surplus properties.[246]

Without TARP and the bailout of GM, what would have happened to Detroit, a city that already relies on federal aid and federal subsidies just to pay the bills and keep its 89 percent Black population feed, housed, and semi-educated? Could the passing of TARP have been the last gasp of the federal government to keep Detroit on life support, considering that the GM Renaissance Center is now has a 93 percent occupancy rate? With Urban Pioneering on the rise in Detroit – and with the impending takeover of the city's finances by the state of Michigan – could we actually see a renaissance in Detroit that looked oh so bleak back in 2008?[247]

As stated, *Overhaul* reported this conversation between Fredrick "Fritz" Henderson, then COO, about the possibility of moving from the GM Renaissance Center to a suburban location. On p. 237-238:

---

[246] http://online.wsj.com/article/SB122523360218877781.html

[247]   http://gmauthority.com/blog/2010/08/blue-cross-blue-shield-to-move-into-gms-renaissance-center/

The politics around GM, with its great size and complexity, not mention its iconic status, promised to be even more intense. Our loving to-do list was full of pitfalls. One day Fritz called me to propose moving GM headquarters from the Renaissance Center to GM's Tech Center in suburban Warren, where we had driven the Volt back in March.

The move would cuts costs, he said, as well as symbolize the leadership's determination to become more to down-to-earth and hands-on. I thought the idea was great, just the kind of action I was hoping to see from Fritz. But when I described it to Deese , he went nuts. "Are you out of your mind?" he said. "Think what it would do to Detroit."
Though small in financial implications for the company – the headquarters was worth perhaps $165 million – compared to the $626 million that GM had paid for it just a year earlier (Sic … GM would spend only $76 million to buy the building in 1996, but spend $500 million renovating the complex) – GM's departure would be a major blow to Detroit. In a one-year period, the once proud city was already suffering with one of the worst unemployment rates in the country, and among the worst murder rates, would see two of its biggest employers go bankrupt, its flamboyant ex-mayor Kwame Kilpatrick convicted of perjury, and its NFL franchise, the Detroit Lions, become the first in football history to go 0-16.

Deese had some people analyze what a mostly vacant RenCen would mean to Detroit real estate. The estimate: a double-digit hit on already deflated real estate prices. Fritz proposed donating the RenCen to the city- though who actually use it was unknown.

The debate, not surprisingly, soon moved beyond Team Auto. Gene Sperling was one of the many to fight the move. "It's over for Detroit if you do this," he yelled in a meeting at [The United States] Treasury. "Don't do this to Dave Bing" – the city's new mayor, a former NBA star and successful auto-supplier entrepreneur. "He's a good man trying to do a good thing." The city relied on GM for $20 million a year in tax revenue, Gene pointed out, and the blowback would be fierce. Deese checked with Larry, who in turn spoke to Rahm [Emmanuel], and word came down that the move would be a bridge too far.

Fortunately, this unique intervention into a specific GM matter was never leaked to the press, saving us from having to explain how it comported with our policy of letting GM and Chrysler manage their own affairs.

Mayor David Bing is poised to ask for an emergency $150 million from the state of Michigan (white taxpayers) instead of being taken over by the financial martial law imposed by the state. GM management wanted to find ways to restructure instead of taking the TARP money (what amounted to a government take-over of GM), and considered heading to the lily-white suburbs.

The government of America (and corporate America) is dedicated to the idea of Black-Run America (BRA), and abandoning America's Black Metropolis would have been disastrous and against official operating procedure. Forcing GM to stay based in Detroit, at the Renaissance Center, was the government's way of mandating the continuation of BRA. Funny that only a year later more than 30,000 Black people would line up in the streets of Detroit after a "rumor" of Obama stimulus checks being based out went viral.[248]

248

http://www.mlive.com/news/detroit/index.ssf/2009/10/thousands_flood_homeless_preve.html

The Renaissance Center was always a mistake – like the hilarious People Mover transit system in downtown Detroit, which can only be compared to the Monorail in Springfield from *The Simpson's* in terms of its absolute superfluous nature and financially wasteful manner- and the government forcing GM to remain in this monument to "wishful thinking" is a reminder of the power of BRA.[249]

In the book "The Rough Road to Renaissance: Urban Revitalization in America, 1940 -1985" John C. Teaford describes for us the failure of the Renaissance Center on p. 271-272:

> Even when by all objective standard a downtown office project proved a failure, messiah mayors and their booster allies could use their ample powers of hype and transform it into a symbol of success. For example, Detroit's mammoth Renaissance Center was both the city's most noteworthy debacle and its most ballyhooed landmark of revitalization. When it opened in 1977, with 2.2 million feet of office space and a 73-story hotel, the Detroit Free Press described it as "the towering symbol of what is hoped to be Detroit's new lease on life." At the lavish dedication ceremony with free champagne for all 800 people present, its principal developer, Henry Ford II, was confident of the invigorating qualities of the center, claiming that it and other construction projects were indications "that the flow of business and commercial operations to the suburbs {had} slowed down very considerably and might well be in the process of reversing itself.
>
> In his 1979 state of the city address, Mayor Coleman Young similarly asserted, "The Renaissance Center has led the way in bringing our down area back."

---

[249] http://en.wikipedia.org/wiki/Detroit_People_Mover

In fact, the center drew tenants from existing downtown office buildings, the main target of the rental agent's sales pitch being firms already located in the central business district. Thus, by 1978 the occupancy rate of the 47-story Cadillac Tower was down to 40 percent, and its woes were not unusual. Moreover, the Renaissance Center itself suffered serious financial ills, losing $140 million by 1983, when its debt and ownership had to be restructured.

A towering, gleaming beaming skyscraper does not by osmosis make the city's primarily Black inhabitants budding entrepreneurs. But there weren't any of the cities esteemed citizens working in the RenCen; it was primarily built as a fortress for suburban workers to – begrudgingly – commute into the city to work in.

The Renaissance Center has received scant praise from Detroit's architecture critics. Several block s from the heart of downtown, separated from the city's edge by a broad ten-lane boulevard and two-story bunkers, the dramatically modern RenCen towers are detached and aloof above their surroundings. The RenCen has been called a "fortress for whites to work in while the rest of the city goes to hell around them."Keeping those "whites" safe in the RenCen, at full strength, the building has a larger security staff than half the nation's police forces.[250]

The Renaissance Center was an instant failure, losing money from the start. In 1978, the RenCen partnership lost $27.2 million, in 1979, $30.3 million; in 1980, $33.3 million, in 1981, $40 million.[251]

---

[250] Darden, Joe. *Detroit: Race and Uneven Devolpment,* Philadelphia : Temple University Press, 1987. p. 51-52

[251] Ibid.

Worse, Ford's prediction was grossly inaccurate: the government of the United States would stop GM from abandoning Detroit in 2008 as the companies stewards tried to find ways to reinvent the corporation.

E. Michael Jones notes in his book "Slaughter of the Cities" that the RenCen project required the largest private investment group ever assembled for an American real-estate venture. "Financing involved a $200 million loan from a consortium of banks and insurance companies as well as at least $300 million from the Ford Motor Company." (p. 599) Without a doubt, the RenCen is a monument to Black-Run America, a structure that thrusts into the Detroit sky, remaining a piercing reminder to the folly of the belief that equality is the natural state of man.

Even Dan Georgakas and Marvin Surkin's "Detroit: I Do Mind Dying" (a study of urban revolution), a radically left-wing book, admits the failure of the Renaissance Center:

> Strategies for reforming even local governments have also become more complex. Despite occasional victories and achievements, if one compares Detroit of the 1960s with Detroit of the 1990s, the city has deteriorated. Where once white neighborhoods at the city's rim surrounded a mainly black inner city, primarily white suburbs now surround a primarily black metropolis. The Renaissance Centre, widely heralded in the 1970s as the engine for revitalizing the city, has proven a disaster.

> From the onset, RenCen had remained viable on paper only because considerable staff from Ford headquarters in Dearborn had been transferred to fill its office space. Built at the cost of $350 million in the 1970s, RenCen sold in 1996 to the General Motors Company for $73 million.

The failure of Detroit to revive and rebuild after the Great Rebellion in 1967 is often attributed to the mercurial mayoralty of Coleman Young or some lacking the city's 80 percent black population. The explanation, however, lies elsewhere.[252]

No, it doesn't. It lies directly with the Black population of Detroit, and the federal government of the United States. The answer to all of Detroit's problems – post-1967 Black riot and the abandonment of the city by white people to be run by Black people – comes in the question found in Wilbur Rich's embarrassing hagiography of Mayor Young in "Coleman Young and Detroit Politics: From Social Activist to Power Broker." It revolves around that wasteful project called The People Mover:

> One of the most widely held and rarely articulated issues during the People Mover construction was, in fact, whether blacks were ready to manage and govern. Simply put, the question was whether or not blacks were competent enough to manage a multi-million dollar corporation - the city of Detroit. Somehow the question had not been answered sufficiently, and it needed to be put forth again, yet no seemed to be prepared to raise the real issue. Silence was broken in a local newspaper interview, when U.S. District Court Judge John Feikens, a man with some liberal credentials, asserted that blacks need time "to learn how to run the city government." He added that black people "talk about a problem and don't know how to solve it."[253]

---

[252] Georgakas,Dan and Surkin, Marvin. *Detroit: I Do Mind Dying.* Cambridge, Mass. : South End Press, 1998. p. 199

[253] Rich, Wilbur. *Coleman Young and Detroit Politics: From Social Activist to Power Broker.* Detroit : Wayne State University Press, 1989. p. 200

No one has ever dared answer Judge Feikens. Indeed, modern American life requires that this question never be asked by anyone in any position of power.

The story of the rise, fall, and the federal government mandating GM stay in the Renaissance Center tells the tale of the tragedy of life – both physically, moral, and intellectual – in Black-Run America (BRA).

Perdition Comes to Detroit, America's Black Metropolis: A Box of Condoms Worth Dying Over?

The AARP recently published the list of the five most dangerous cities in America. Two (Flint and Detroit) are found in Michigan. St. Louis, New Haven (CT), and Memphis round out the list.[254]

Notice any correlation here? This writer from the *New Haven Register* does.[255]:

(Deleted)
> A 2010 crime breakdown shows 23 of the city's 24 homicide victims were black. One was Latino. None were white.

---

[254]   http://www.aarp.org/travel/destinations/info-02-2012/five-most-dangerous-cities.html?cmp=NLC-WBLTR-CTRL-030912-F1-1&USEG_ID=14748510714

[255]

http://www.nhregister.com/articles/2009/08/06/opinion/doc4a7a5350b0103427090509.txt

---

Why was that?

Police Chief Frank Limon and Mayor John DeStefano were asked that question Wednesday at an annual crime data press conference at 1 Union Ave.

They announced that murders rose from 12 to 24 from 2009 to 2010. Twenty-two victims were black males, one a black female, and one Hispanic male.
Of 124 non-fatal shooting victims, 99 were black men; seven were black females; seven Hispanic males; one Hispanic female; eight white males; one white female; and 1 "other male."[256]

St. Louis and Memphis both see Black people enjoying a complete monopoly on the violent crime category. Complete, as in owning Park Place and Boardwalk with the maximum number of hotels the game allots. You land in the wrong neighborhood in either of these cities, and you are mortgaging your life to being a potential - unwitting - participant in a game of "Knockout King."[257]

It is these five cities that showcase, once again, the veracity of the claim, "guns don't kill people, dangerous minorities do."

Detroit, however, is America's Black metropolis. As E. Michael Jones points out in "The Slaughter of the Cities," it's the most racially homogenous big city in America. And to think, in 1960 - before the Black insurrectionary riot of 1967 - Detroit was 76 percent white:

---

[256]

http://www.newhavenindependent.org/index.php/archives/entry/another_year_no_white_/

[257]   http://www.stltoday.com/news/local/metro/the-knockout-game-case-that-shocked-st-louis-and-how/article_cdf5032a-b65e-51e0-a84e-de0f0ce0c5f8.html

After Coleman Young became mayor, Detroit, as part of its attempt to make sense of out of the social chaos which social engineering had brought to the city, "developed a quasi-official ideology that regards the pre-Young era as a time of white colonialism ended by the 1967 insurrection and its aftermath. The situation in Detroit, according to Ze'ev Chafets, who lived there as a boy before moving to Israel, "is very similar to postcolonial situations in the Third World."[258]

No other city in America has come to represent Black America and its potential then in Detroit, where one can see what happens to a metropolis when Black people assume complete control of a city's destiny.

Consulting Chafets book "Devils' Night and Other True Tales of Detroit" (published in the early 1990s, a period when the historic American majority population almost decided to win via the ballot box), we find this passage:

> ...but to Arthur Johnson and the rest of Detroit's black intelligentsia, something is being born in Detroit - a new black metropolis.
>
> "We are engaged in the most determined , feverish effort to save Detroit. Why? Because Detroit is special. It's the first major city in the United States to have taken on symbols of a black city. It has elected a strong, powerful black mayor, powerful in both his personality and his office. Detroit, more than anywhere else, has gathered power and put it in black hands."[259]

Go on step farther than Chafets, William Robertson Boggs dared to write this in 1991 when Coleman Young was still alive, one of the only direct challenges to Actual Black-Run America (ABRA) Detroit published during his lifetime:

---

[258] Jones, E. Michael. *The slaughter of cities: urban renewal as ethnic cleansing*. South Bend, Ind.: St. Augustine's Press, 2004. 410

[259] Chafets, Ze'ev. *Devil's night: and other true tales of Detroit*. New York: Random House, 1990. 28

Show piece Detroit fell apart in 1967. That summer, as they had in so many other cities, black neighborhoods erupted in a frenzy of violence and rapine. Detroit's riots were the worst the country has seen this century. They went on for five days and left 43 people dead. The 101st and 82nd Airborne divisions had to be called in to restore order.

Detroit never recovered from those five days in 1967. Whites have fled the city; in the 20 years following the riots, Detroit lost 600,000 people. The 70 percent white majority of 1960 dropped so quickly that in 1973 Detroit had both a black majority and a black mayor. Now, no other city in the United States has a character or identity that is so clearly black. Mayor Coleman Young calls himself "the black mayor of a black city."

This is scarcely an exaggeration. The police chief and all four police commissioners are black. The school superintendent is black, as are the heads of virtually every city department. Both of the city's congressmen and most of its judges are black.

While federal and state subsidies keep Detroit from complete collapse, Mayor Young operates his city much as an African potentate might. His picture hangs in every city office building, and his name graces the municipal letterhead. The personal business cards of every city employee bear the mayor's name. At every opportunity, he names parks and civic centers after himself. Even the city zoo is now named for Coleman A. Young.

The very history of the city now has something of a colonial-African hue. The period of prosperity before the riots is now officially viewed as analogous to colonization. A city document describes the pre-1967 police force as "a hostile white army, entrusted by white authorities with the job of keeping nonwhites penned up in ghettos."As the riots recede further into the past, they are increasingly seen as a glorious insurrection, in which the oppressed black man threw off his shackles and wrested control from the white man.

Detroit even has its own anthem, which is also the unofficial anthem of black America: *Lift Every Voice and Sing*. The people of Detroit still sing the *Star Spangled Banner* when the presence of whites makes it necessary, but it is invariably followed by an enthusiastic chorus of what Detroiters call "our"anthem. No city in America is more self-consciously black, no city more clearly and completely governed by blacks than Detroit.[260]

One doesn't need to travel to Africa to see what happens when "colonization" ends, though Detroit is an example of what happens when a white civilization is colonized by Black people. We can bid *adieu* to Western Civilization anytime you enter the perdition known as modern Detroit, a city not destroyed by liberalism, but by a consistent application of Black power in every sphere of public and private life. Right Sheila Cockrel?[261]

---

[260] http://www.amren.com/ar/1991/08/index.html

[261] http://www.time.com/time/nation/article/0,8599,1947779,00.html

---

The most dangerous zip code in America is found in Detroit (48205)[262], an area that 100 percent Black - though the downtown Detroit area is 89 percent Black - and a fertile ground for future Whole Foods shoppers once the city gets a national grocery chain again.[263]

In the waning days of ABRA in Detroit, perhaps no story encapsulates the shocking hilarity of Detroit's demise then the tale of woe concerning the shooting death of a Black gas station patron merely trying to purchase a pack of condoms (doesn't Planned Parenthood give these away for free - especially in Detroit?)[264]

We know that life is worth exactly what it costs to buy a pack of condoms in America's Black metropolis:

> A man was shot and killed Friday night after an apparent dispute over the price of condoms at a Detroit gas station.
>
> WWJ's Beth Fisher spoke to an employee at the BP gas station on Fenkell and Meyers, where the shooting took place on the city's westside overnight. The employee said the argument was apparently over the price of a box of condoms.

---

[262] http://detroit.cbslocal.com/2011/09/29/law-enforcement-targets-detroits-deadliest-zip-code/

[263] http://online.wsj.com/article/SB124510185111216455.html

[264] http://www.detroit-stdtesting.com/2011/11/29/detroit-std-testing-critical-for-young-adults/

He said the customer bought a box of condoms, but made a comment that he was overcharged and could have bought them somewhere else for a cheaper price. After being told he couldn't get a refund, the customer allegedly began tossing items off the shelves. That's when, according to the employee, the overnight clerk came out with a gun and fired a warning shot, which struck the customer in the shoulder.

Police say the customer was taken to a local hospital where he later died from his injuries.

Ron Scott, with the Detroit Coalition Against Police Brutality, said they are working on conflict resolution between gas station owners and Detroiters, something they will be discussing at a meeting on Sunday.
"We can't have this kind of attitude and this kind of disrespect for life. Whether it happens to people who work in the gas station or definitely if it happens to people in the community. From what I'm understanding, the price of a condom should not be somebody's life," said Scott.

Police say the store clerk, whose name has not been released, is in custody. An investigation is ongoing.[265]

[265]   http://detroit.cbslocal.com/2012/03/10/man-shot-at-detroit-gas-station-reportedly-over-price-of-condoms/

In Black-Run America (BRA) we are taught to reflexively celebrate the accomplishment of one individual Black person as representative of the entire Black race; conversely, those rules don't apply to white people.

In BRA, we are taught not to notice individual Black failure (reporters won't even mention Black people in crime stories), nor consider it representative of how Black people behave. Those are stereotypes.

For whites, the reverse is true: any negative action of a white person - especially if it is in dealing with a minority group member - is representative of the entire white population of America.

What do you do with Detroit? Since 1973, Black people have been in charge of the government and tasked with maintaining infrastructure there, which they inherited from the white population that fled to the suburbs to build cities, neighborhoods, and infrastructure anew.

The state and condition of a city - or neighborhood - is only a reflection of its majority population. AARP's five most dangerous cities all have one thing in common: in the case of Detroit, America's Black metropolis, there is a distinct absence of white privilege to blame.

Perdition has come to America. Nominally, it's still known as Detroit.

We call it "The Mogadishu of the West."

Detroit Mayor David Bing to ask for $150 million in aid; Detroit's Received More Than a Trillion in Aid Since the Inception of Black-Rule in 1973

"Detroit, the place where capitalism failed."

This quote comes from the book *63 Alfred Street: Where Capitalism Failed* by John Kossik, which blames the failures on Detroit for the inability of capitalism to work in a city where the immutable laws of the Visible Black of Economics have been at work for decades. [266]

Kossik focuses his thesis on the tragic ruins of a Venetian Gothic mansion, built more than 130 years ago when white people were more than 99 percent of population there.
Capitalism didn't fail Detroit, for it is capitalism that has allowed the lily-white suburbs to thrive, courtesy of the ingenuity of the people living there to innovate and produce something of wealth and value. Their labor is rewarded; in Detroit, the exact opposite is on display, courtesy of the Black population (89 percent of the city) found there.

Though it is not formal yet, Detroit's beleaguered mayor is going to do what the first Black mayor of Detroit – Coleman Young – did so well: beg, plead, and pray for federal grants, federal aid, and or a loan to help keep the city moving forward. The Detroit News reported:

> Mayor Dave Bing is seeking $125 million to $150 million in a short-term loan from the state to help fix the city's fiscal crisis, Bing's office confirmed Thursday night.

---

[266] http://www.63alfred.com/

Bing's request follows his State of the City speech Wednesday night where he vowed to keep an emergency manager out of the city and called for "tangible support" from the state, including financial and operational support.[267]

To stave off the collapse of the city – the Detroit School System has already been taken over by the state[268], a system that spends $15,000+ per pupil[269] but produces the lowest big city standardized test scores in all of America and a population that is nearly 50 percent illiterate[270] – and the implementation of an emergency manager to assume control of the city's finances[271], Mayor Bing is resorting to playing the role Coleman Young made famous: Demand more money, and have absolute no return on investment to show for the federal aid, federal grant, or money borrowed to help Detroit move forward.[272]

Wilbur Rich's book *Coleman Young and Detroit Politics: From Social Activist to Power Broker* was basically a running apology for the mismanagement of federal aid that Young was able to convince the government to keep sending Detroit's way.

267

http://www.detroitnews.com/article/20120309/METRO01/203090383/Bing-wants-state-loan-city-150M?odyssey=tab%7Ctopnews%7Ctext%7CFRONTPAGE

268   http://www.newsmax.com/US/Michigan-detroit-poorschools-poorly-performingschools/2011/06/20/id/400725

269 http://cbsdetroit.files.wordpress.com/2011/05/basicskillsreport_final.pdf

270   http://www.outsidethebeltway.com/study-finds-47-of-detroit-residents-are-functionally-illiterate/

271   http://www.nytimes.com/2012/03/08/us/mayor-of-ailing-detroit-resists-outside-takeover.html

272

http://books.google.com/books?id=xl3fiNVcQxQC&q=federal+grants#v=snippet&q=federal%20grants&f=false

Between 2009 – 2011 alone, Detroit Public Schools snagged $200 million in federal stimulus money (the largest amount given to any school system in the state of Michigan)[273]. The test scores and graduation rate produced by these Black scholars (96 percent of the K-12 student body in Detroit is Black) didn't magically go up, though the drop-out rate did. Worse, Wayne County – home to Detroit – received a total of $2.4 billion in stimulus dollars between that same time.[274]

Where did that money go?

The same place that the $11 million grant to help low-income job seekers[275]. Enriching their wardrobes with appropriate attire for interviews (of which only two people were helped). The same place where the $50 million that is sent each year by the federal government for Head Start went:

> Following complaints that the Detroit Human Services Department fostered an environment of nepotism, reckless spending and corruption to the detriment of the early childhood education program Head Start, the federal government plans to stop sending $50 million a year to the city to fund the program, the Free Press learned Thursday.[276]

Head Start has been declared a failure, by the way. Meaning that the $50 million given to Detroit each year for more than 30 years has been a monumental waste of taxpayer money.

---

[273]   http://www.detroitpolitico.com/2012/02/detroit-public-schools-snagged-200m-in-federal-stimulus-money-did-it-help-students/

[274]   http://www.pbs.org/newshour/bb/education/july-dec11/detroitgrad_11-25.html

275

http://www.detroitnews.com/article/20120307/METRO01/203070333/Audit-Part-11M-grant-Detroit-job-seekers-only-aided-2?odyssey=tab%7Ctopnews%7Ctext%7CFRONTPAGE

[276]   http://www.freep.com/article/20120309/NEWS01/203090401/No-more-Head-Start-cash-for-City-of-Detroit?odyssey=tab%7Ctopnews%7Ctext%7CFRONTPAGE

In July of 2011, the Detroit Free Press reported on another city department mismanaging $75 million in federal funds:

> The FBI is investigating the city's Human Services Department over misspent tax dollars and its handling of $100 million in federal grants. There's been a continuing police investigation into how the city's Department of Health and Wellness Promotion has handled about $75 million in state and federal funds. And Detroit Mayor Dave Bing fired the department's director, Yvonne Anthony, in May.
>
> More than 25 of Bing's top appointees have left the city in the last two years, and Bing has pleaded with Detroit's corporate community to be more active in helping to revitalize the city.[277]

Federal grants are needed to keep the police on the streets[278] even though they've stopped responding to 911 calls. The Federal grants are needed to keep firefighters employed.[279] Indeed, federal grants to the tune of millions of dollars are even needed to keep neighborhoods stabilized, though no evidence for stability exists.

There is no tax-base in Detroit anymore. The wealth producers (i.e. white people) fled when the threat of criminality – almost entirely by Black people – became too great in the late 1960s. Those Black people who are in the middle-to-upper-middle class in Detroit are there because of intense affirmative action in the city's government (and in the distribution of contracts to private contractors).

Fitting that Lyndon B. Johnson designated Detroit a "Model City" in the early 1960s, where hundreds of millions of dollars were poured into The Motor City to help alleviate poverty and help the growing Black population get off their knees and onto their feet.

---

[277]   http://www.freep.com/article/20110709/NEWS01/107090375/Federal-workers-help-financially-ailing-Detroit-spend-wisely

[278]   http://www.wxyz.com/dpp/news/region/detroit/federal-grants-will-keep-dpd-officers-on-the-street

[279]   http://www.myfoxdetroit.com/dpp/news/local/detroit-seeks-federal-dollars-for-fire-department-20120110-ms

Helping them with hundreds of millions of aid[280], Detroit's progressive white Mayor Jerry Cavanagh could only watch in horror as Black people engaged in the most destructive riot in American history, burning significant parts of the city, helping convince hundreds of thousands of white people to move into the suburbs immediately.[281]

The New York Times reported in 1997, 30 years after those devastating riots that Detroit never recovered from, that the misery of Black-rule in Detroit was still better than what they had rioted against:

> There were nearly four dozen riots and more than 100 smaller cases of civil unrest in the United States in 1967, but Detroit's riots were the deadliest. A Presidential commission later attributed most of the 43 deaths to police officers and National Guardsmen who, in the commission's view, had gone out of control.The long-simmering anger of black residents at an abusive, mostly white police force erupted here in the early morning hours of July 23, 1967, and lasted five days. The flash point was a raid by white police officers on an after-hours drinking and gambling club at the corner of 12th and Clairmount Streets, in a heavily black neighborhood. By the time the smoke cleared almost a week later, 683 buildings across the city had been damaged or destroyed and tanks had rolled through the streets. But the riots exacerbated demographic shifts that had begun a decade before in many big cities.
>
> Around 1940, many Southern blacks, like various immigrant groups before them, moved to Detroit for the work in the automobile factories. The city's population at the time of the riots was one-third black, and by 1990 that percentage had grown to 76 percent.Even before the riots, many middle-class Detroit residents, particularly whites, had begun moving to the newly built suburbs, commuting to work on the broad highways being built.

---

[280]   http://www.michigan.gov/documents/dnr/mhc_mag_phooie-on-louie_308397_7.pdf

[281] http://muse.jhu.edu/books/9781609170295

238

But the riots turned the steady stream of people moving to the suburbs into a torrent. Businesses followed their customers. Thousands of houses were abandoned as the city's population plunged to 992,000 from 1.6 million at the time of the riots. Even today, some black residents refer to the upheaval here 30 years ago as a rebellion against racist white authority rather than a riot. The site where the troubles began, 12th Street, was renamed Rosa Parks Boulevard in 1976, after the civil rights heroine from Montgomery, Ala., who refused to give up her bus seat to a white man and who later moved to Detroit.[282]

What happened in Detroit is a strangely mirrors what happened in South Africa. The Great Migration of Blacks from the South in the early decades of the 20th century eventually overwhelmed the white population of Detroit. Black people had nothing to do with building Detroit; but they have had everything to do with destroying it.

Same goes with South Africa.

Since 1973, when the city was roughly 50 percent white and 50 percent Black (and boasting a population almost double– of which 89 percent are Black today – the 770,000 it is today), the various – all have been Black – mayors of Detroit have had to rely on grants, borrowing funds, and federal aid to keep the city going.[283]

Fitting that the white residents of Detroit in 1973 – before packing their bags and heading to the suburbs to thrive – tried to save the city via the ballot box. Charles M. Carey's *African-America Political Leaders* tells us this about the year Young was first elected:

---

[282]   http://www.nytimes.com/1997/07/23/us/5-days-in-1967-still-shake-detroit.html?pagewanted=all&src=pm

[283]

http://www.mlive.com/news/detroit/index.ssf/2011/03/detroit_must_accept_grim_popul.html

In 1973 Young declared his candidacy for mayor of Detroit. His opponent was John F. Nichols, the white commissioner of the police who was running on a "law and order" platform. Young stole his thunder by promising to get rid of all kinds of crime, including police brutality. The polls indicated that more than 90 percent of whites favored Nichols, while more than 90 percent of the blacks favored Young. Since African Americans barely outnumbered white in Detroit, Young won by a few thousand votes.[284]

Young didn't get rid of crime, with Detroit instantly becoming one of the most dangerous cities in the world, known as the "Murder Capital" of America in the 1970s. Today, the police don't even report – nor respond to 911 calls – the crime rate.

The floodgates for hiring Black people to get back at whitey began, with Young hiring more Black officers, firefighters, and municipal clerks. No longer could city employees live in the suburbs, they were forced to live in the city.

According to *The Quotations of Coleman A. Young*, this employment of affirmative action hiring policies had a purpose, with the newly elected Young saying:

> "Some people say affirmative action is discrimination in reverse. You're damned right. The only way to handle discrimination is to reverse it."[285]

The past is never past. The lesson of Detroit is the lesson for America; once in power, the presumed inequities of the past will be rectified. In the case of The Motor City, the lingering – dwindling – white population was severely discriminated against, and yet they were asked to pay the bill for their own dispossession.

284

http://books.google.com/books?id=EUVXKwkHuaQC&pg=PA5&lpg=PA5&dq=coleman+young+federal+grants+to+keep+detroit+going&source=bl&ots=Atjo8jB0HQ&sig=0WxE_ANjf2mLGoVXjTjP5lnmY38&hl=en&sa=X&ei=dVNaT7fgH8GrsQLVwcHFDQ&sqi=2&ved=0CFEQ6AEwBw#v=onepage&q=young%2C%20coleman&f=false

[285] Young, Coleman A.. *The quotations of Mayor Coleman A. Young*. New ed. Detroit: Wayne State University Press, 2005.

240

They deserve no pity. The citizens of Detroit deserve no mercy.

The state of Michigan has created 16 "Michigan Renaissance Zones" in Detroit, which are virtually free of any taxation. The whole concept of "enterprise zones" is that instantly – without government intrusion through taxes – capitalism should flourish.[286]

But capitalism hasn't flourished. It would not be far fetched to state that trillions of taxpayer money (via federal loans, grants, and stimulus aid) over a span of fifty-sixty years has poured into Detroit. Whether it was to fight poverty, improve the test scores and graduation of primarily Black students, fight crime, maintain infrastructure, stimulate economic growth, or just pay city bills, the aid has been a waste.

Elliot Washington in 2008 wrote these words about Detroit, with have no basis in reality:

> Since the early 1930s and FDR, Detroit has had a tragic love affair with liberalism, the consequences of which have to a degree been comparable to the sieges by the cruel superpowers of antiquity – Egypt, Babylon, Assyria, Persia, Greece, Rome, the Huns, the Mongols. True, in Detroit there are no siege works here, no boiling oil, flaming arrows, catapults or battering rams, yet the barbarian hoards are not only at the gates, but are *within* the city gates, and these people, infected by a stubborn liberal mindset, are surely killing this town.[287]

The white citizens of Detroit left, after being electorally defeated in a true racial election in 1973. This was after most had left because of the Black riot in 1967 and the high rates of Black crime that white citizens encountered in Detroit.

286

http://www.detroitmi.gov/DepartmentsandAgencies/RenaissanceZones.asp
x

[287] http://www.wnd.com/2008/04/60620/

They built flourishing suburbs wherever they went, leaving behind a city they built to be ruled by Coleman Young and his Black friends.

Liberalism didn't destroy Detroit anymore than capitalism did. It has been the ingenuity of others and the wealth they have created, which has been taxed by a government dedicated to the advancement of Black-Run America (BRA), and sent as federal aid and federal grants that have kept the city of Detroit going to this day.

In the Batman story *No Man's Land*, Gotham City is hit with a massive earthquake that destroys the city. The cost of rebuilding is so great, the United States government decides to blow up every bridge out of Gotham and build a wall around the city, with 24/7 armed guards keeping everyone in the city (via huge walls) and preventing anyone from entering. Even members of the clergy and philanthropic organizations are barred from entering.

This could be one of the solutions to the Detroit problem.

Or, like the plan in *Robocop*, a private company could bailout the city, privatizing all of the agencies (police, fire department, waste, public transit, etc.) there in the process.

Knowing that neither of these two options would ever be implemented, it must be stated that Detroit must never be bailed out again.

Taxpayer money shouldn't continue to support a city built on reversing the perceived racism of the past, blaming whitey for every problem that Black people encounter along the way.

It's time Black people take responsibility for their actions. In this case, we are talking about the demise of one of the great American cities. Scratch that, one of the great cities of the world.

Black people forced white people out of Detroit, who in turn rebuilt the city in their image in the surrounding lily-white suburbs.

Commerce, innovation, and economic activity flourish there.

Detroit? Regression to the mean.

The Visible Black Hand of Economics on display for the world to see. Pumped with a continuous infusion of federal grants and federal aid (your taxpayer money that could have gone to space exploration or cancer research), Detroit has continued to deteriorate under Black rule.

Mayor Bing must be told "no" when he formally requests the $150 million in aid. For the sake of all Americans – Black and white, Hispanic and Asian – the citizens of Detroit must be told why the answer is "no" as well.

"Don't Get Detroit-ed": An Introduction to a New Series

No one wants to admit the reality of *Climate Change*. Real Climate Change.

Cities where the effects of Climate Change have been most overwhelming and noticeable include Camden, New Jersey; Birmingham, Alabama; and Baltimore, Maryland.[288]

What happened in Detroit is far worse. This is why we dub the warning of Climate Change "Don't be *Detroit-ed*."

And this isn't being an alarmist, as a long list of cities across the United States are in jeopardy of being *Detroit-ed*, perhaps the worst fate to befall a metropolitan area in the world.

---

[288]   http://stuffblackpeopledontlike.blogspot.com/2011/08/what-is-climate-change.html

No, that's no severe enough. What has happened to Detroit goes beyond the 10 plagues of Egypt listed out in the book of Exodus. Plagues of blood, frogs, lice, wild animals, pestilence, boils, hail, locust, darkness, and the death of the firstborn... these pale in comparison to what has happened to Detroit since 1973.

In 1990, Primetime Live on ABC aired one of the most damning news stories on what it means to be Detroit-ed. Titled *Detroit's Agony*, the venerable Diane Sawyer introduces the 14-minute story, with Judd Rose reporting, stating:

> "Our first story is not about a city. It's about a warning. Detroit... Once a symbol of US competitive vitality. Some say Detroit it is still a symbol of the future, the first urban dynamo to fall. "

Newsweek reported on the Primetime Live special back in 1990, noting:

> The program was not overtly racist. But it only nodded to the city's black middle class and stable residential neighborhoods. It also lapsed into gratuitous stigmatizing shorthand. To stigmatize the racial divide, producers juxtaposed blacks dancing to M.C. Hammer with suburban whites sipping tea. "So now when it's Hammer time in the city, it's tea time in the suburbs. ' Rose said.[289]

The best quote comes courtesy of Mayor Coleman Young, who stated that any criticism of Detroit is code for attacking "Blacks." That Detroit in 1950 had a population of two million (and was 80 percent white), and in 1990 – 17 years after his election – had a population of less than a million and was 70 percent Black is one of the most ominous signs of *Climate Change* available.

It's not a faulty or fraudulent science. When a city goes from one extreme (80 percent white) to the other (70 percent Black), you'll see discernible Climate Change.

Young was quoted as telling Rose in *Detroit's Agony*:

---

[289]   http://www.thedailybeast.com/newsweek/1990/11/25/desperation-in-detroit.html

---

In this country, Black people are victims of racism. It's not accidental that the cities around the nation that have the largest percentage of Blacks, have the largest percentage of poverty, have the largest percentage of crime, and the largest percentage of unemployment.

Immediately after making this assertion (which is true, because once a city goes majority Black, the Visible Black Hand of Economics takes over), Rose points out:

But in Detroit, Blacks aren't just the majority. They're the authority. They run the police, the police, the courts, the schools, and city hall. But Black political power hasn't meant Black economic prosperity.

When Young claims that other big cities have similar problems (to which Rose didn't state also our courtesy of the Black population), Rose – with a burnt-out home in the background and the 73-story Renaissance Center towering in the distance – said this:

Most big cities do have the same problems. In some cases worse. Washington has more murders, Los Angeles has more gangs, New York City has more racial violence. America's cities are on a dark and dangerous road. But you come here [Detroit], and you get the feeling that this, this is what the end of the road looks like.

Mr. Rose was correct back in 1990. Detroit is the end of the road for American cities. And Mr. Rose was astute to make the observation that Detroit in 1990 was completely run by Black people; he was correct to point out that this did not automatically translate to economic prowess (recall the Black woman who famously said that Obama would pay her mortgage and gas once he was in office; Black people really believe that under a white controlled government, economic gains are created solely by the government and that this is the cause for such deep economic divisions between the races).

Now, imagine 22 more years of uninterrupted Actual Black-Run America (ABRA) in Detroit. It's the point now where the state government of Michigan will step in and assume authority of the Black-run city (now with a population of less than 775,000 and 89 percent Black).

This is what we mean by being Detroit-ed.

Precious metal thieves running wild[290]; no tax-base to even afford keeping the lights on; 911 calls no longer being responded too by police[291]; vigilante justice rising with the police effectively giving up; ambulance drivers abandoned and forced to stay in their vehicles as New Year's[292] revelers fire their guns all around them; corruption and fraud in every level of government and city service; crime statistics no longer kept and actually actively covered-up; paramilitary patrolling the 'nice' neighborhoods as 'guards'; and toddlers being killed left and right, this is what civilization looks like once *Climate Change* has occurred and the Black Undertow assumes power.[293]

The Black mayor of Detroit, David Bing, has asked for $150 million bailout to save the city, without acknowledging that it is largely federal grants and federal aid that has kept the city on life support since Coleman Young assumed office.

Michigan Gov. Rick Synder has removed this option, stating that every struggling city in Michigan (all more than 50 percent Black in population, though Michigan is only 16 percent Black) can't be bailed anymore. [294]

290

http://www.crainsdetroit.com/article/20080609/SUB/806090335/precious-metal-as-thefts-increase-tougher-laws-are-being-mined

291   http://www.theblaze.com/stories/detroit-unveils-new-9-1-1-policy-no-serious-danger-youll-get-transfered/

292   http://www.myfoxdetroit.com/dpp/news/local/detroit-ems-rig-stranded-as-gunfire-rings-in-the-new-year-20120103-ms

293 http://www.crainsdetroit.com/article/20120314/FREE/120319952

294 http://www.detroitnews.com/article/20120315/POLITICS02/203150503/

All the while, the Black people in Detroit warn [and whine] of impending "colonialism" by the 'white' government...[295]

This, to borrow a phrase from Mr. Rose in *Detroit's Agony*, is truly life at the end of the road.

Strange that Detroit's lily-white suburbs – where it's still Tea-time and not "Hammer Time" – thrive. How is that possible again? Though the Black Undertow slowly seeps into these suburbs, they still thrive.[296]

Detroit's Agony should have been a wake-up call. It wasn't. The call went unheeded.

Now, other cities are racing to see which one will be the next to join the ignoble ranks of Detroit, and represent the end of America.

To be Detroit-ed means for Climate Change, real Climate Change, to completely incapacitate a city in every quantifiable category. It means: once you go Black, you never come back. The life the city knew when it was majority white will be replaced with the type of community Black people create regardless of the county or state.

From sea to shining sea, it's always the same outcome.

Unless your Washington D.C., but that's a story for another day.

Tonight, we induct the first city into the "Don't Get *Detroit-ed*" Watch List.

So sit back and prepare to learn about cities where property value is inevitably plummeting, school districts are failing, crime is skyrocketing, and federal aid dependency is higher than the price of a gallon of gas.

---

[295]   http://michigancitizen.com/white-supremacy-surges-in-state-government-p10816-76.htm

[296]   http://blogs.metrotimes.com/index.php/2011/10/how-did-metro-detroit-get-so-segregated-david-freund-has-answe/

It wasn't unions that killed Detroit; it wasn't progressives espousing some utopian form of liberalism; it was Black people.

21,000 Murdered in Detroit since 1969; Who Speaks for them?

It should be known the only way to deal with high rates of Black criminality – in a community where they represent 10 percent of the population or 90 percent - is with force exercised by the police. This is why, in the waning days of white rule (in a city they built) in Detroit, efforts were made to curb rising rates of Black violence – the primary reason housing segregation patterns emerge in any community – by creating the STRESS police task force.

In 1973, Coleman Young would be elected the first Black mayor of Detroit – pushing the domino that would eventually turn a city that was 80 percent white in 1950 to 89 percent Black in 2012 – by campaigning to get rid of STRESS.

Lawlessness and disorder are now the rule in Black-run Detroit, with the new documentary *Deforce* – showcasing what happened in Detroit after the Black "rebellion" of 1967 – letting slip this fascinating detail about why The Motor City should henceforth be known as the land of "murders and executions":

The documentary chronicles key portions of the city's history, ranging from the automobile boom and former Mayor Coleman Young's Poletown Plant to the July 1967 riots and subsequent STRESS police task force's sometimes lawless actions. "DEFORCE" touches on the corruption in Kilpatrick's tenure as mayor, shows a panoramic view of the differences on the border at Grosse Pointe Park and looks at the well-publicized crime statistics and how they got to that point.
"It's bad to other people because other people didn't grow up over here," said "Nod," a Detroit resident in the film. "But to us, it's just regular. ... It's nothing to us."

In 2006, an estimated $1.3 billion to $2.5 billion in drugs was trafficked through Detroit, as chronicled in the film. Of the 21,000 murders that have occurred in the city since 1969, many are drug related. In the first six months of 2004, 65 percent of 800 shootings in Detroit were drug related. In the same time span, 100 U.S. soldiers were wounded in Afghanistan.

"The most disturbing statistic that I'm always (repeating) is more than 21,000 people have been murdered since 1969. That's the population of Birmingham or Sterling Heights," Rodney said. "We've desensitized to the violence in the city. ... If there were a shooting at Groves, it would just turn peoples' worlds upside down and they'd pull their kids out of schools."
They also put it this way: Spanning the three decades of the Northern Ireland Civil War in the late 20th century, Detroit's murder rate was more than six times that of Northern Ireland during that same time period.[297]

Yes, many of these murders probably were drug-related; almost all were just "Black-related" killings. This is why STRESS was so necessary, to stop the fratricide in the Black community; but Black people would rather have lawlessness and disorder in their communities and cities; protecting criminals in their midst's; blaming "whitey" and poverty for their continued problems, then admit the problem rests with them.

---

[297] http://www.candgnews.com/news/local-filmmakers%E2%80%99-doc-analyzes-detroit%E2%80%99s-struggles

Especially in a city that has been so thoroughly re-made into the image of a Black-metropolis as Detroit, where 21,000 murders have happened since 1969 – two years after the Black "rebellion" of 1967.

The most dangerous place for a Black person isn't the womb; it's Detroit, a metropolis who's every level of government, police, and public services are run entirely by Black people.

21,000 murders since 1969; this is the legacy of America's version of the Revolution in San Domingo. Detroit is both "The Mogadishu of the West" and the manifestation of John Brown's dream, which came true in the Republic of Haiti.

White people fled the ashes and ruins of Detroit after the Black insurrection in 1967, when a raid of a Blind Pig turned into massive Black riot in response to what they deemed "police brutality."

Since 1969, 21,000 people are dead now, victims of wanton criminality in Detroit.

The Color of Crime report showcases why white people chose not to live in areas with high levels of integration. The reason? Their life might just depend on it:

> Of the nearly 770,000 violent interracial crimes committed every year involv- ing blacks and whites, blacks commit 85 percent and whites commit 15 percent.• Blacks commit more violent crime against whites than against blacks. Forty- five percent of their victims are white, 43 percent are black, and 10 percent are Hispanic. When whites commit violent crime, only three percent of their victims are black.
> • Blacks are an estimated 39 times more likely to commit a violent crime against a white than vice versa, and 136 times more likely to commit robbery.
> • Blacks are 2.25 times more likely to commit officially-designated hate crimes against whites than vice versa.[298]

---

[298] http://www.colorofcrime.com/colorofcrime2005.pdf

Newsone.com, the Baghdad Bob of Black news web sites, had the audacity to publish a story claiming white-on-Black killings are rampant in the new millennium. Of the eight profiled, the vast majority involve a police officer using lethal force to put down a Black criminal. [299]

Those 21,000 murder victims in Detroit from 1969 to today have no voice. After the Black "rebellion" of 1967, the battle of Detroit had been effectively won; there is no need to pay attention to what happened once Black-rule commenced, for "whitey" had been dethroned.

That 21,000 people have been murdered – and that nearly all of these have been Black – isn't cause for national concern.

For it to be, we'd have to admit that Black-rule has been a failure, and that Black people lack the capacity to govern themselves and create safe communities.

21,000 murdered in Detroit since 1969. And yet the murder of Trayvon Martin is somehow worth crying over.

Who speaks for the dead in Detroit? No one. There is no money in it, for it would only bring national attention to the disorder rampant in Black-run Detroit; there is a money shot in Organized Blackness running to the defense of a Black kid shot by a Cuban outside of Orlando.

The key to understanding Black-Run America (BRA) is Detroit; to unlock the madness that our modern era is entirely based upon resides in this one city, which could topple the egalitarian nonsense that dominates conventional wisdom (mandated by Disingenuous White Liberals – DWLs - of course).

After the fire and smoke subsided in Detroit following the 1967 Black "rebellion", and the 82nd Airborne and National Guard units left, President Lyndon B. Johnson set-up the Kerner Commission to find out what went wrong.

---

[299]   http://newsone.com/newsone-original/tjstarr/black-men-killed-by-white-people/

Whitey was, of course, blamed.[300] Bill Moyers of PBS would comment on the 40th anniversary of the commission in 2008, publishing this:

> Forty years ago race and class was on the minds of Americans too — when The National Advisory Commission on Civil Disorders released its report on the urban riots of 1967. That report, more commonly known as the Kerner Report, with its stark conclusion that "Our nation is moving towards two societies — one white, one black — separate and unequal" — was a best-seller. It was also the source of great controversy and remains so today. Referencing the Kerner Commission report has become rhetorical shorthand in some ways.
> For critics it suggests wasteful federal spending programs — for others, societal goals and potentials not yet met. In covering the 40th anniversary report USTODAY headlined its 40th anniversary coverage "Goals for Black America Not Met." The article raised some ire when quoting Robert Rector of Heritage Foundation: "Rector says the report ignores a major cause of poverty: single-parent homes. He says 70% of black children do not have a father in the home." That sentiment earned this response from Elliott Currie, a member of the Kerner Commission, 40th Anniversary Task Force: "The implication is that it's the heedless behavior of black men — rather than the strains of a blighted economy and a legacy of discrimination — that is responsible for the continuing crisis of poverty and racial disadvantage 40 years after the Kerner Commission."[301]

Why yes Mr. Currie, it is the fault of heedless Black men. It's really that simple. It was heedless Black males who primarily pulled the trigger of the gun that ended the lives of more than 21,000 primarily Black people since 1969 in Detroit; it is Black people's inability to create businesses in Detroit – after white people left and creating thriving suburbs – that would enable the city to have some tax-base for city services.

---

[300] http://historymatters.gmu.edu/d/6545/

[301] http://www.pbs.org/moyers/journal/03282008/profile.html

But we can't blame Black people in BRA for anything, let alone the collapse of what once was "The Arsenal of Democracy"; were we to blame Black people for their actions, the world DWLs have created evaporates into the air like a small puddle on a hot, southern summer day.

Disproving Walter Williams Theory of Liberalism Behind Majority-Black Cities Collapse: A Look at Detroit Public Schools

This is a two-part series, a look at a recent column by Walter Williams – white conservatives favorite Black columnist because he writes what so many of them wish they could say – that states Black Democrat mayors are the reason a city like Detroit has collapsed and that crime is the result of the liberal agenda.

That Pittsburgh, controlled by continuous line of Democrat mayors since 1934, isn't a city overwhelmed with crime completely obliterates Mr. Williams theory; so does the state of Vermont, the most liberal in all of America. That Pittsburgh, considered one of the best places to live in America, is also one of the whitest big cities left in America is just a coincidence right, when Detroit is the most homogeneous big city in all of the US (and, coincidentally, the Blackest)?[302]

---

[302] http://en.wikipedia.org/wiki/List_of_mayors_of_Pittsburgh

Wrong. The reason that Detroit is the way it is, and so many other American cities are on the verge of being *Detroit-ed* are related to three things: high levels of Black crime, lower levels of collective intelligence (a thriving city requires an abundance of above-average intellects; a dying city requires the reverse, as below-average intellects are incapable of maintaining the infrastructure); and affirmative action policies which replace white bureaucrats in all levels of public office with unqualified Black employees. High levels of crime in poverty-stricken Black neighborhoods do not correlate to the same scenario transpiring in poverty-stricken white neighborhoods, which as Williams correctly pointed:

> Crime imposes a hefty tax on law-abiding residents of black neighborhoods. Residents bear costs of having to shop outside of their neighborhoods; criminals have driven many businesses out. Children can't play safely in front of their homes. Fearing robberies, taxi drivers, including black drivers, often refuse to accept telephone calls for home pickups and frequently pass black customers by on the street. Neighborhood property values are lower as a result of crime. Plus, there's the insult associated with not being able to receive pizza or other deliveries on the same terms as people in other neighborhoods.[303]

Walter Williams is describing – in succinct detail – the Visible Black Hand of Economics theory, which has constantly been validated wherever Black people become the majority population in America. No greater example of this criminally understudied phenomenon can be found than Detroit, Michigan.

We start this journey to invalidate the beloved Walter Williams theory that liberalism is the cause for Detroit's collapse by looking directly at the education system in The Motor City, which is responsible the more than 90 percent Black student body there with learning the "three R's" and understanding the importance of civic virtue so that they will become custodians of the cities bright future.

---

[303] http://www.wnd.com/2012/03/what-black-dem-mayors-have-wrought/

Sadly, though per-pupil-spending in Detroit is some of the highest in all of the nation ($15,000 per student), most students leave high school only equipped with an education worthy of earning a vocation as a custodial attendant.[304]

It was in 1971 that disgraced former mayor of Detroit, Jerome Cavanagh, surveyed the scene of fleeing white businesses owners from Detroit and said, that he planned trips to "Detroit's sister cities -- Nagasaki and Pompeii."

Two years later, Coleman Young would be elected mayor Detroit and the conversion of Detroit from an overwhelmingly white metropolis with a Black crime problem to an overwhelmingly Black metropolis with an even bigger Black crime problem was complete.

Cavanagh, like all Disingenuous White Liberals (DWLs), knew that Black people were incapable of maintaining the city that whites were leaving behind; he knew that the bulk of Black children in schools would grow up to take jobs as barbers, nurses, security guards, postal clerks or postal service mail sorters, taxi drivers, bus drivers, or parking lot attendants, and that this would be no way to sustain a city in need of entrepreneurs and new business.[305]

Outside investors would be scared off because of the high rates of crime found in the city, leaving Detroit with a shrinking tax-base of largely illiterate Black individuals, more than 30 percent (50 percent of Black children) living under the poverty line.[306]

Cavanagh, aware of the high rates of Black crime, knew that a city destroyed by an atomic bomb and one destroyed by a volcano would be the perfect twosome for a city destroyed by Black people.

---

[304] http://www.mackinac.org/10743

[305]

http://www.allgov.com/Unusual_News/ViewNews/10_Occupations_with_Largest_Percentage_of_African_Americans_100905

[306]   http://www.outsidethebeltway.com/study-finds-47-of-detroit-residents-are-functionally-illiterate/

It all starts with the children, and in the Detroit Public School system,[307] more than 40 armed police officers and 300 security officers patrol the hallways in a fruitless quest to quell the violence; after seeing more than 800 on-campus assaults since 2009,[308] every high school has high-tech security systems[309] in place that all students must walk through daily to check for concealed weapons; students are required[310] to go through metal detectors, metal wand checks, pat-downs, and random searches because of fears of weapons and drugs; and all of this so that Detroit Public Schools – the beneficiary of $200 million in stimulus money from 2009 – 2011 – can graduate 21 percent of its students![311]

What's the good news out of the TSA-level security at Detroit Public Schools? Violent crime is down![312]

So, when the more than 90 percent Black DPS school system isn't staging UFC quality exhibition bouts, what type of learning and, ultimately, test results do we see?:

307

http://www.redorbit.com/news/education/429029/detroit_public_schools_ne w_security_efforts_begin_cops_get_training/

308   http://loop21.com/content/detroit-public-schools-now-have-metal-detectors

309   http://www.clickondetroit.com/news/Detroit-High-Schools-Get-High-Tech-Detectors/-/1719418/1787472/-/4atht9z/-/index.html

310   http://detroit.blogs.time.com/2009/12/17/do-detroit-public-school-students-deserve-4th-amendment-protection/

311   http://www.google.com/#hl=en&sclient=psy-ab&q=200+million+stimulus+detroit+public+schools&oq=200+million+stimu lus+detroit+public+schools&aq=f&aqi=&aql=&gs_sm=3&gs_upl=44117924l 0l8088l49l42l1l4l4l0l177l4738l17.25l50l0&gs_l=hp.3...44117924l0l8089l49l 42l1l4l4

312

http://www.mlive.com/news/detroit/index.ssf/2012/02/crimes_down_at_detr oit_public.html

Detroit Public Schools' students recently won the award of the worst math scores in the National Assessment of Educational Progress' 40-year history. Couple the disheartening standardized test scores with the nation's lowest graduation rate, according to NPR, and you have a public school system that has utterly failed its students. [313]

Worse, those students who take standardized tests in DPS perform at historic lows for not just the state of Michigan, but the entire nation:

The data released Tuesday also shows no more than 33 percent of students met or exceeded the state's standards in any given category. Math was the district's worst category with less than 600 students making passing grades. The best was reading, which 32.6 percent of students passed the test.

June 29, The Detroit News: The news also is grim for other predominantly poor districts in Metro Detroit, including Ecorse, River Rouge, Inkster and Pontiac, where two-thirds to 90 percent of the students are eligible for free and reduced lunches.

In all of those districts, students who took the MME this spring were well below state averages in math, reading, social studies, writing and science. In Ecorse, just one of the district's 81 juniors was considered proficient in writing and math.

Also, despite a district-wide academic plan adopted last year for ACT scores, DPS scored dropped to 15 from 15.5 last year.[314]

An average of a 15 on the ACT (out of 36)? And you expect these students to be prepared for college, let alone run a once mighty city – and sustain an economy there - that was called the "Arsenal of Democracy?"

---

[313] http://www.publicschoolreview.com/articles/195

[314]

http://www.mlive.com/news/detroit/index.ssf/2011/06/detroit_public_school
s_merit_e.html

In 2009, the sons and daughters of America's first Black metropolis produced results in a national standardized test that confirm the bleak prediction of Cavanagh from way back in 1971:

> Most Detroit Public Schools' fourth- and eighth-graders were unable to score at a basic math level on a national test this year — marking the lowest performance in the history of the National Assessment of Educational Progress.
>
> Taken by about 1,900 fourth- and eighth-graders, Detroit's fourth-graders scored 200 against the national average 239 on a scale of 500. Just 18 urban districts participated in the NAEP.
>
> While the test scores hit a historic low in the nation, the test also indicates the movement toward reform. More than a year ago, DPS voluntarily decided to take part in the NAEP in order to see how its progress compared to other districts nationally. Reform efforts underway will include an emphasis on reading, preschool and new technology in classrooms districtwide.[315]

Even the conservative wet-dream alternative to public schools (the only way to end the racial gap in learning!), charter schools, show embarrassingly low results in Detroit, further proof that the collapse of Detroit goes far beyond liberalism and might fall squarely on the problem of one-party rule in the city. That being the party of Black-rule, courtesy of men and women whose sons and daughters produce the lowest NAEP test scores in American history.[316]

130 schools in Detroit have closed since 2005; mostly because of the low test scores compiled by the students in the schools. These scholars will be tasked with helping save Detroit and ushering in an era of prosperity rivaling that of Henry Ford's 1920s Detroit, when the city boasted the tallest selection of skyscrapers in the entire world.[317]

---

[315]   http://www.freep.com/article/20091208/NEWS01/91208020/Detroit-students-scores-record-low-national-test

[316] http://www.crainsdetroit.com/article/20110707/FREE/110709948/report-charter-high-schools-often-lag-detroit-public-schools-test-scores

[317]   http://www.usatoday.com/news/nation/2011-07-06-Atlanta-schools-standardized-test-cheating_n.htm

But hey, the graduation rate is trending upwards[318] (really has nowhere else to go), while the drop-out rate seems on the decline too![319]

But what percent of these graduates are college ready upon completion of their studies in DPS?:

A quick perusal of the database that the Detroit Free Press provides shows some heartbreaking figures.

> In Detroit, the numbers were downright abysmal. Only Renaissance High, the district's top high school, broke even that 10 percent threshold. Of course, Renaissance's graduation rate in 2010 was an impressive 95.5 percent. At Cass Tech, which also graduated 95.5 percent of its students last year, only 4.4 percent of this year's expected grads are prepared for the next level academically.
>
> Meanwhile, at every other Detroit public high school, the portion of students deemed college ready was less than 1 percent.
>
> The local charter schools, hailed by many as a key component to Detroit's educational turnaround, also reflected pathetic numbers. At Winans Academy High School, for instance, the 2010 graduation rate was 88 percent. The percent of student deemed college-prepared? Zero. Same for Detroit Academy of Arts and Sciences, which boasted a 92 percent graduation rate last year.[320]

---

[318]   http://detroitk12.org/content/2011/02/22/dps-reaches-62-percent-graduation-rate-the-highest-since-state-began-new-cohort-methodology-in-2007/

[319]   http://www.pbs.org/newshour/bb/education/july-dec11/detroitgrad_11-25.html

[320]

http://www.mlive.com/news/detroit/index.ssf/2011/02/state_education_stud y_finds_th.html

Oh well; at least most of the Black male students received the proper training in how to go through security, since the odds are most will wind up in prison at some point in their life. If they go into public service in Detroit, the odds are even higher they'll face jail time.

Don't cry for the students in Detroit, though, as every one of them receives a free lunch courtesy of the tax-payer.[321]

So, Mr. Williams, these are the individuals whose parents are tasked with running Detroit. This is what happens when you affirmative action an entire city, driving white people to the suburbs, and installing a one-party (Black-rule, not Democrat) system of government into city hall.

Lower levels of intelligence, when compared to the rest of the state, pace Black-run Detroit, with the children of these leaders showing the apple doesn't fall far from the tree.

And what of those who attend college at Wayne State University in Detroit?:

> Wayne State is located in America's largest black-majority city, yet is one of the nation's worst at getting degrees into the hands of African Americans. Only one in 10 black students who enroll at Wayne State earn a degree within six years -- a startling rate that is less than one-fourth the national average for African Americans and one-fourth Wayne's own graduation rate for white students.
>
> Wayne's black-white graduation gap is the widest among all public universities in United States, but many other Michigan schools aren't far behind. The state's public and private universities have the sixth-highest racial graduation gap in the country in 2010, according to Education Trust.

321

http://www.mlive.com/news/detroit/index.ssf/2011/08/all_detroit_public_sch ools_stu.html

More than half of white students get a degree within six years at Michigan's public universities, compared to a third of African-American students. [322]

Jerome Cavanagh, who was elected mayor of Detroit because of promises to the city's Black population (only 26 percent of the population in the early 1960s, yet responsible for 65 percent of the violent crime) that he'd implement affirmative action polices in hiring, foresaw that Black-rule translated to an atomic blast over the city or a spontaneous volcanic eruption. [323]

And that has occurred. Just take a look at the "Ruin Porn" coming from Detroit, which rivals the actual porn coming from Los Angeles.

From the pages of Playboy magazine comes the most damning report of Detroit Public Schools, which in turn is a damning report of those Black students, who comprise 88 percent of the DPS enrollment.[324]

Frank Owen writes:

> Beyond the murder rate, there are three statistics that tell you a lot about what's happening in Detroit: More than half the residents don't have high school diplomas, 47 percent of the adults are functionally illiterate, and 44 percent of people between the ages of 16 and 60 are either unemployed or not looking for work. Half the population is disqualified from participating in the official economy except at the lowest levels.[325]

---

[322]

http://www.mlive.com/news/detroit/index.ssf/2012/02/at_wayne_st_easy_to _get_in_dif.html

[323]   http://www.michigan.gov/documents/dnr/mhc_mag_phooie-on-louie_308397_7.pdf

[324] Characteristics of the 100 Largest Public Elementary and Secondary School Districts in the United States: 2008–09

[325] Owen, Frank. "Detroit, Death City." Playboy. August. 2004: 60-65

The Kerner Report as Blueprint for Black-Run America (BRA)

The days of democracy in the Black metropolis of Detroit are dwindling, denoting a truth that pierces the heart of the esteemed Walter Williams theory that liberalism is at fault for the failure of Black people. Portland, Austin (Texas), Boulder (Colorado), Silicon Valley (California), Seattle, and Burlington (Vermont) all thrive while they have the same progressive liberalism that Williams believes is the root cause for the collapse of Black-run cities like Philadelphia, Cleveland, and Detroit.

But these Stuff White People Like (SWPL) run cities aren't mismanaging hundreds of millions of dollars in state grants over a 20-year period[326]; they aren't having their credit rating downgraded by Fitch Ratings and Moody's Investor Services; no, they are some of the nicest places in America to live, in spite of the overwhelming whiteness and liberalism found in these cities.[327]

In Detroit, the most homogenous big city in America (89 percent Black – at it's height in 1950, it was 80 percent white), the state of Michigan is on the verge of repossessing the city:

> A state-appointed review team unanimously agreed Wednesday that a "severe financial emergency" exists in Detroit and that some form of a consent agreement is necessary, but did not recommend a specific plan.
> The Rev. David Murray, a former Detroit school board member, said he feels sorry for the state panel because they are being used.

---

[326]   http://www.freep.com/article/20120322/NEWS01/120322085/Detroit-City-Council-hopes-to-reach-compromise-with-state-on-grants?odyssey=tab%7Ctopnews%7Ctext%7CFRONTPAGE

[327]   http://www.freep.com/article/20120322/NEWS01/120322074/Detroit-s-credit-rating-downgraded-by-second-agency

"It's a racist attack. I don't care what color face they put in front of us," the Rev. Murray said. "We don't want a review team (or) a financial manager. We want our money. I'm asking if you will stand up against this tyranny and resign."[328]

What money? Detroit lost all of its wealth-producing tax-base after the 1967 Rebellion, when 10 percent of Detroit's 500,000 Black population joined in the five-day riot that cost the lives of more than two score people, convincing the white citizens that it was time to evacuate the city.

Since, Detroit has limped along via generous federal grants to sustain a city where the sons and daughters of those who comprise the majority of the police, fire fighters, civil servants, city employees, and government officials produce the lowest standardized test scores in all of the nation.

This is what happens when you have an entire city whose political power is entirely in the hands of Black people, with massive affirmative action policies in place since the early 1960s replacing actual merit-based hiring.

One need only look at the student's performance in Detroit Public Schools (DPS) to get a glimpse of the intelligence of those actually running the city's government and in charge of sustaining the economy.

But why was all of this allowed? Why is all of this tolerated? The Detroit Riot of 1967 (described proudly as an "insurrection" or "rebellion" by the Black residents against the occupying white political establishment, though Black people were the ones who colonized the city via wave after wave of The Great Migration and eventually forced whites out because of high levels of crime) was one of hundreds of Black uprisings in the 1960s, largely due to the perceived police brutality the Black communities in cities with nearly all-white police forces faced.[329]

328

http://www.detroitnews.com/article/20120321/METRO01/203210437/Review-team-Severe-financial-emergency-Detroit-Dillon-gets-plan-from-city?odyssey=tab%7Ctopnews%7Ctext%7CFRONTPAGE

[329] http://www.pbs.org/wgbh/amex/eyesontheprize/story/13_detroit.html

The reason for this extra-scrutiny: Black people were the ones, just as now, committing the vast number of the crimes:

> Throughout December 1960 and January 1961 both the *Detroit Free Press* and *The Detroit News* focused heavily on "black crime." The *News* reported, for example, that although "blacks con- stituted 26 percent of the city's population, they were responsible for almost 65 percent of serious crime." The paper also blamed African American leaders and their communities for not doing enough to stop crime.[330]

When white cops (95 percent of cops in Detroit were white in 1967) raided a speakeasy in late July 1967, Black people in Detroit protested the incursion of law into a lawless part of their neighborhood.

"This is a racial incident... it represents one simple thing: black people want control of black communities," the Rev. Albert Cleage, a Detroit religious leader proclaimed.

Well, Rev. Cleage got his wish; white people ceded power to Black Detroiters by voting with their feet. Now, the state of Michigan wants Detroit back because Black people defaulted on Martin Luther King's dream. They have been judged by their collective inability to display quality fiduciary character (the average credit score in Detroit is 619) in administering the budget and maintain the infrastructure of the first major American Black metropolis – thankfully built by white people who only needed a riot and continued high rates of Black criminality to convince them all to leave.[331]

But what keeps people from admitting the true reason for the failure of Detroit, and instead has them blame "liberalism" when this same ideology is practiced and espoused by the primarily white citizens of Boulder, Colorado as they walk down the pristine avenue of Pearl Street?

---

[330]   http://www.michigan.gov/documents/dnr/mhc_mag_phooie-on-louie_308397_7.pdf

[331]   http://www.bizjournals.com/washington/news/2012/03/15/area-credit-scores-debt-higher-than.html

---

Why does Walter Williams continue to blame "Liberalism" for the failure of Detroit, when other cities flourish under the same political mindset?

To state otherwise, that the Black citizens of Detroit are responsible for the fate of the city, would invalidate the official mission of the United States of the America since the smoke was still clearing in The Motor City in 1967.

Lyndon B. Johnson, having already spent billions to improve the lives of Black people in major cities throughout the nation, commissioned a report on the root cause of the Black riots that swept America in the 1960s.

The Kerner Report.

To understand why we live in what we have dubbed Black-Run America (BRA), the starting point for researching why Black people's failures (especially why the complete collapse of Black-run Detroit) must never be blamed – and their choices, actions, decision, and thinking - on them can be traced to this one document.

What does the Kerner Report actually state?:

> "This is our basic conclusion: Our nation is moving toward two societies, one black, one white – separate and unequal. Reaction to last summer's disorders has quickened the movement and deepened the division. Discrimination and segregation have long permeated much of American life; they now threaten the future of every American."

The future for every American is jeopardized because of the existence of what we call BRA; to continue to live under the delusion that Black people aren't responsible for their actions threatens the future competitive nature of the United States, because of the misallocation of trillions of tax-dollars to fight so-called "white racism" as the fundamental cause of Black failure. This is what the Kerner Report blamed Black failure upon:

Despite the complexities, certain fundamental matters are clear. Of these, the most fundamental is the racial attitude and behavior of white Americans towards black Americans. Race prejudice has shaped our history decisively; it now threatens to affect our future.

White racism is essentially responsible for the explosive mixture which has been accumulating in our cities since the end of World War II. Among the ingredients of this mixture are: 1. Pervasive discrimination and segregation in employment, education, and housing, which has resulted in the continuing exclusion of great numbers of Negroes from the benefits of economic progress.

2. Black in-migration and white exodus, which have produced the massive and growing concentrations of impoverished Negroes in our major cities, creating a growing crisis of deteriorating facilities and services and unmet human needs.

3. The black ghettos where segregation and poverty converge on the young to destroy opportunity and enforce failure. Crime, drug addiction, dependency on welfare, and bitterness and resentment against society in general and white society in particular are the result.

The document offers the blueprint for which our entire society has been based upon, going so far as to blame undesirable nature of the jobs available to Black people as the cause of poverty (instead of their intellectual ability, when the current vocations with the highest rate of Black employment 43 years after affirmative action went into overdrive to promote Black people above their station include barber, postal worker, taxi driver, and bellhop); blaming slavery and long periods of unemployment for the "Negro" family structure to be more matriarchal; and the criminality found in Black areas completely on poverty.

From the ashes of American cities, the fires started by Black people upset that white police dared focus extra-attention on their communities because of higher rates of crime found within, spawned this report which findings still permeate throughout every level and operation of both the public and private sector life.

In 1988, The New York Times published an expose on how progress had been made to curb that white racism which was to blame for Black kids throwing bricks through windows and looting businesses all across the nation (burning them to the ground after absconding with stolen goods):

> The National Advisory Commission on Civil Disorders, headed by Gov. Otto Kerner of Illinois, blamed "white racism" for the "continued polarization" of American society, and argued that only a "compassionate, massive, and sustained" Government effort could reverse the overall trend.
>
> Cleveland and other American cities show the mixed record that has been compiled over the two decades. The worst-case prognosis of the Kerner report - the division of American into separate but unequal societies - has not come about, but the general direction predicted by the report and the stubborn persistence of the race problem in America have endured.
> Black progress is a difficult thing to measure, particularly in the current paradoxical situation, where some succeed as entire communities descend deeper into failure. But among the ingredients of change most often noted by scholars is the extraordinary increase of black political power, in Congress and other parts of the Federal Government and especially in the major cities.About 300 cities, including many of the nation's biggest, have black mayors. The Rev. Jesse Jackson is a serious Presidential candidate. Mayor Andrew Young of Atlanta was the United States representative to the United Nations under President Carter. Representative William H. Gray 3d, a Pennsylvania Democrat, is chairman of the important Budget Committee.[332]

---

[332] http://www.nytimes.com/1988/02/29/us/20-years-after-the-kerner-report-three-societies-all-separate.html?pagewanted=all&src=pm

Those big cities that Black people became mayor of have all largely collapsed (outside of Denver).

The New York Times would publish another article that relied heavily on the finding of the fabled Kerner Report to explain the Los Angeles Riots of 1992:

> One of the report's most famous and controversial findings was its conclusion that: "White racism is essentially responsible for the explosive mixture which has been accumulating in our cities since the end of World War II." To some critics, the emphasis on racism, in both the report and the national civil rights debate, has obscured the degree to which the answers to the problems of the ghettos must come from within.
> "The assumption was that white America was the problem and therefore white America was the solution," said Robert Woodson, a black who heads the National Center for Neighborhood Enterprise in Washington, which calls for conservative, self-help solutions to inner-city problems. "It set up the proposition that the destiny of black America rested with what white America did."
> Representative Gary Franks of Connecticut, the only black Republican in Congress, said welfare dependency, crime and drugs are far more of a threat to the urban poor than white racism.[333]

The destiny of America rests in the hands of the continued application of the findings of the Kerner Report or the outright rejection of them. It is Black individuals choice to take drugs, became a welfare dependent, or commit a crime; not the looming specter of white racism or slavery.

Black people were victorious in the 1967 Battle of Detroit, with white people fleeing the ashes of their city and awarding the Black rebels (colonizers would be the apt word) with the keys to "The Paris of the West" their parents and grandparents helped build.

---

[333] http://www.nytimes.com/1992/05/08/us/after-riots-riots-60-s-riots-90-s-frustrating-search-heal-nation.html?pagewanted=all&src=pm

It is in the decaying remnants of that city, one whose infrastructure that Black people were incapable of sustaining – even after they achieved total political power – that we see the fallacious nature of the Kerner Report findings.

But political power didn't translate into economic success.

Brick by brick falls to the ground in neglect while Black people complain of persistent racism for the failure of Detroit under their control demonstrates that the Kerner Report got it wrong.

Completely wrong.

America has been held hostage by Disingenuous White Liberals and Black Rage (think Organized Blackness) for too long. To abandon the official position of the American government as delineated in The Kerner Report, which ascribes all Black failure to the legacy of white racism and slavery, would represent a complete capitulation to the reality that the past 44 years of attempted social programming to the deny that nature does trump nurture would represent an event on par with the collapse of the Soviet Union or the Cultural Revolution in China.

The dogma of equality dies with the fall of Black-run Detroit.

The Kerner Report acted as a shield to hide the truth that nature consistently throws back in our face with each report of racial disparities in any measurable test (save the 40-yard-dash for NFL skilled position players).

Had Detroit flourished in the absence of white people and under the august and benevolent rule of Black people, we'd have to conclude the Kerner Report was correct. Blaming barriers to education, housing, and employment all died when the city became more than 80 percent Black in the 1980s.

Black people should have flourished economically without the impediment of white racism keeping them from reaching their potential; the only thing that flourished in Detroit post-1967 Rebellion was Black crime.

But the city did not.

Democracy dies in Detroit, with the impending appointment by the state of Michigan of an emergency manager to preside of the budget of "The Mogadishu of the West."

Not only Democracy dies, but the Kerner Report has been invalidated.

The legitimacy of BRA has always been through the voluntary belief that eventually Black people would succeed; for BRA to continue, millions of people will have to be involuntary forced to believe this now.

It's Time to Play the Game: All-In on a STRESS-free Detroit vs. Rudy's Post-Dinkins NYC

You may have noticed a trend growing here at *Stuff Black People Don't Like*: an all-out assault on Detroit, the greatest representation of Actual Black Run America (ABRA) available for study.

No, not the Detroit that has come to symbolize the Big Three Automakers, entering our lexicon as some synonym for the combined fortunes of Ford, General Motors, and Chrysler. We aren't talking about the Detroit that has been rebuilt in the Whitopia's surrounding the city, a place where commerce lives on, school systems produce college-ready graduates, and innovation is a daily reminder of what was lost to The Motor City once the Black Riots of 1967 turned a majority white city, majority Black in less than five years.

Any discussion about the decline of Detroit - not the fortune of the Big Three motor companies, but of the 82 percent Black city - must have race at the center of the discussion.

Consider that 20 years, New York City under its first Black Mayor David Dinkins appeared headed to a similar fate as Detroit. It took the election of a proto- fascist Rudy Giuliani[334], who basically worked to resurrect the policing methods once implemented in cities with horrible rates of Black crime (hmm, think Detroit, where Black people in 1960, though only 26 percent of the overall population, were responsible for 65 percent of serious crime) to once again ensure that the *City that Never Sleeps* could rest peacefully when its citizens dared shut their eyes.[335]

The book *Violence in the Model City: The Cavanagh Administration, Race Relations, and the Detroit Riot of 1967* by Sidney Fine reports this on page 15:

334

http://www.nytimes.com/2007/07/22/us/politics/22giuliani.html?pagewanted=all

[335] http://nymag.com/print/?/anniversary/40th/50652/

It was crime and its association with blacks that triggered a major crisis in race relations in Detroit in 1960. Four days after the Civil Rights Commission concluded its hearings in the city, the *Detroit News* noted in an editorial that although blacks constituted 26 percent of the city's population, they were responsible for almost 65 percent of its serious crimes. Asserting that the black community bore "a share of responsibility" for this fact, the *News* complained that the black leadership had "not pressed as hard" on this issues as it should have. "A wave of murders, rapes and purse snatching," with blacks identified as the perpetrators, culminated that same month in the murder of a white nurse's aide, a twenty-eight-year-old mother of three.

The policing methods implemented as a last ditch effort to maintain law and order in Detroit - where Black crime was tearing apart the social fabric of the city - were epitomized in a unit called STRESS: Stop the Robberies, Enjoy Safe Stress:

> In the 1960s and 1970s the Detroit Police Department was notorious for its violence, particularly against minority youth. One police unit, dubbed STRESS—Stop the Robberies, Enjoy Safe Streets—carried out the execution-style killings of a more than a dozen black men in the space of a few years.
> Coleman Young, the city's first black mayor, was elected in 1973 by pledging to disband STRESS and integrate the police force. Young and other Democratic officials oversaw the appointment of black police chiefs and the hiring of thousands of minority officers. But as social inequality grew in the 1970s and 1980s—particularly as the mass layoffs and plant shutdowns in the auto industry turned Detroit into the poorest big city in America—Young strengthened the powers of the police and embraced the politics of law and order.[336]

---

[336] http://www.wsws.org/articles/2000/may2000/det-m17.shtml

Nothing like a little affirmative action to shake-things up, and make Detroit a STRESS-free city. Of course, Detroit became one of the world's infamous cities for murder, crime, and other mayhem - courtesy of Black elements within the majority Black population - but had the fictional Black Detroit Detective Axel Foley of *Beverly Hills Cop, Beverly Hills Cop II, and Beverly Hills Cop III* (portrayed by Eddie Murphy) helping out the PR effort for the city.

As Detroit quickly became a majority Black city, a study was commissioned in 1973 by New Detroit, an organization founded in the ashes of the 1967 Black Riot, that showed 78 percent of white Detroit citizens approving of STRESS; 65 percent of Detroit's Black citizens disapproved of STRESS.[337]

Knowing that the dwindling Black population is resorting to vigilante justice or the hiring of private security firms - mercenaries - to stop criminality from being the No. 1 vocation and avocation in Detroit (with the embarrassingly inept affirmative-actioned majority Black Detroit police force incapable of providing even the basic fundamentals of protection), you have to wonder how many Black citizens would favor a return of STRESS.[338]

How bad was affirmation action in Detroit, and what role did it play in dismantling the police department's overall effectiveness? Well, the answer shouldn't surprise you:

337

http://books.google.com/books?id=4VgEAAAAMBAJ&pg=PA15&lpg=PA15 &dq=stress+police+detroit+black&source=bl&ots=bsh5CFxF6c&sig=glKW WO3w67G0-Zttbln9rd8Usck&hl=en&sa=X&ei=R7UxT7e-LZKKsALCn5ySBw&ved=0CGcQ6AEwCA#v=onepage&q=stress%20polic e%20detroit%20black&f=false

338   http://stuffblackpeopledontlike.blogspot.com/2012/02/life-after-white-people-detroit-glimpse.html

---

Many police department entrance exams, especially in the prelitigation years, were aptitude tests akin to the verbal SAT. Detroit administered a three-hour I.Q. test (the "Otis") to applicants in the 1960s and into the 1970s. Over the same period, the District of Columbia used a civil service examination designed for positions in the federal bureaucracy. This test comprised 80 questions on vocabulary, reading comprehension, and analogies. These questions clearly measure aptitude, but are not related in any obvious way to police work. (Deleted)

African American applicants, historically as well as today, do not perform as well as white applicants on police department entrance examinations. For example, in the Detroit, Michigan, exams of 1967 to 1971, the African American pass rate was 44.3 percent, and the white pass rate was 80.7 percent. The Memphis, Tennessee, tests administered from 1981 to 1989 had a similar impact on black applicants. The pass rate for whites was a high 96.7 percent, but that for African Americans was 69.2 percent.[339]

So these tests might not have been related to police work, but judging by the inability of the majority Black police force in place in Detroit now (all of whom were afforded the right to their position based on their race, and not their sterling academic credentials) you can see they were important.[340]

But what was most important for Mayor Coleman Young was the removal (in his quest to remake the Detroit police in his own corrupt image) of the nefarious applicant tests that potential Black police officers - all across the nation - had trouble passing:

---

[339] http://emlab.berkeley.edu/%7Ejmccrary/mccrary2007.pdf

[340] http://openjurist.org/824/f2d/512/detroit-police-officers-association-v-a-young-morgan

In New York City, Chicago, Minneapolis, New Orleans, San Francisco, and other cities, filed lawsuits on size and height requirements for new recruits, on the content of entrance and promotion examinations, and on patrol assignments. They demanded to be hired in greater numbers. Their gains were impressive: in 1972 there were only 7 women in the United States assigned to patrol work; by 1974 there were 900, and women made up 4 percent of police forces in cities and towns throughout the country. Advocates of affirmative action on the basis of race claimed even more success. In Chicago, for example, the percentage of blacks on the force climbed from 13 percent in 1962 to over 20 percent by the late 1970s. In Washington, D.C., it went from 13 to 42 percent, and in San Francisco, from 2 to 20 percent in the same period. In the 1970–1990 period blacks accounted for 41 percent of all new police hires nationwide. By the end of the 1980s, 130 cities in the United States had black police chiefs, including New York City, Chicago, Baltimore, Philadelphia, and Houston.[341]

Now you can begin to understand why crime is so bad in all of these cities. But in Detroit, it all goes back to STRESS and what Mayor Coleman Young - that fighting Tuskegee Airmen - did to the city's police force. In Bridging the River of Hatred:The Pioneering Efforts of Detroit Police Commissioner George Edwards, author Mary Stolberg practically orgasms in writing about the removal of embedded white racism in the Detroit police force, and its replacement of an affirmative-actioned, Disingenuous White Liberal (DWL) approved Black force:

---

[341] http://www.umass.edu/legal/Hilbink/250/Dennis A. Deslippe - Do Whites have Rights.pdf

Wayne County Sheriff Roman Gribbs replaced Cavanagh in the mayor's seat. After two years in office, Gribbs instituted a controversial undercover, anticrime campaign called Stop the Robberies, Enjoy Safe Streets (STRESS). Critics complained that the STRESS program's unorthodox tactics, including the use of decoys, unfairly targeted African-Americans. Other problems exacerbated objections to STRESS. As author William Rich wrote, "During a thirty-month period in the early 1970s, there were an estimated four hundred warrantless police raids and twenty-two related deaths (mostly of blacks). Detroit had the highest number of civilian killings per capita of any American police force." Just as they had in 1961, police excesses galvanized the city's African-American voters behind Coleman Young, who won the 1973 mayoral race.

Significant change in the department also came with passage of the City Charter of 1973, which gave more impetus to Edward's belief in civilian control of the police department. Under the new system, the commissioner was replaced by a board of five commissioners appointed by the mayor and approved by city council. A chief replaced the superintendent. To appease worried white Detroiters, Young appointed Douglas Fraser of the UAW to chair the police board. He also retained FBI Agent Phillip Tannian as police chief. To meet supporters demands, Young appointed Frank Blount, an African American, as deputy chief. Three months into office he disbanded the STRESS program.

Like Edwards, Young recognized the importance of recruiting and promoting more black officers. In September 1975, he appointed Detroit's first African-American police chief, William Hart. In 1991, when Hart was convicted for embezzlement and sentenced to prison, Young replaced him with another African American, Stanley Knox.

Young also moved quickly to hire black officers. The department opened recruitment offices in inner-city neighborhoods and scrapped test that smacked of racial bias.

Young also called for enforcement of the city's residency requirement and instated an affirmative action program that required promotion of one black officer for every white officer promoted. His efforts eventually bore fruit. By 1990, Detroit was far ahead of of the nation's other large cities; its force was 58.7 percent African American. The next closet was Philadelphia, where 25.7 percent of police were black.[342]

Wait a second: doesn't Detroit's proud majority Black police force still lead the nation in both rates of police brutality[343] and police killings?[344] The only variable that changed was Black police officers shooting Black criminals, instead of white cops shooting the Black criminals that made so many DWLs and representatives of Organized Blackness irate.

So STRESS wasn't that bad after all. It was just a last ditch effort to save the city from the Black criminality that now occupies all seats of government power, frightens away investors, and, more importantly, keep Black criminals on the streets in check.

NYC faced a similar crisis back in the earlier 1990s.

Isn't the application of STRESS in New York City basically what saved the city?:

342

http://books.google.com/books?hl=en&lr=&id=5T15dbjzSnsC&oi=fnd&pg=PA9&dq=stress+police+detroit+racist&ots=jt5eNuxQbQ&sig=X42eAgTuDu4IKsuPIT2-e0rSktk#v=onepage&q=stress&f=false

[343] http://www.ottawamenscentre.com/news/20030629_police_brutality.htm

[344] http://www.wsws.org/articles/2000/may2000/det-m17.shtml

New York's Republican Mayor Rudolph Giuliani waged his successful campaign in 1993 on an aggressive law and order platform. A former federal prosecutor, he denounced the Democratic incumbent, David Dinkins, as soft on crime. In office, Giuliani's proudest boast has been the declining crime rate, which he attributed to his "get tough" policy.[345]

By the way, getting tough on crime means getting tough on racial minorities, because they represent the groups most likely to be criminals:

The color of murder and gun violence in New York
Lo and behold, Capehart learned something he apparently hadn't known before: *Blacks and Hispanics commit essentially all the violent crime in New York*. They are also the most likely crime victims.
Capehart quoted the report for 2010 directly:

"Murder and Non-Negligent Manslaughter victims are most frequently Black (67.0%) or Hispanic (28.1%). White victims account for (3.2%) of all Murder and Non-Negligent Manslaughter victims while Asian /Pacific Islanders account for (1.8%) of all Murder and Non-Negligent Manslaughter victims. The race/ethnicity of known Murder and Non-Negligent Manslaughter suspects mirrors the victim population with Black (65.3%) and Hispanic (30.6%) suspects accounting for the majority of suspects. White suspects account for (1.8%) of all Murder and Non-Negligent Manslaughter suspects while Asian/Pacific Islanders accounted for (2.4%) of the known Murder and Non-Negligent Manslaughter suspects.

"The Murder and Non-Negligent Manslaughter arrest population is similarly distributed. Black arrestees (53.8%) and Hispanic arrestees (36.4%) account for the majority of Murder and Non-Negligent Manslaughter arrestees while White arrestees (7.1%) and Asian/Pacific Islander (2.2%) arrestees account for the remaining portions of the Murder and Non-Negligent Manslaughter arrest population."[PDF]

---

[345] http://www.wsws.org/articles/1999/apr1999/dial-a06.shtml

Seeing the news so starkly distressed Capehart. He writes:

"In short, 95.1 percent of all murder victims and 95.9 percent of all shooting victims in New York City are black or Hispanic. And 90.2 percent of those arrested for murder and 96.7 percent of those arrested for shooting someone are black and Hispanic. I don't even know where to begin to describe the horror I still feel looking at those numbers. But the word 'hunted' comes to mind."[346]

New York City could have ended up like Detroit (though the only criminals left in NYC - it seems - share a common bond with Detroit's majority population), but instead of capitulating to ABRA, the citizens of The Big Apple rejected it.

For those failing cities where Black crime is driving away white residents, businesses, and investors - think Philadelphia, New Orleans, Baltimore, Atlanta, Milwaukee, Cleveland, St. Louis, Birmingham, Richmond, etc. - understand that being STRESS-free is only a precursor to becoming another full-fledged Detroit.

It's that simple.

---

[346]   http://www.vdare.com/articles/crime-in-black-and-white-wapos-jonathan-capehart-vs-nyts-al-baker

Life After White People: Detroit, a Glimpse of How Civilization Dies

Life After White People.

The grass isn't always greener on the other side.

Life After White People.

Law and order no longer remain.

Life After White People.

A land where only madness reigns.

Without a constant infusion of federal dollars to stimulate the economy of Detroit (EBT, TANF/Welfare, Section 8 Housing), it's not hard to speculate that the city would have come to resemble Mogadishu, with rival warlords fighting for the remaining populations allegiance.

Seriously. If you remove the lifeline of federal and state financial support, Detroit would look like something out of *Black Hawk Down*. Well, even with this aid, the remains of the Motor City is simultaneously a glimpse at America's Atlantis, a lost city whose greatness can only be spoken about through the eerie silence of photography and the decaying remains of civilization, and America's Mogadishu. Just read this story from Time magazine in 2009, about the last White City Council Member, Sheila Murphy Cockrel:

But in some ways, Cockrel is a relic of Detroit's past. She is the only white member of the city council and, when her term ends in late December, she could well be its last. Even though she is personally popular, she is leaving the council partly because she is tired of the scandals that have rocked the city lately. Her departure is a significant moment in the history of Detroit, the largest majority-black city in America. In the 1950s, when Detroit's population reached its 2 million peak, nearly 1.6 million white people lived here. In 1990, though whites were still represented in several major elected posts, they comprised only about 20% of the population. Now, whites make up barely 8% of the city's estimated 912,000 residents. [347]

A more profound paragraph about why Detroit was once one of America's greatest cities - if not the world - and now its unquestionable worst could scarcely be written.

---

[347]

http://www.time.com/time/nation/article/0,8599,1947779,00.html#ixzz1leVg pfhA

Detroit is Actual Black Run America (ABRA) and but a few generations removed from being "the Arsenal of Democracy," Detroit has become a living, breathing representation of the type of Black History you'll never learn about during the month of February.

The police have lost control of Detroit[348], giving up on patrolling 20 percent of the city. Who knows... the coming months could see an emergency call placed to the National Guard - just like in 1967 during the Black Riots - in a last ditch effort to bring peace and some form of stability to the city. [349]

Those few remaining Black professionals still clinging to some semblance of law and order - specifically in Palmer Woods area of Detroit [350]- have turned to Recon Security (a paramilitary organization) to keep them safe, paying tribute to a legal type of warlord in exchange for peace:

[348]   http://www.huffingtonpost.com/2012/01/13/detroit-police-precinct-business-hours_n_1204069.html

[349]   http://articles.businessinsider.com/2010-12-13/news/30065559_1_mayor-dave-bing-police-patrols-street-lights

[350]
http://online.wsj.com/article/SB10001424052748704292004575230532248715858.html

A Detroit neighborhood association has brought in high-profile private security patrols with paramilitary-style personnel to help fight crime.

The Palmer Woods Association in March hired Detroit-based Recon Security, which is owned by a Highland Park police lieutenant, the Detroit Free Press reported Monday. The decision followed a rash of break-ins and property crimes in the upscale neighborhood.

The neighborhood association has been working with the city to limit traffic access through the neighborhood as part of efforts to reduce crime. The association also works with police to improve security and says the patrols are another way to reach that goal.

Recon Security's Threat Management Division patrols the neighborhood and stops nonresidents to make sure they have legitimate business or a connection to residents. If they see suspicious or criminal behavior, Recon Security's staff members call police.

The patrols include a black Hummer H2 pickup rolling through the area. On the front doors, a silver seal reads: "THREAT MANAGEMENT SPECIALISTS DETERRENCE DETECTION DEFENSE." Inside, Dale Brown patrols wearing camouflage pants and combat boots.

"You can create a positive environment for families to exist," said Brown, 42, who served in the Army in the early 1990s.

Brown is part of Recon Security's Threat Management Division, a partnership between Recon Security, owned by Highland Park Police Lt. Robert Howard, and Brown's Threat Management Centers. Howard describes the division as something similar to a SWAT team.

Karoy Brooks, a retired Detroit Public Schools principal who has lived in Palmer Woods for 25 years, was among those initially apprehensive about the patrols.

"I had some questions, and I was wondering how the neighbors would react," she said. "I think everybody's definitely on board."[351]

For those Black Detroit residents - still smarting from the failed 2004 attempt to create "Africa Town"[352] in downtown Detroit, which would have earmarked city money to the tune of $38 million specifically for Black entrepreneurs - without the monetary ability to pay for private paramilitary squads to patrol their streets, an ancient form of justice is flourishing in a city where the absence of police has created a vacuum for power:

---

[351]

http://www.mlive.com/news/detroit/index.ssf/2011/06/palmer_woods_neighborhood_in_d.html

[352] http://www.washingtontimes.com/news/2004/oct/8/20041008-123152-7116r/?page=all

The people of Detroit are taking no prisoners.

Justifiable homicide in the city shot up 79 percent in 2011 from the previous year, as citizens in the long-suffering city armed themselves and took matters into their own hands. The local rate of self-defense killings now stands 2,200 percent above the national average. Residents, unable to rely on a dwindling police force to keep them safe, are fighting back against the criminal scourge on their own. And they're offering no apologies.

"We got to have a little Old West up here in Detroit. That's what it's gonna take," Detroit resident Julia Brown told The Daily.

The last time Brown, 73, called the Detroit police, they didn't show up until the next day. So she applied for a permit to carry a handgun and says she's prepared to use it against the young thugs who have taken over her neighborhood, burglarizing entire blocks, opening fire at will and terrorizing the elderly with impunity.

"I don't intend to be one of their victims," said Brown, who has lived in Detroit since the late 1950s. "I'm planning on taking one out."

How it got this bad in Detroit has become a point of national discussion. Violent crime settled into the city's bones decades ago, but recently, as the numbers of police officers have plummeted and police response times have remained distressingly high, citizens have taken to dealing with things themselves.

In this city of about 700,000 people, the number of cops has steadily fallen, from about 5,000 a decade ago to fewer than 3,000 today. Detroit homicides — the second-highest per capita in the country last year, according to the FBI — rose by 10 percent in 2011 to 344 people.

On a bleak day in January, a group of funeral directors wearied by the violence drove a motorcade of hearses through the city streets in protest.

Average police response time for priority calls in the city, according to the latest data available, is 24 minutes. In comparable cities across the country, it is well under 10 minutes.

Citizens like Brown feel they have been left with little choice but to take the law into their own hands.

The number of justifiable homicides, in which residents use deadly force in self-defense, jumped from 19 in 2010 to 34 last year — a 79 percent rise — according to newly released city data.

Signs that vigilantism was taking hold in the city came earlier, around Memorial Day 2009, when former federal agent Alvin Davis decided he'd had enough of the break-ins at his mother's home on the east side. She called the police again and again, but the brazen robberies continued. Davis, then a 32-year-old Immigration and Customs Enforcement officer, snapped.

Prosecutors said he spent days chasing and harassing the teenagers who were allegedly robbing his mother, even shoving his federally issued firearm into one of their mouths. No one was killed, but by the time he was done, Davis had racked up charges of unlawful imprisonment and assault. In August 2010, he was convicted and sentenced to four years in prison.

But many residents in his mother's Jefferson-Chalmers neighborhood are sympathetic to Davis, whose case is on appeal.

"He basically did what a lot of us wished we could do," said Ken Gray, 58, who lives down the street from Davis' mother.

One high-ranking official in the county legal system, speaking to The Daily, said the rise in justifiable homicides mirrors a local court system that's increasingly lenient of the practice.

"It's a lot more acceptable now to get your own retribution," the official said. "And the justice system in the city is a lot more understanding if people do that. It's becoming a part of the culture."

Detroiters are arming themselves with shotguns and handguns and buying guard dogs. Anything to take care of their own. And privately, residents say neighborhood watch groups in Detroit are widely armed.

"It's like the militiamen who stepped up way back when. That's where the neighborhood folks are," said James "Jackrabbit" Jackson, a 63-year-old retired Detroit cop who has patrolled the Jefferson-Chalmers neighborhood for years.

"They're ready to fight," Jackson said. "We don't hardly see police anymore." The city's wealthier enclaves have hired private security firms. Intimidating men in armored trucks patrol streets lined with gracious old homes in a scene more likely seen in Mexico City than the United States.

That kind of paid protection can run residents anywhere from $10 to $200 per month, and companies say business is good.

"We're booming," said Dale Brown, the owner of Threat Management Group, which along with Recon Security patrols neighborhoods like Palmer Woods in black Hummers.

"We're paramilitary, but we're positive. I'm not a vigilante. I'm an agent of change."

The Detroit Police Department, grappling with deep funding cuts in a city with a spiraling budget crisis, acknowledges that response times are high and says it is working on a plan to lower them. But a spokeswoman for the department insists the rise in justifiable homicides is unrelated.

"It's not about police response time because often the act has already taken place by the time the police are called," said Sgt. Eren Stephens. She said citizens have a right to defend themselves.[353]

How long will it be until a form of Somali ~~"land pirates"~~ marauders arise from the ashes of Detroit, with desperate gangs of Black people banding together to kidnap fellow citizens and hold them for ransom? With public services collapsing into a sea of anarchy - who can forget the story of the stranded Detroit EMS unit on New Year's Eve, as gunshots were heard all around - stories like the one the *Detroit Free Press* reported on January 8, 2012 will be increasingly commonplace:

> A man and woman died in a house fire in Detroit on Saturday night that was caused by extension cord misuse, fire officials said today.
>
> The blaze at Burlingame and 12th broke out around 9 p.m. Firefighters called for help from police when extended family and neighborhood residents insisted on entering the home, said Detroit Fire Arson Investigator Patrick McNulty.
>
> "It was an ugly scene," McNulty said, adding that close to 100 police officers were there when he arrived at 9:45 p.m. "The firemen felt like they were close to turning the water on people. They're outnumbered. There were a lot of people out there. And once police arrived, things calmed down pretty quick."
>
> Dan McNamara, head of the firefighters union, said Saturday night that no police officers were initially available when firefighters called for help.
>
> "We're unprotected out here," McNamara said Saturday night.
>
> McNulty said the crowd would have been interfering with the firefighters if they were allowed to walk in and out of the scene.

---

[353]   http://www.thedaily.com/page/2012/02/05/020512-news-detroit-vigilantes-1-5/

"Sometimes emotions get the best of people, and I think that's what happened," McNulty said.[354]

This is what it looks like when civilization collapses. Detroit, Michigan. Firefighters stating that their unprotected from the criminals whose fire they try and put out. What happened there post 1967 is the kind of real Black History that should be taught during the month of February.

The game is over for Detroit, Clint Eastwood.

It is up to those American patriots capable of discerning the cold truth from what remains of Old Detroit to start deciding the type of nation they wish to leave their children and grandchildren. To decide what type of world they want to leave for their unborn children.

Detroit of 2012? A world where the greatest growth industry is in private security, like some third world nation?

This scenario will come to any major city that goes the route of Detroit.

Atlanta, Memphis, Birmingham, Baltimore, Cleveland, Chicago, Kansas City, St. Louis, Milwaukee, New Orleans, Nashville, Charlotte, Miami, Cincinnati, Newark, Indianapolis, Philadelphia, Harrisburg... this is your future.

Life After White People.

A land where only madness reigns.

---

[354] http://www.freep.com/article/20120108/NEWS01/120108018/Extension-cords-Detroit-house-fire-deaths?odyssey=tab%7Ctopnews%7Ctext%7CFRONTPAGE

"It will rise from the ashes": Detroit's Motto Needs Changing

Detroit is the Black capital of America. This statement is indisputable. Which is why the next two months are going to be extremely interesting, with the city of Detroit slated to run out of money and be taken over by the state of Michigan in the hopes of curbing monetary mismanagement.[355]

The decline of Detroit was only cemented when Black people rioted in 1967, forcing whites to flee to the suburbs. Since that time, the Big Three car companies - Ford, GM, and Chrysler - have survived (reorganizing with each challenge), while Actual Black-Run America Detroit has become the case study for post-colonialism in America.

The Great Migration of Black people from the North were the colonizers (they now return back South, defeated, the cities they leave in ruins), and Detroit's demise is courtesy of these individuals - when taken as a whole - whose civilization was incompatible with that of the one white people created.

Detroit is now the poster child for welfare/TANF entitlements, Section 8 Housing, EBT/Food Stamps, and free lunches at schools for all children. If it were not for the generosity of white taxpayers, it's hard to imagine were the money would come from to support the citizens of Detroit. Philanthropy? Churches? Not anymore:

---

[355] http://www.historydetroit.com/stats.asp

Detroit's struggling neighborhoods stand to lose far more than just a church -- they'll lose a lifeline
On the east side of Detroit, the Nativity of Our Lord Catholic Church is the anchor of a neighborhood that has seen the addition of 14 new homes and a 62-unit senior center.

Joyce Anderson, an administrative assistant for the Wayne County Prosecutor's Office, moved into a new house two years ago, in part, because of Nativity's outreach in the neighborhood.

Now Nativity is fighting a recommendation that calls for the parish, and three others on the east side, to close.
"The church is really the reason I'm here. They were building up the community," said Anderson, 56, who is not Catholic. "If they closed, all the positive energy would go with them."
"If Nativity leaves," Anderson said, "I'm gone."

Detroit Archbishop Allen Vigneron is reviewing recommendations to close up to 20 churches in Detroit, Highland Park and Hamtramck, and about 30 more in the suburbs. The pending closures -- which are expected to be finalized this month -- could shrivel the church's urban footprint to nearly one-third of the 112 parishes that existed in Detroit and its enclaves in 1988.

Since 2000, about 25 parishes have closed in Detroit and the surrounding suburbs. Recently, at least seven parishes in the suburbs have decided to close or merge in the next year or two. But unlike the pending suburban closures, many of the urban parishes didn't ask to be closed.

Many of the threatened urban parishes provide services to poor and homeless people. They are beacons of stability. And they are fighting to stay open.

"If it is providing food services, helping the homeless, closing (a church) is really a symbolic death knell of a neighborhood," said demographer Kurt Metzger, who directs Data Driven Detroit and shared population trends and statistics with the Archdiocesan Pastoral Council, which made the closure recommendations.[356]

Detroit is a dying city, deprived of all hope and a future. It's fitting that Detroit's city flag has a Latin motto describing how it will rise from the ashes:

> The two Latin mottos read *Speramus Meliora* and *Resurget Cineribus*, meaning "We hope for better things" and "It will rise from the ashes," which was written by Gabriel Richard after the fire of 1805. The seal is a representation of the Detroit fire which occurred on June 11, 1805. The fire caused the entire city to burn with only one building saved from the flames. The figure on the left weeps over the destruction while the figure on the right gestures to the new city that will rise in place.[357]

Detroit isn't going to rise from the ashes. It's settling into them, letting the dust settle over buildings and an infrastructure that Black people have no ability to maintain.

It is being abandoned. Completely. Is this what those who are Pro-Life want? The death of one of the world's greatest cities, where vigilante criminality is rising because the Detroit Police were the causality of oppressive affirmative action policies in the 1970s (after Mayor Coleman Young took over).

Nolan Finley of *The Detroit News* has written a brave column, asking what can be done to save Detroit. The answer is, of course, nothing:

---

[356]   http://www.freep.com/article/20120212/NEWS01/202120557/As-churches-close-hope-help-are-lost-with-them?odyssey=mod%7Cnewswell%7Ctext%7CFRONTPAGE%7Cp

[357] http://en.wikipedia.org/wiki/Flag_of_Detroit

Since the national attention is on birth control, here's my idea: If we want to fight poverty, reduce violent crime and bring down our embarrassing drop-out rate, we should swap contraceptives for fluoride in Michigan's drinking water.

We've got a baby problem in Michigan. Too many babies are born to immature parents who don't have the skills to raise them, too many are delivered by poor women who can't afford them, and too many are fathered by sorry layabouts who spread their seed like dandelions and then wander away from the consequences.
Michigan's social problems and the huge costs attached to them won't recede until we embrace reproductive responsibility.

Last year, 43 percent of the babies born in Michigan were to single mothers. And even though Medicaid pays for birth control, half of the babies born here were to mothers on welfare. Eighteen percent were born to teenagers who already had at least one child. And nearly 1-in-5 new babies had mothers with no high school diploma.

In Michigan, poverty is as much a cultural problem as it is an economic one.

I spoke with an educator who is dealing with a single mother, mid-30s, with 12 children and a 13th on the way. The kids have an assortment of fathers with one thing in common — none married their mother. This woman's womb is a poverty factory.

It wouldn't matter if Michigan's economy were bursting with jobs, the woman and her children would still be poor.

Who's supporting these kids? If you're a taxpayer, you are. The roughly 45,000 children a year born onto the welfare rolls is a major reason Medicaid will consume 25 percent of next year's budget.

Those kids are more likely to grow up to be a strain on Corrections spending or welfare recipients themselves. And they'll drain money from the schools and universities that could help break this cycle.

In the 1990s, Michigan considered penalizing women who had more babies while on welfare, but pro-life groups killed the idea out of fear it would lead to more abortions.

Now, says state Human Services Director Maura Corrigan, the state is trying other measures, including attacking school truancy and the new four-year limit on welfare benefits, which she says is already increasing participation in work training programs.

"We are trying to get at generational poverty," she says. "We're studying positive incentives to change."
But she says the cultural breakdown is a strong tide to row against.

"We're watching marriage move from being part of the social fabric to being merely optional," says Corrigan, who devotes her personal time to working with disadvantaged children. "The kids I mentor don't know people who are married."

They do know people whose irresponsible behavior is being subsidized by their neighbors.
And as long as the taxpayers of Michigan keep paying for them, those babies will keep on coming.[358]

358

http://www.detroitnews.com/article/20120212/OPINION03/202120303/Michigan-breeding-poverty

Detroit is the future for all big cities in America. How many other cities have property values that mirror the titanic fall of residential properties in Detroit, all courtesy of the Black Undertow? We ask this not to endorse what Finley has prescribed, but to debate it.

Life in Detroit is worthless. A feckless reminder that nature is brutal, and nurture is a pipe-dream. Now, the nightmarish existence of Detroit of 2012 is a glimpse of what is to come for all cities that suffer under ABRA.

An MSNBC host, Melissa Harris-Perry, has a theory that Black people tend to be elected mayors of cities only after they've tipped into economic decline. Sadly, she doesn't point out that only when Black people - who vote nearly 97 - 99 percent for a Black candidate - become either a numerical majority of a city's population or the majority in a plurality, the economic decline is only a reality of the majority:

> Week seven of Melissa Harris-Perry's introductory course in African-American studies at Tulane University includes a lecture about "the hollow prize" — a theory that African-Americans tend to be elected as mayor only after a city has tipped into economic decline.
>
> One day last summer, when Ms. Harris-Perry was filling in for **Rachel Maddow** on MSNBC, she recast the class lecture as a television segment, invoking Detroit; her adopted home, New Orleans; President Obama; and tax policy.
>
> "I've given that lecture a million times — a million times," Ms. Harris-Perry said in a recent interview. "But I do it once on Rachel's show, and it was everywhere the next day. It was up on Web sites, people were e-mailing me — that, for me, was a really clear indication of how powerful television is."[359]

---

[359] http://www.nytimes.com/2012/02/13/business/media/host-of-msnbcs-melissa-harris-perry-is-a-professor.html?pagewanted=1&_r=3

Peter Eisinger wrote *The Politics of Racial Economic Advancement* in 1979. It details Newark, Gary, Detroit and discusses Atlanta, all under the harsh rule of Black mayors. Only Atlanta ever recovered, and it's collapse is inevitable.[360]

We know that New York City almost died in the mid-1990s, until the Black mayor was displaced by Rudy.

Dr. Perry's, whose PhD in African-American History is only valuable in Black-Run America (BRA), this thesis is embarrassing. It is only when the Black Undertow becomes too great a menace to maintain businesses, civil society, law and order, top-notch school districts, and a flourishing tax-base that white flight occurs in rapid enough numbers to ensure a Black mayor can be elected. Once this happens, the trickle of white people from the city becomes a torrent.

Once this occurs, it is rare that a city will survive. Coleman Young in Detroit enacted affirmative action policies throughout the city government positions, with the consequences still being felt today. The ramifications of these pro-Black, anti-merit policies can be seen in the abandoned sections of a city settling into... into the silence of indifference.

Rise from the ashes? Detroit needs a new motto.

---

[360] http://www.irp.wisc.edu/publications/dps/pdfs/dp55879.pdf

No League of Shadows Destroyed Detroit; It was Black People

This summer, *The Dark Knight Rises* will set the box office ablaze. The third and film in the Director Christopher Nolan's *Batman* trilogy, we will see the culmination of Bruce Wayne's efforts to save Gotham City from the criminals and corrupt.

In the imagination of comic book writers, authors of fiction, and those in Hollywood working on the scripts of movies and television shows, magnificent heroes can be created to save the day. Defeat the bad guy, restoring peace and stability to a city where anarchy and chaos would have otherwise ruled without their benevolent sacrifices.

Nolan's first film in the trilogy – *Batman Begins* – sees a younger Bruce Wayne seek out the means to fight evil and injustice. The League of Shadows trains him; a group of men who we learn have existed for centuries to fight corruption and decadence ("because no courts will try men entrenched in bureaucracies that exist merely to perpetuate themselves, to paraphrase the leader, Ra's al Ghul), and, once a society has reached a point of no return, ensure that harmony and balance are ultimately restored by destroying said city. We learn that the League of Shadows sacked Rome when it became too decadent and corrupt.

It is in this exchange of dialogue between Ra's and Wayne the true function of the League of Shadows is delineated:

> Ra's al Ghul: Tomorrow the world will watch in horror as its greatest city destroys itself. The movement back to harmony will be unstoppable this time.
>
> Bruce Wayne: You attacked Gotham before?

Ra's al Ghul: Of course. Over the ages, our weapons have grown more sophisticated. With Gotham, we tried a new one: Economics. But we underestimated certain of Gotham's citizens... such as your parents. Gunned down by one of the very people they were trying to help. Create enough hunger and everyone becomes a criminal. Their deaths galvanized the city into saving itself... and Gotham has limped on ever since. We are back to finish the job. And this time no misguided idealists will get in the way.[361]

The real world has no League of Shadows. It has no heroes either, costumed and jumping from one rooftop to another at night to fight criminals and keep the city streets safe.

Ours is a world where no secretive cabal needs to organize in the shadows to see some of our greatest cities (at least in the United States) brought to their knees. Were the fictional League of Shadows smart, to destroy Gotham City they'd simply implement the exact same policies that have been enacted in the United States of America, and the bureaucrats in charge of the metropolis where Bruce Wayne's parents were gunned down by the white criminal Joe Chill wouldn't have to worry about criminal offenses such as the murder of its most illustrious citizens.

The ruling of restrictive covenant being unconstitutional meant the death of not just major cities, but every city in America will eventually happen. Were the world of Gotham City in Nolan's *Batman* trilogy to operate under the rules of our world, Gotham would have been long ago been destroyed.

The League of Shadows would have unleashed a more destructive force upon a city than a weaponized aerosol hallucinogenic to bring about mass hysteria (as they did in *Batman Begins*): A majority Black population.

No, all the League of Shadows would have to do to destroy Gotham City is change the racial complexion from a majority white, economically thriving city into a majority Black city, where the only thing thriving is a high crime rate and blight.

---

[361] http://www.imdb.com/title/tt0372784/quotes

Sure, it might take 20 – 30 years for this plan to mature, but the League of Shadows has been around for over an millennia. Civilizations come and go, but looking at the history of 20th century America, the fate of Birmingham, Memphis, Baltimore, Newark, Camden, Prince George's County, Atlanta, and, of course, Detroit, is inexorably tied to going from a majority white city or county to a majority Black city or county.

In the case of Detroit, the corruption of the elected Black officials is but a microcosm of the day-to-day corruption and criminality found in its population (82 percent Black now; at the height of the city's influence, it was more than 75 percent white when it was dubbed "The Arsenal of Democracy" in the 1940s).

Virtually all of the crime that drove white people from Detroit in the 1960s and 1970s was committed by Black people, who never ceased killing and robbing one another.[362]

Even as Detroit has ceased being a functioning city – when it was once of the world's most revered cities for its daring architecture, culture, arts, and industrious population – the misery found there hasn't subsided.

Once the center of economic ingenuity based upon being the manufacturing hub behind America's ascension to superpower status, Detroit is now a city – courtesy of a tax-base of barely literate Black people[363] – that will soon be without a payday:

> The city is fast running out of money, with only $76 million reported on hand last month, and could be headed toward payless paydays this spring unless union concessions and other cuts are implemented soon, new financial numbers show.

---

[362]

http://www.detroitnews.com/article/20100902/METRO/9020418/Murders-young-black-men-rise

[363]   http://detroit.cbslocal.com/2011/05/04/report-nearly-half-of-detroiters-cant-read/

The cash flow numbers; as of Jan. 27 also show the city would be $46.8 million in the hole at the end of the fiscal year on June 30. The city would officially run out of cash in mid-to-late April, the figures posted on the city's website predict, a fiscal reality that first prompted the governor to consider sending in an emergency manager.

At the end of November, the city had a cash balance after required distributions of $109.9 million. That fell to $53.7 million in December and jumped back to $76 million last month. The city is forecasting a steady drop in cash this month to $55.9 million, then $42.2 million in March and $2.5 million in early April. It's unclear why the numbers jumped in December.

"Things are going down, down, down," said Edward Rago, the former city budget director under Mayors Coleman A. Young and Dennis Archer.

"All the evidence points to the fact that things are bad, they are getting worse, they are going to be negative in eight weeks or so."

The city also was forecast to receive $97 million in revenue through the end of January but was $21 million short of projections.

Rago said that cash flow trend soon will signal a payless payday for Detroit.[364]

Unlike the city of Pittsburgh, the majority Black population of Detroit that inherited the city once they chased away white people after the Negro Revolt of 1967 (and subsequent introductions of massive affirmative action policies in the 70s and 80s) they couldn't restructure the economy to sustain the city – even as its population dwindled away– and completely failed to innovate or find ways to secure new investments from entrepreneurs or corporations. The tax roles dwindled as crime, prostitution and drug dealing made the concept of a "Black" market an oxymoron.

364

http://www.detroitnews.com/article/20120227/METRO01/202270342/Detroit-running-out-cash?odyssey=mod%7Cmostview

We read about the brutality in Detroit, when a nine-month old Black baby died in a hail of bullets from an AK-47, fired from a Black individual upset from the events at a wedding shower. We read about an 86-year-old Black veteran, beaten and carjacked, who crawled in search of help, but no good Black Samaritan was to be found.

Now, news of two Black teens utilizing an AK-47 in their car-jacking's has broken.[365]

Life is so little valued in Detroit, that the Black 14-year-old son of a Black mother opened fire on her while she slept, because she denied him the opportunity to hang with his friends:

> Family members say a 14-year-old boy shot his mother to death as she was sleeping early today because he was mad she wouldn't let him hang out with friends.
>
> Tamiko Robinson, 36, died around 3 a.m., according to her brother, Leshaun Roberts.
>
> Detroit Police spokeswoman Sgt. Eren Stephens would not release any information about the case.
>
> "He just wanted to hang with the thugs," Roberts said, sitting on the front porch of the home on Burns, just off Gratiot Avenue, as he was holding a family picture of them. "The first thing that came to mind was he did it because of what they were going through."
>
> Roberts said the boy, who is on the swim team and ROTC at Kettering High School, broke into an office in the home to get a gun owned by his mother's fiance.

365

http://www.detroitnews.com/article/20120227/METRO01/202270365/Detroit-Police-Two-suspects-caught-attempted-carjacking-shooting-boy-6?odyssey=tab%7Ctopnews%7Ctext%7CFRONTPAGE

As she slept in the living room and her fiance slept in an adjacent room with their 5-year-old daughter, Roberts said her son shot her on the couch and when she fell to the floor.[366]

Mayor David Bing has taken to scolding the Black people of Detroit[367] (remember, Detroit is 82 percent Black) for failing to raise their children correctly, though the Black people of Detroit who reared them weren't exactly paragons of virtue considering they are the ones responsible with creating an environment that is considered the most dangerous in America:

> Mayor Dave Bing today called on parents to better raise their children in the wake of a disturbing spate of violence involving young people in Detroit.
>
> His voice rising at times, Bing said what was especially jarring to him were crimes in which youngsters attack their parents. He said those kinds of incidents hurt him deeply and are simply "unacceptable."
>
> "When you've got parents afraid of their kids, you know you have not done a good job as a parent," Bing said in a news conference in his 11th floor conference room at City Hall. "You need to start disciplining those young people when they come out of the womb. Mothers and fathers ... you can't start disciplining a kid at the age of 12 or 14, it's too late." "What we are living with today is totally unacceptable," Bing continued. "And we're going to deal with it, we're going to solve the problem and we're going to make our streets and our homes safe again."

---

[366] http://www.freep.com/article/20120227/NE WS02/120227043/14-year-old-boy-shoots-mo m-in-Detroit?odyssey=tab%7Ctopnews%7Ctext%7CFR ONTPAGE

[367] http://www.detroitnews.com/article/20120227/METRO/202270428/Bing-Parents-need-step-up-stem-crime-Detroit?odyssey=tab%7Ctopnews%7Ctext%7CFRONTPAGE

Police Chief Ralph Godbee said his department will solve the recent crimes. The string of violence in the past few days includes the shooting death of an infant, a carjacking that left a 6-year-old in critical condition and a 14-year-old who is accused of killing his mother. But they can't do it alone, he said.

"We're not standing idly by. What closes the loop for us is community involvement," Godbee said. "If you don't have the community closing that loop and turning over criminals that will kill our young people and maim our senior citizens, then we don't have a true community policing system. To that end, we're going to do our part."Godbee said his department has "the resolve to get the job done."

"The fact that we're afraid of our own children is a commentary right there," Godbee said. "I don't want to wax philosophical, but when I was growing up I was more afraid of my father than I was the police. That element is missing in our community." Bing said that a "very small percentage of our population" is committing the crimes, but he stressed citizens "cannot just stand idly by and accept this." Even though admitting he doesn't have all the answers, Bingpledged to do "whatever I can to eradicate the kind of thinking and action that is now taking place in our community.""I was taught to respect my elders, and I was taught to protect the young," the mayor said. "And for whatever reason, we have a culture that doesn't accept that anymore."[368]

---

[368] http://www.detroitnews.com/article/20120227/METRO/202270428/Bing-Parents-need-step-up-stem-crime-Detroit?odyssey=tab%7Ctopnews%7Ctext%7CFRONTPAGE

Fitting that he gave this speech at the Coleman A. Young Municipal Center[369], named for the first Black mayor of Detroit who denuded the city of its white police force.

Wait a second. Isn't another one of America's formerly great cities seeing the exact same scenario of white people leaving in droves and Black people taking over every public institution in the city? Why yes, Philadelphia is seeing the Detroiting of *The City of Brotherly Love* take place as we speak.

It was just last summer that Mayor Michael Nutter took the Black people of Philadelphia (responsible for virtually all the violent crime in the city) to task, in a heavily promoted speech:

> As violent mobs of young men continued to wreak havoc in Philadelphia for a second summer in a row, Mayor Michael Nutter has taken a hard line against the roving "flash mobs," tightening weekend curfews, endorsing stiff "stop-and-frisk" polices, and blasting the mostly black teenagers involved in the violence with fiery words from the pulpit this weekend. About 50 teenagers were arrested Friday for violating the newly enforced weekend curfew. It is aimed at cracking down on mobs of young people responsible for random attacks on people and property.
>
> The mayor's crackdown has placed him in the center of a simmering debate about how black community leaders should respond to violence within their own community. On one side are those who admire the mayor's take-no-prisoners rhetorical style and use of police force, while others say this approach lets the mayor off the hook for failing to address the needs of young black

---

[369]   http://www.myfoxdetroit.com/dpp/news/local/detroit-mayor-dave-bing-and-police-chief-ralph-godbee-talk-about-city-violence-20120227-dk

Philadelphians. In a combative speech on Sunday at Mount Carmel Baptist Church in Philadelphia, Mayor Nutter said that young black men have to stop acting like "sperm donors" and "human ATMs." He admonished parents for failing to supervise and expect good behavior from their children. And he directly implicated habits and styles of some young black men in the city.

"If you walk into somebody's office with your hair uncombed and a pick in the back, and your shoes untied and your pants half-down, tattoos up and down your arms and on your neck, and you wonder why somebody won't hire you?" Nutter told the congregation "They don't hire you 'cause you look like you're crazy. You have damaged your own race."

"I am a proud black man in this country," Nutter said in a subsequent interview with the Associated Press. "It was a message that needed to be said. It needed to be said at this time . . . People have had enough of this nonsense, black and white."
[370]

Strange that so many of the formerly great cities in America have turned into breeding grounds for criminality, pathetic school systems (which are only a reflection of the students in the schools) and depressed property values.

Gotham City could have been easily destroyed in *Batman Begins* by the introduction of Black people into positions of power and a slow rise in the overall Black population of the city as a percentage of the whole population. White flight would have happened and the effects would be nearly irreversible.

No Batman could save the city then from the crime, decadence, and corruption found merely in City Hall (does Batman even have a Black guy in his rogues gallery?), let alone the thugs and gangs that roam the streets of Detroit, New Orleans, or Philadelphia.[371]

---

[370] http://www.csmonitor.com/USA/Society/2011/0815/Philadelphia-flash-mobs-black-mayor-takes-aim-at-black-community

[371] http://www.freep.com/article/20120227/NEWS01/120227032/Kilpatrick-Never-stolen-anything-his-life-says-Detroit-s-spirit-damaged-by-his-affair

No Blackman can save them either.

The League of Shadows had it all wrong. Strange they could sack so many other civilizations but fail to understand the racial dynamics of America in the 20th and 21st century to understand why so many of our great cities have collapsed.

Stranger still that the liberalism so many claim to be the cause of Detroit and other majority Black cities' decline can't say the same about Burlington, Vermont; Missoula, Montana; Boulder, Colorado; or Portland, Oregon, where liberalism thrives amid a sea of tranquility, courtesy of whitey.

Misguided idealists refuse to look at the ruins of Detroit and blame the current occupants for its condition. The same goes for the declining city of Philadelphia. The same goes for Milwaukee. The same goes for St. Louis. The same goes for Orlando.

The same goes for… well, you get the picture.

Is corruption, crime, misery, decay, and failure the ultimate fate of any city that comes from transitioning from majority white to majority Black population?

Yes. The League of Shadows' failure in bringing Gotham City to its knees – with or without a Batman to protect it – was in not introducing Black people into the metropolis to facilitate immediate white abandonment.

Once this occurs, the fate of the city is sealed. To understand where Philadelphia is headed, look no further than Detroit.

Our world has no League of Shadows to incapacitate a city through a veil of secrecy and surreptitious, clandestine machinations. The Visible Black Hand of Economics, an action that is available for all to see without any shadows blocking the view, destroyed Detroit.

Life is Balance: Another Romney in Office While America Burns

Looking across the political landscape, it should be obvious that we are preparing for a Mitt Romney - Barack Obama showdown in November.

An e-mailer recently asked why we haven't been covering some of the recent criminal actions of Black people from such exotic locations as Portland, St. Louis, and Philadelphia. Because the impending collapse of Detroit (and the takeover by the state of Michigan) will be the biggest story of the first quarter of 2012.

Long-time SBPDL readers should know that once a target is acquired, we attack it. Completely. Last summer, this site along with View from the Right, Unamusement Park, OD, TakiMag, OneSTDV, GL Piggy, and a few others began documenting the trend of Black people targeting whites in vicious attacks. Some call it Knockout King; in Milwaukee, it was just Black people (more than a hundred) attacking whites. In Philadelphia, well, it was Black people waging war with one another (and white people) that illustrates why liberty is really cracked in Black-Run America (BRA).[372]

This needs to be made clear right now: If you notice that it is Black people attacking white people nationwide; if you notice that Black people are waging a war on the profitability of public transportation by attacking whites and driving them to car pool to work; that Black children are attacking white kids on school buses; if notice that the government seems to favor Black people; well, you my friend are an ENEMY OF THE STATE.

You don't have to advocate the superiority of the white race. All you have to do - to be considered an ENEMY OF THE STATE - is notice collective Black failure and the government's (both state and federal) to endless promote Black people above everyone else.

Perhaps it's fate that we enter a race for the President of the United States between Mitt Romney, the son of former Michigan Governor George Romney. After all, it was George Romney who was the Republican governor of the state when Black people rioted in the summer of 1967 and burned it to the ground, scaring the remaining white people to the suburbs and solidifying that *Climate Change* would totally ruin The Motor City:

------

[372] http://articles.philly.com/2012-01-06/news/30598180_1_black-on-black-killings-murder-big-cities

------

A massive race riot erupted in Detroit. The summer of 1967 was a turbulent time in American history. The Detroit rioting began near 12th Street and Clairmount in a predominantly African-American, overcrowded, and low-income neighborhood. Early on the morning of July 23, Detroit police officers raided a "blind pig," which was an establishment that illegally sold alcohol after hours. A crowd gathered as those arrested were put in a police wagon. Riots erupted and quickly spread. Detroit Mayor Jerome Cavanagh asked Michigan's governor, George Romney, to send in the State Police. Eventually, Romney called in the National Guard. After eight dangerous and unfortunate days, the riot came to an end. The riot's immediate effects were disastrous. Forty-three people had lost their lives. 1,700 stores had been looted. In all, 7,231 people were arrested and over 1000 buildings were burned. Damages to property amounted to about $50 million. As a result of this debacle, President Lyndon Johnson set up the Kerner Commission to investigate the causes of civil disorder in American cities. New taxes were eventually adopted to bring increase revenue for education, welfare, and other government services. In 1972, a state lottery was also established to help raise money and alleviate the dire conditions of inner-city living. [373]

It should be noted that Gov. Romney (the elder) had designs for the White House, but those all ended when he claimed he was "brainwashed" into supporting the Vietnam War:

Governor George W. Romney of Michigan was a leading contender for the 1968 Republican presidential nomination until September 4, 1967, when he told Detroit television newsman Lou Gordon that he had been "brainwashed" by American generals into supporting the Vietnam war effort while touring Southeast Asia in 1965.

---

[373] http://blogpublic.lib.msu.edu/index.php/july-23-1967-detroit-race?blog=5

Though Romney tried in earnest to explain himself, he became the target of blistering press and partisan attacks. Romney's candidacy never recovered from the furor he created with his statement.[374]

The day will come when Black-Run America ends, that never-ending pursuit to promote Black people above everyone else (even at the expense of the nations overall health) which is the official governing policy of the government, the court system, the private sector, the military, the media and entertainment industry, and academia.[375]

Many white politicians will claim, like Romney the Elder, that they were "brainwashed" into believing it. The summer of 2011 was a prelude to the sparks that will fly in the summer of 2012, courtesy of ~~packs of youth~~, ~~flash mobbers~~, Black people.

After all, both Camden and New Orleans have requested the National Guard to patrol the city streets in a last-ditch bid to keep Black people from killing one another.[376]

Life is Balance. The moment that Mitt Romney is elected POTUS, it won't just be Detroit that could go up in flames, but every American city (think St. Louis, Philadelphia, Baltimore, Chicago, Birmingham, Portland, Buffalo, Memphis, Cleveland, Cincinnati, Atlanta, etc.) that feels the defeat of Mein Obama is yet another reminder that The Man wants to keep the The Brother forever down.

---

[374] http://www.washingtonpost.com/wp-srv/politics/special/clinton/frenzy/romney.htm

[375] http://www.vdare.com/posts/minority-occupation-govt-forces-pepsi-to-hire-possible-criminals

[376] http://www.myfoxphilly.com/dpp/news/local_news/camden-asks-national-guard-for-help-120611

The Dream Deferred: Marching on Michigan Gov. Rick Synder's Home in the Name of Defending Black-run Detroit

There's no need to sugar coat what is about to happen in Detroit. Arguably the greatest city in America as recently as 60 years ago, a massive Black riot in 1967 sparked the demise of the city. Courtesy of white flight helping decimate the white voting base, radical Black racialist Coleman Young was elected mayor in the early part of 1970s, and the Africanization of Detroit was cemented in stone.

We are mere weeks (maybe even days) away from the culmination of Young's true legacy: that being the takeover of 82 percent Black Detroit by the state of Michigan. Perhaps it's fate that Young served with the 477th Medium-Bomber Group during World War II, part of the famed Tuskegee Airmen Though he would never be deployed overseas to bomb Germany, it would be difficult to convince anyone who visited Detroit in 2012 that a massive aerial bombing campaign didn't occur there. (Deleted sentence)

Comparing Detroit 2012 to Dresden in 1945 isn't a logical leap, knowing that Young was a trained bombardier. Only that could explain the burned-out buildings, abandoned portions of the city, and demoralized population. Instead, the circumstance we find Detroit in is due primarily to the power of Black-Run America (BRA), a ruling ideology that mandates

Black people are never responsible for their actions (or the consequences of those actions).

Well, that or years of the greater social experiment in the history of mankind finally ending (though the usually sound scientific method's conclusions will be disregarded) with a whimper, as Black-run Detroit ends. The conclusion should be that removing the population that created, innovated, built, and sustained a city and its infrastructure and replacing it with one whose sole claim to fame is the invention of the supersoaker isn't sound advice for the health of community.

MSNBC's own Rev. Al Sharpton's livelihood revolves around being one of the primary agitators for Organized Blackness, so in the final days that equality-derived freedom reigns in Detroit, it's no surprise that he is leading the lynch mob to save The Black City:

> The Rev. Al Sharpton on Sunday joined the chorus of opponents to the emergency manager law and pushed plans for a peaceful protest in front of Gov. Rick Snyder's <u>home</u> on Martin Luther King Day.
> Sharpton, who joined U.S. Rep. John Conyers, D-Detroit, ministers and members of the Occupy Detroit movement, said Public Act 4 is a "sick" law that unfairly targets urban cities. He said protestors who gather at Snyder's Ann Arbor home should be peaceful but resolute in their opposition to the law.
> "Just like Wisconsin started union busting and then it went to Ohio and Indiana, " he said, "…This will be the beginning of governors nullifying the rights of people and they will say municipal elections don't mean anything," said Sharpton at a news conference at the King Solomon Baptist Church on the city's near west side. "You can vote for who you want but the governor will remove them if he wants to. This precedent must be stopped.
> "If Snyder gets away with it here, it will spread nationally."
> The 4 p.m. march on Snyder's home is expected to draw busloads from urban centers all over the state and organizers say they have cooperation from the Michigan State Police to have streets blocked off.

Sharpton and the Rev. Charles E. Williams II, pastor of King Solomon Baptist Church, planned on visiting a couple of church congregations Sunday to help gather signatures to repeal the law. Williams said they have more than 170,000 signatures, more than the 161,000 minimum required to freeze the law and place it on November's ballot.

So far, cities such as Benton Harbor, Flint, Ecorse, Pontiac and Detroit Public Schools are under emergency managers. The state is considering placing Detroit under an emergency manager and is currently conducting a fiscal review of the city's troubled <u>finances</u>.

Conyers, who has been a fierce opponent of the emergency manager law, said he's still waiting for U.S. Attorney General Eric Holder to respond about the constitutionality of Public Act 4 but to him it's a clear violation and should be repealed. "I think my case of unconstitutionality is clear," Conyers said. "If he has a different view, he's going to have to express it and we'll have to draw our own conclusions."

Zachary Steve, a member of the Occupy Detroit movement, said the law is a clear affront to hard-working citizens who have the right to elect their officials to make their own decisions.

"We have the governor taking away the consent of the government from local communities and school boards and giving that absolute power to one individual," Steve said.

"The constitution established a credo for divided power, a legislative, an executive, a judiciary branch. This law removes that divided power. It takes away the consent of the government."[377]

---

[377]

http://www.detroitnews.com/article/20120115/METRO/201150334/Critics-emergency-manager-law-target-Snyder-s-Ann-Arbor-home?odyssey=tab%7Ctopnews%7Ctext%7CFRONTPAGE

Eric "My People" Holder will probably agree with Conyers that Public Act 4 is a "sick law" and it's not inconceivable to see the Department of Justice intervening on behalf of 82 percent Black Detroit. Indeed, the Department of Justice has been intervening on behalf of 13 percent of the population for more than half a century.

Like his wife, Conyers should be in jail. The fact that for almost a century, Wayne County residents have helped reelect this man again and again to represent them in Washington D.C. shows you why the concept of democracy is a failure.

Then again, Holder might have more in common with Conyers then were he in jail:

> According to Department of Justice whistleblower J. Christian Adams, AG Eric Holder has a certain something in his wallet. It is a quotation — and he has carried it for decades. It essentially says, to quote Adams, "Blackness is more important than anything, and the black US attorney has common cause with the black criminal." It's not surprising that Holder would feel this way about black lawyers and criminals.
>
> Because in his case they're one and the same. [378]

---

[378] http://www.freerepublic.com/focus/f-news/2790533/posts

Not one major conservative will use the collapse of Detroit (nor will they take on Eric "My People" Holder) to broach the subject of race, though The Motor City has been a veritable Petri Dish for Disingenuous White Liberals (DWLs) to watch their beliefs unfold in real-life, to their melancholy conclusion.

Though Coleman Young protested this next sentence throughout his hilariously triumphant autobiography *Hard Stuff*, Black people were incapable of sustaining the civilization that whites left them (well, abandoned to them) in Detroit.

Memo to Al Sharpton: it was Black people who ruined Detroit, once a city that was the shining example of American ingenuity, where a true middle-class flourished and thrived; where arts and culture abound; and where dreams of the city's inhabitants for the Detroit their children would inherit resembled the world of the cartoon *The Jetsons*, as opposed to the nightmarish existence that Black people have brought to the city, making it resemble an almost all-Black version of *The Flintstones*.

The dream of equality was never deferred. At the tip of Federal guns, it came true in America. Look no further than the fate of Detroit, to see where every city in America is eventually headed.

Courtesy of the only Climate Change that truly poses a threat to mankind's future.

Coleman Young's Detroit: The Real Legacy of the Tuskegee Airmen

Coleman Young International Airport in Detroit is perhaps the most aptly named airport in the world. After all, Young was the mayor of Detroit from 1974 – 1993, whose tenure can best be described as one long eulogy for the city.

In his autobiography *Hard Stuff*, Young describes himself as an MFIC (Mother Fucker in Charge), and peppers his sentences with the descriptive *mother fucker* after seemingly every other word. It's perhaps the most honest look into a Black politicians thinking that has ever been published.

Fitting that in 1972, two years before the election of the city's first Black mayor, the Tuskegee Airmen, Inc. was founded in Detroit. It would be this organization that would strive to motivate and inspire America's young to become participants in our nation's democratic process, while working to spread the word on the enormous contributions those brave Nubian airmen gave to the victory in Europe during World War II.

After all, the MFIC himself was a Tuskegee Airmen.[379] One of the lesser known stories regarding the Tuskegee Airmen – save that they did lose a number of bombers they escorted – is what transpired stateside with these brave Nubian soldiers of God:

> By 1945, B-25 bomber squadrons with the 447th were deployed to Freeman Army Air Field outside Seymour, Ind., where Second Lieutenant Lawrence served as a navigator/bombardier. Although officers' clubs were officially desegregated under military regulars, commanders at Freeman Field refused to serve black officers.

---

[379] http://library.ucr.edu/?view=tuskegee/tuskegeeairmen.html

In April 1945, Tuskegee Airmen, led by 2nd Lt. Coleman Young, who went on to become the mayor of Detroit, decided to challenge base authorities. Young was among 19 Airmen initially arrested after refusing to leave the club. Two other civil disobedience actions followed during a two-day protest, resulting in the arrests of 161 officers, including Lawrence.

Ultimately, the military secured only one conviction, nailing Lt. Robert Terry on a charge of jostling another officer during the protest. Terry was drummed out of the Army Air Corps with a $150 fine, loss of rank and a dishonorable discharge. But in 1995, Terry received a full pardon, a refund and restoration of rank. Other participating Tuskegee Airmen had letters of reprimand removed from their files.[380]

That MFIC... always in the forefront of change! Fitting that his name graces scores of buildings in the town that freedom failed (under his watch) in, where concepts such as Democracy, self-government and equality took a fatal nosedive from which they shall never recover. Well, at least when the pilot flying the plane is Black.

Detroit is a ruined city now (the Visible Black Hand of Economics), where no grocery chain can stay open because the once might metropolitan, now blessed with an 84 percent Black population can't sustain one:

Ninety-two percent of food options in the city come from party and liquor stores, forcing residents into making nutrition choices in unsafe and unsanitary conditions, according to a report released Thursday.

---

[380]

http://www.heraldtribune.com/article/20120112/ARTICLE/120119843?p=2&tc=pg

In 2008, the city's last two Farmer Jack stores closed, leaving Detroit without a major chain grocery store. Independent stores such as Mike's Fresh Market or Foodland are among the options some city residents use for groceries. Still, city residents spend nearly $200 million a year on groceries in stores outside the city, according to the report.[381]

This is the true legacy of Tuskegee Airmen. There advancements for "freedom" destroyed Detroit. Fitting that the MFIC Coleman Young himself was elected mayor of The Motor City when its fate was sealed happened to have been a Tuskegee Airmen.

Talk about poetic justice!

Even more fitting, the Tuskegee Airmen National Museum is found in Detroit, for the former "Arsenal of Democracy" owes it dilapidated and ghostly state to the existence of these Black airmen. That Detroit is on the verge of being taking over by the state of Michigan while the movie *Red Tails* debuts in theaters is more proof that God has a sense of humor.

In fact, let's allow the president of that museum a moment to explain the significance of the airmen:

> The Red Tails — the nickname comes from the paint job on their planes — finally got their chance at the big time in 1944, escorting heavy bombers over German territory. With their new orders, the Tuskegee Airmen not only lodged the war's most-successful track record in protecting long-range bombers from enemy attack, a feat even Pentagon brass couldn't overlook, but they also demolished notions of inferiority.

381

http://www.detroitnews.com/article/20120120/METRO01/201200377/1409/METRO/Group-Detroit-lacks-healthy-food

"It used to be said that the Tuskegee Airmen never lost a bomber to the enemy," says Brian Smith, president of the Tuskegee Airmen National Museum at Detroit's Fort Wayne. "But research shows we lost about 25 bombers in 205 missions. All the same, nobody else can brag about that kind of success rate."[382]

In that same article, we learn this, which cuts like a dagger the heart of the Tuskegee Airmen story out of its still beating chest:

Like much of the country, in World War II, the U.S. military was segregated with white and black servicemen on separate bases, and the latter mostly relegated to menial tasks far from the front lines. In particular, African-American pilots for much of the war were prevented from engaging the enemy in the air — instead doing "mop-up" operations far from the front, taking out Nazi trains and trucks.[383]

Who were these Black fighter pilots facing in the air? Foo Fighters?

One article published recently about the fledging national museum states that 10- 20 of the original surviving Tuskegee Airmen currently call Detroit home. "Original?" Has a thriving circuit of impersonators popped up?[384]

But let's get back to Brian Smith, the president of the national museum. Here's what he told the *Sun-Sentinel*:

"These men were superheroes," said Brian Smith, director of the Tuskegee Airmen National Museum in Detroit. "They actually did superhuman things during the war."
Smith, 54, said he was 12 when his father first told him their story. He called it inspirational and said a Tuskegee Airman taught him to fly.

---

[382] http://www.detroitnews.com/article/20120120/ENT02/201200319/Air-legend-local-audience-embraces-Tails-?odyssey=mod%7Cnewswell%7Ctext%7CFRONTPAGE%7Cs

[383] Ibid

[384] http://www.freep.com/article/20120112/ENT01/201120637/Tuskegee-Airmen-film-hoped-to-boost-Detroit-efforts

More than 990 men trained at Tuskegee before it was shut down. About 400 of them flew missions over Europe and North Africa during the war, with ground fire or routine accidents killing 78 of them.

Many credit HBO's groundbreaking 1995 movie "The Tuskegee Airmen," for highlighting their historical feats. There have been several documentaries made, as well, including "Double Victory" and "Silver Wings & Civil Rights: The Fight to Fly."[385]

"Superheroes?" Considering that the 'groundbreaking' 1995 film established one lie after another as fact, perhaps the day will come when we learn these Black fighter pilots used telepathy to steer the planes and some form of mutant power to deflect incoming missiles from the bombers they escorted.

In a hilariously inaccurate column by *The Detroit Free Press* Rochelle Riley (she claims that the Airmen never lost a bomber – a fact that is still in most American text books), Smith is quoted yet again:

Dr. Brian Smith, director of the Tuskegee Airmen National Museum at old Ft. Wayne in southwest Detroit, couldn't wait to see the film at a Saturday screening.

"The main thing we hope the movie will do is portray the Airmen as superheroes," Smith said. "I feel they are superheroes. And with superhero status, people, we hope, will research and find out who they were, what actually happened to them, what kinds of racial things they had to go through ... and in doing that, they'll search out the museum and find out about our youth programs and want to support us."[386]

---

[385] http://www.sun-sentinel.com/news/broward/fl-tuskegee-pilots-20120120,0,7618424.story

[386] http://www.freep.com/article/20120115/COL10/201150539/Rochelle-Riley-Tuskegee-Airmen-deserve-a-better-home?odyssey=mod%7Cnewswell%7Ctext%7CFRONTPAGE%7Cp

"Superheroes?" Really. It's fitting that these 'superheroes' have drifted to Detroit, living out their remaining days in a city that fellow Tuskegee Airmen – the MFIC himself – Coleman Young inflicted the final fatal blow that has led to Detroit slowly bleeding out (though few dare give the real reason why).

Superheroes the Tuskegee Airmen were not. But like Coleman Young, the current craze over a bunch of pilots whose only true accomplishment revolves around their tributes in helping us understand that freedom has failed, the Red Tails are an elaborate hoax.

Life is balance. In the final days of "free" Black-run Detroit - where Coleman Young International Airport, with the Tuskegee Airmen National Museum but a stones throw away rest – you now know the true heritage of what the Red Tails represents.

Detroit died, because Black could fly.

But perhaps Smith is right, maybe these men our superheroes…

While watching the previews for *Red Tails*, it finally dawned on me what this movie represents: *300* for Black people. Remember Zack Snyder's 2008 film? Based on Frank Miller's graphic novel, *300* tells the tale of King Leonidas and the brave Spartans who were slaughtered fighting Xerxes massive army.

The movie was laughed at by critics, but it sparked a nerve with moviegoers earning huge box office receipts, turning Gerhard Butler (who played Leonidas) overnight into an "A" list star.

I've long wondered why this movie was made. It depicts white men kicking some serious ass (largely non-white ass mind you) in a time when white actors (primarily Americans) are being phased out of being projected as bad-asses. Just ask Thomas Jane or that goofy white guy from *Fast and the Furious* franchise.

Juxtapose this thought with the question of why *Red Tails* was made: outside of Black people, who really wants to see a movie about Black pilots? Though it was fraught with errors, the casting of *Top Gun* was nearly flawless from a racially correct standing of who actually flies the fighters in our military.

Red Tails even shows the Black fighter pilots engaging in some contemporary pre-sports competition Nubian ritual (where the team comes together to get pumped up), where they huddle together and shout in unison, "We Fight! We Fight."

How inspiring!

The New York Times Stephen Holden wrote these words in a review of the film:

> This much-decorated squadron of African-American pilots, whose P-51 Mustangs were painted with red tails, flew thousands of missions between 1943 and 1945. They discredited an outrageously racist 1925 Army War College study that asserted that blacks lacked the intelligence, ambition and courage to serve in combat. The mere existence of this movie and Mr. Lucas's imprimatur could be seen as significant morale boosters for African-American men whose World War II service still remains woefully underrecognized.[387]

Hate to burst your bubble Steve, but the reality is only in a segregated unit could Black pilots succeed against other Black pilots. The learning curve was only against other brothers. As we have seen since integration, few Black pilots in flight training can compete with the learning curve set by white pilots.

No matter, *Red Tails* is the attempt to create superheroes out of the Black fighter pilots of World War II (because no other war can provide anything but a few token Black pilots).

With this post, I'm done writing about *Red Tails* at SBPDL. What we are told is such an obvious lie, that someone had to write about it.

But I'm reminded of the last lines from *300*, when Dilios tells the story of Leonidas death to inspire the Spartans and Greeks to wage one last war against Xerxes:

---

[387] http://movies.nytimes.com/2012/01/20/movies/red-tails-george-lucass-tale-of-tuskegee-airmen-review.html?ref=stephenholden

"This day we rescue a world from mysticism and tyranny and usher in a future brighter than anything we can imagine."

In a nutshell, that sums up what SBPDL has become: we wage a war against the concept of Black-Run America (BRA), which has made improving Black people's lives at the expense of the nation's health a religion, with anyone who dares question this concept a heretic, who is immediately excommunicated.

BRA is tyranny, and it must be opposed. But BRA is the MFIC (to borrow Coleman Young's favorite term), so we too must work to rescue a world from mysticism and tyranny, if we are to ensure that our future is not one big Detroit.

And never forget, it was a vaunted Tuskegee Airmen who steered Detroit into the ground. Soon, she'll officially be six feet under.

Detroit's status in 2012 is their true legacy.

Detroit's Destiny

Remember the time you were in class and knew the answer to a question posed by your teacher, but didn't raise your hand out of fear you might be wrong? Or the time you had a crush on a beautiful girl, but were too afraid to ask her on a date because she might say 'no'?

Well, we are reaching the political equivalent of that moment— where that self-induced fear and trepidation which precludes us from doing what is rational and natural because of the negative consequences we perceive could arise from such action—with the impending financial collapse of Detroit.

"Impending" is the wrong word. "Imminent" would be, too. "Inevitable" is the apt word.

Why the insolvency of Detroit is inevitable now must be stated, because others will raise their hand and supply the wrong answer. *The American Thinker* will try and blame Democrats and Unions without mentioning that America's most liveable big city, Pittsburgh, is filled with both.

Free Republic won't allow anyone to even mention the word "Black" in the strange color-blind world the owners of that site have cultivated (with a religious zeal and intensity normally seen in a cult).

Beloved conservative economist Thomas Sowell can state it is due to "liberal social policies," without acknowledging these same policies are in place in cities that attract corporate investments, like Portland, Seattle, Boulder, and Denver. Others will state that a city under "total Democrat hegemony" for 50 years was bound to collapse, maintaining a desire to stay color-blind even in the face of economic Armageddon.[388]

Michael Barone, famous for stating that Hispanics will save the Republican Party, was in Detroit during the Black riots of late July 1967, still the worst riots this nation has ever seen. He wrote an article for the American Enterprise Institute stating how his politics were shaped by this event. Considering that he advocates the continued mass immigration of a people who in 2006 marched in major American cities waving the Mexican flag defiantly, we have to wonder what exactly Barone learned.[389]

The Weekly Standard published Matt Labash's ode to Detroit's collapse back in 2008, where he only in passing pointed out the racial significance of a city's collapse. (In 1960, Detroit was 76 percent White. Though at the time Blacks represented only 24 percent of the population, there were responsible for 65 percent of the violence crime there):

> Somewhere along the way, Detroit became our national ashtray, a safe place for everyone to stub out the butt of their jokes.

[388] http://rightwingnews.com/uncategorized/metro-detroit-no-longer-most-segregated-because-of-kumbayah-song-and-black-people-fleeing-liberal-utopia-detroit-but-mostly-because-of-black-people-fleeing-liberal-utopia-detroit/

[389] http://www.american.com/archive/2008/january-february-magazine-contents/present-at-the-destruction

It happens, though, when you're from Detroit. In the popular imagination, the Motor City has gone from being the Arsenal of Democracy, so named for their converting auto factories to make the weapons which helped us win World War II, and the incubator of the middle class (now leading the nation in foreclosure rates, Detroit once had the highest rate of home ownership in the country), to being Dysfunction Junction. To Detroit's credit, they've earned it.

How bad is Detroit? It once gave the keys to the city to Saddam Hussein.

Over the last several years, it has ranked as the most murderous city, the poorest city, the most segregated city, as the city with the highest auto-insurance rates, with the bleakest outlook for workers in their 20s and 30s, and as the place with the most heart attacks, slowest income growth, and fewest sunny days. It is a city without a single national grocery store chain. It has been deemed the most stressful metropolitan area in America. Likewise, it has ranked last in numerous studies: in new employment growth, in environmental indicators, in the rate of immunization of 2-year-olds, and, among big cities, in the number of high school or college graduates.

Men's Fitness magazine christened Detroit America's fattest city, while *Men's Health* called it America's sexual disease capital. Should the editors of these two metrosexual magazines be concerned for their safety after slagging the citizens of a city which has won the "most dangerous" title for five of the last ten years? Probably not: 47 percent of Detroit adults are functionally illiterate.

Precisely what caused all this mess is perhaps best left to historians. Locals' ideas for how it happened could keep one pinned to a barstool for weeks: auto companies failing or pushing out to the suburbs and beyond, white flight caused by the '67 riots and busing orders, the 20-year reign of Mayor Coleman Young who scared additional middle-class whites off with statements such as "The only way to handle discrimination is to reverse it," freeways destroying mass transit infrastructure, ineptitude, corruption, Japanese cars--take your pick.[390]

We no longer have the luxury of such utopian dreams of taking our pick when it comes to placing the blame for Detroit's monumental collapse; we must deal with the facts as they are and point out that Detroit has become the best friend of budding photographers hoping to publish the next best-selling coffee table book because it is a city that most resembles the dangerous foreign landscapes pictured in *National Geographic*. (For an actual coffee table book on modern Detroit, check out *The Ruins of Detroit*, by French photographers Yves Marchand and Romain Meffre.) Detroit is 82 percent Black. The Great Migration to Detroit of Blacks from the South (exacerbated by Henry Ford's promise to hire 10 percent of his employees from the Black population) inexorably created White Flight from that city, turning the city once known as "The Paris of the West" into the American version of the Paris Suburbs. Much of the rest of the city been torn down due to neglect.[391]

That Democrat hegemony bemoaned for ruining the city has been overwhelmingly Black for 40 years, starting with the election of Coleman Young, the first Black mayor in the history of Detroit. The mass exodus of people from the city was primarily White back in the 1960s and '70s (which turned a majority White city into the majority Black mess you have now), but is currently a torrent of Black people fleeing in hopes of finding a place to live with a national grocery chain.

White people fled Black crime then; Black people flee Black crime now.

Mike Brownfield of The Heritage Foundation has said Detroit is "a liberal's worst nightmare," but fails to point out that it is Black people

390

http://www.weeklystandard.com/Content/Public/Articles/000/000/015/945ay nyk.asp

391

http://www.freep.com/article/20100401/NEWS01/304010003/1318/3000-buildings-to-be-torn-down fleeing a liberal Black city to the tune of a 25 percent population decline in 10 years.

What are you afraid of saying Mr. Brownfield? Why can't you just say Detroit is in trouble because of its majority population (why doesn't the *Detroit Free Press* ever run an article that asks, In changing world, Detroit remains overwhelming black?)? Why can't Dr. Sowell? Why can't *The American Thinker*? Why can't *National Review*?[392]

The decline of Detroit (and America's major cities such as Baltimore, Milwaukee, Memphis, Philadelphia, St. Louis, Cleveland, Newark, New Orleans, Atlanta, Birmingham, Chicago, etc.) is completely racial in nature. Michael Walsh of *National Review* laments that "some day, we'll all live in Detroit" without mentioning the fact that Detroit's lily-white suburbs--where the White descendants of the War of Detroit (the 1967 Black riot) retreated to-- are perhaps the nicest in America.[393]

Conservatives must understand that is the Black residents of Detroit who have helped depreciate what was once some of the highest property value in the country to the majority of zip codes in America with the lowest property value.[394]

The Black press seems to understand understands this: The Atlanta Post published a story in 2010 stating that to Abandon Detroit = Abandoning Black America; Detroit post-1967 is a direct representation of Black America.

One mustn't forget that every student in Detroit now eats for free (courtesy of the state) so that the stigma of being on the free lunch program won't affect the self-esteem of Black children. As of 2009, more than 300,000 Black residents of Detroit were on food stamps, which equates to 38 percent of the citizenry. One can only guess what that number is now.

---

[392] http://blog.heritage.org/2011/03/24/morning-bell-detroits-liberal-nightmare/

[393] http://www.nationalreview.com/corner/288012/some-day-well-all-live-detroit-michael-walsh

[394] http://www.businessinsider.com/cheapest-zip-codes-america-home-prices-2011-10?op=1

With news that Detroit could run out cash by December, Mayor Dave Bing has had to announce massive cuts to the city that contradict the *USA Today's* triumphant, front-page, above the fold claim in October of 2011 that Detroit was back! Just a few months ago The Detroit Free Press reported:

> Delivering on his pledge to avoid an emergency manager, Mayor Dave Bing said today he will lay off 1,000 employees, implement a hiring freeze and increase his demands on unions to accept 10% pay cuts and deep concessions in health care and pension benefits.

This follows an earlier proclamation from Bing that stopped garbage removal, police patrols and other government services in 20 percent of the city. Who can forget that more than 100 Detroit Department of Transportation bus drivers refused to work and stayed at the Rosa Parks Bus Terminal because of rampaging Black youth (who have helped earn Detroit the honor of America's Most Dangerous City) attacking them.

That same bus system is so unreliable that LaWanda Flake, a disabled mother of six, recently bartered her home on Craigslist for a van to get her children to school on time. That house once belonged to one of the top Mo' Town artists (The Supremes), but has since come to represent how quickly property depreciates once Black people assume control of a city.[395]

If Detroit fails, then the unthinkable could happen: Michigan recently passed a "financial martial law" bill which allows the state to assume control of a bankrupt city. Once Detroit fails, an Emergency Manager will put in charge of the city and *The American Interest* warns us a 21st Century version of a "Plantation" will be created in America:

That's not the only problem: if the review determines that the city is broke, white Republican officials could end up making decisions that change the fate of a predominantly African American city — imposing cuts in employment, pay, benefits and services that will affect almost everyone who lives in Detroit.

---

[395]   http://news.yahoo.com/blogs/sideshow/mother-six-trades-98k-house-used-minivan-152424777.html

Detroit Free Press columnist Jeff Gerritt lays out what the governor will face if the takeover goes forward:

> "Plantation" is a word he'll hear a lot — in fact, Councilman Kwame Kenyatta already invoked it to describe what would happen if the state took control of the city's finances in an effort to keep it from running out of money by spring...
>
> Nothing happens in this region outside the context of race. Our often-painful history is the oxygen we breathe, even when we choke on it. We're all finding it a little hard to breathe just now.[396]

"Plantation" is the wrong word. On actual plantations, people worked. In the case of Detroit, the White Republican "owners" will labor away on behalf of their "slaves."

As Black people flee Detroit and head into the prosperous lily-white suburbs surrounding the city, they ensure that the middle-class areas will continue to shrink.[397]

The classic 1980s film *Robocop* teased at that truth when the CEO of OCP said, "Old Detroit has a cancer. That cancer is crime." In Hollywood's Detroit, multi-racial gangs, made up primarily of White males, prevailed.

Detroit faces a dual problem of spiking murder rates and a police force that is either incompetent or, increasingly, *absent*. This has led many residents to take the law into their own hands. *The Daily* reports, in an article entitled "911 is a Joke":

Justifiable homicide in the city shot up 79 percent in 2011 from the previous year, as citizens in the long-suffering city armed themselves and took matters into their own hands. The local rate of self-defense killings now stands 2,200 percent above the national average. Residents, unable to rely on a dwindling police force to keep them safe, are fighting back against the criminal scourge on their own. And they're offering no apologies.

---

[396]   http://www.freep.com/article/20111203/OPINION01/111203002/Jeff-Gerritt-Detroit-residents-wonder-Who-has-our-back-

[397]   http://news.yahoo.com/middle-class-areas-shrinking-us-study-000732421.html

Black dysfunction has, ironically, realized the dream of *Reason* magazine and Anarcho-Capitalists—a *laissez-faire* city with few government services. In Detroit, the dream is a nightmare.

In the span of only a few months, two of the former industrial giants that represented America's once mighty manufacturing base will have become virtually insolvent. Sad that 72 percent Black Birmingham, Alabama, was responsible for the bankruptcy of Jefferson County.

Now, it is precisely those who comprise the 82 percent share of Detroit's population that will be responsible for the financial ruin of that city, because they were incapable of sustaining the civilization that was left behind to them.

Only a few people will raise their hand and give the correct answer as to why "the Motor City" is finally out of gas.

To admit that Detroit is a failure because of its majority population is not possible in the political climate of 2012 America. To do so would undermine the political aim and drive of what this writer has dubbed "Black-Run America" (BRA).

This does not mean that Black people run actually America—far from it—but that America (corporate, religious, government, legal system, entertainment, etc.) is run for the advancement of Black people, and that to publicly say anything negative about Black people is, more or less, against the law of the land.

The National Question can't be properly answered until we have the courage to proclaim the truth of Detroit's demise. "Liberalism," "socialism," the "Democrat-controlled political class" are all partial, insufficient answers at best.

It's about race, stupid.

Burning Down the House: Detroit, Affirmative Action, and the end of Black-Rule in The Motor City

What if you could see a city where the logical conclusion of the consequences of affirmative action play out, where the desire to rectify past inequities in hiring patterns turns into an orgy of trying to add every conceivable Black person in the city onto the public payroll?

What if you could see a city where the founding population was ethnically cleansed after two disastrous race riots (1943 and 1967) and continued high rates of criminality made it impossible to justify living there? Robert Conot's *American Odyssey: A Unique History of America Told Through the Life of a Great City* offers a direct window into why white people fled Detroit. On p. 448 of the book, we learn that in 1960 – when Black people were only 28 percent of Detroit's population – that "the number of crimes reported in the city jumped from 54,700 in 1957 to 68,500, and major economic crimes (Robbery, burglary, and grand larceny) increased 40 percent – from 18,000 to over 25,000. During the latter 1950's black suspects began to outnumber white suspects (in 1960 there were 18,936 black and 13,603 whites arrested), and as a result the spotlight was turned upon "Negro" crime."

It was this increase in crime that drove 1 out of every 4 white people to leave Detroit in the 1950s, as the white population in plummeted from 1,545,847 to 1,182,970 in 1960. At the same time, the Black population increased more than 50 percent.

In *American Odyssey*, we learn the severity of Black crime in the city of Detroit:

"There had been 9,500 Negroes among the 35,000 person arrested in Detroit in 1940. There were 23,000 among the 36,000 arrested in 1963… In 1963 the number of major economic crimes was nearly double what it had been in 1952, and almost four times what it had been in 1939. Most of the victims of crimes committed by Negroes were Negroes. Negroes were one of the most vocal segments of Detroit's population demanding better police protection."[398]

In 1939, Detroit was 9 percent Black; in 1952, Detroit was 16 percent Black; by 1963, the city was 32 percent Black. Funny that Black people would demand better police protection in their neighbors, as Detroit would unveil the STRESS unit that specifically tried to deter crime in these 'hoods but Black people would immediately claim brutality.

In 1973, Coleman Young would run for mayor of Detroit on a platform of ending STRESS, saying this fascistic program unfairly targeted the Black community. He would win (in an incredibly racial election) and immediately disband STRESS. Crime hasn't stopped since, with most of deserted Detroit no longer under the protection of 911 services. And it is Black people being preyed upon by other Black people still.[399]

But what of affirmative action, you ask? Look no further than the police, where more than 63 percent of the Detroit Police Department is Black:

> Currently, twelve of the department's fifteen upper command members including the chief, assistant chief of operations, assistant chief of administration, and all six of the department's district commanders are Black.[400]

What of the rest of the city?

---

[398] Conot, Robert E.. *American odyssey,*. New York: Morrow, 1974. 466

399

http://www.detroitnews.com/article/20120328/METRO01/203280394/Detroit-senior-kills-break-suspect-long-can-fight-back-will-?odyssey=tab

[400] http://en.wikipedia.org/wiki/Detroit_Police_Department#cite_note-16

Todd C. Shaw's *Now is the Time!: Detroit Black Politics and Grassroots Activism* offers this glimpse into the world of public affairs in Detroit, reporting that Detroit's first Black mayor, Coleman Young, solidified by Black monolithic support by implementing affirmative action:

> Nonetheless, Young strongly influenced the dominant contours of public affairs in Detroit. Racial loyalty ensured that Detroit's first black mayor enjoyed support among important sectors of the African American community – for example, senior citizens, churchgoers, civil-rights leaders, and Black Nationalist spokespeople. After all, it was Young who reformed and completely integrated the police force, achieved affirmative action goals, aggressively defended Detroit and black political control against a hostile (white) media and the suburbs, and averted financial collapse of the city in the early 1980s. [401]

Funny, it took an emergency injection from the Jimmy Carter Administration in the 1970s [Black people became the majority population of Detroit in 1972] of $46 million (called the Comprehensive Employment and Training Act) after Young was forced to layoff 4,000 employees of the city in fiscal year 1974-1975 just to keep the city going then.

On p. 79, we learn to the extent of the affirmative action policies in Detroit:

> This mattered to African Americans, for by the end of Young's term [1994] and into the Archer administration, roughly 70 percent of all city employees were African American. The administration was also responsible for administering and dispersing millions of dollars in public contracts and grants in pursuit of affirmative-action goals. In Young's first term alone, city contracts with minority firms rose from a mere 3 percent to 20 percent.
> [402]

---

[401] Shaw, Todd Cameron. *Now is the time!: Detroit black politics and grassroots activism*. Durham: Duke University Press, 2009. Print. 78-79

[402] Ibid

Only Ze'ev Chafets book *Devils Night and Other True Tales of Detroit* offers a more comprehensive look at who exactly has been in charge of Detroit and, more importantly, the group of people responsible for the impending collapse of the city[403]:

> Coleman Young is the black mayor of a black city, a fact never from his consciousness.
>
> As Arthur Johnson observed, in no other place in the country have blacks succeeded in gathering so much political power into their own hands; specifically, the hands of the mayor. After four terms, he has cast the city government in his own image. Five of the nine members of the City Council are black [this book was published in 1990; now, all members are Black]. So were the chief of police, the fire chief, all four police commissioners, and the heads of most city departments (and, although Young does not appoint them, both congressmen, the superintendent of the schools and a majority of the city's judges).
>
> In city departments, where they are a minority, whites often feel like outsiders. One senior official told me that she received bomb threats from colleagues because she was not part of the "black political mafia."

---

[403] City Council Consent Agreement." *Detroit News*. N.p., n.d. Web. 20 Mar. 2012. <www.detroitnews.com/article/20120328/METRO01/203280450/Detroit-City-Council-consider-consent-agreement-state-Thursday?odyssey=tab%7Ctopnews%7Ctext%7C

But Young has done more than broaden access to the pork barrel. Under him, Detroit has become not merely an American city that happens to have a black majority, but a black metropolis, the first major Third World city in the United States. The trappings are all there – showcase projects [Renaissance Center], black-fisted symbols [Joe Louis Statue], an external enemy and the cult of personality. Detroit has even developed a quasi-official ideology that regards the pre-Young era as a time of white colonialism, ended by the 1967 insurrection and its aftermath. An official city publication describes the police department as having been a "hostile white army, entrusted by white authorities with the job of keeping nonwhites penned up in ghettos."[404]

Worse, Michael Goodin, a senior editor at the Michigan Chronicle proudly stated that "Young often declared that neither the city nor the major companies operating in Detroit made any efforts to invest in or support black businesses or black entrepreneurs here. In 1973, the year before he took over, the city and its major companies had spent not much more than $30,000 with black businesses. But by 1993, when he stepped down, more than $200 million was being spent with black businesses each year. Mayor Young was not afraid of letting bigoted white citizens or businesspeople know what they owed black people. And he was also not afraid of telling certain black people what they should be doing."[405]

$200 million a year invested in Black owned businesses by the city of Detroit. What kind of return on investment did we get?

Once those Black people were unleashed, look what they did to the city of Detroit.

This is what happens when you allow the inmates to run the asylum (Patterson Fears Detroit is Headed for Bankruptcy, Unrest, *The Detroit News*, March 27, 2012, Mike Martindale):

---

[404] Chafets, Ze'ev. *Devil's night: and other true tales of Detroit*. New York: Random House, 1990. Print. 176-177

[405] Graham, Lawrence. *Our kind of people: inside America's Black upper class*. New York: HarperCollins, 1999. Print. 297

Oakland County Executive L. Brooks Patterson said Wednesday he is concerned that harsh comments against a possible consent agreement to solve Detroit's financial crisis could foster economic chaos and even civil unrest.

In an interview, Patterson expanded on remarks he made before a Chamber of Commerce breakfast Wednesday morning at Oakland University. During the event, he described Detroit as a "tinderbox" and criticized a minister's comments made at a Detroit town hall meeting.

The outspoken Patterson also predicted Detroit couldn't survive without an emergency manager "yet continues to borrow money in an effort to get out of debt."

"Detroit is in a desperate economic struggle and appears headed towards the cliff we call bankruptcy," said Patterson. "An emergency manager may be the only way out of it. We have seen that in Flint, Pontiac, other cities, struggling with money problems. In Pontiac, we went from hundreds of employees and eliminated police and fire departments, much of city hall, and will probably be down to about 20 before it is all done."

He also criticized Detroit City Council's vote Tuesday to borrow $137 million to allow the city to make two upcoming debt payments.

"Trying to borrow your way out — like trying to sell $135 million (in bonds) like the council is talking — doesn't solve anything," Patterson said. "It just increases your debt. You don't get out of debt by adding to it."

Patterson said an emergency manager is "not pejorative" in his dictionary.

"The (emergency manager) may be all that stands between economic chaos and bankruptcy," Patterson said.

Patterson also criticized comments by the Rev. Malik Shabazz of the New Black Panther Party at a Detroit town hall meeting Monday on the fiscal crisis. Shabazz told state officials, "Before we let you take over our city, we will burn it down first." in reference to any state ordered takeover by an emergency manager.

"That kind of talk is inflammatory and is getting dangerously close to the line of incitement to riot," said Patterson, a former prosecutor. "You don't have to riot. You just have to incite people to riot. "[406]

Riot? Again. Hasn't Detroit had enough Black riots? Charlie LeDuff of Detroit's Fox Affiliate interviewed Rev. Shabazz, getting these hilarious words from the man of the cloth:

"What ... is the matter with you?" LeDuff asked Shabazz.

"I love freedom," he said.

"I know, but dude, like freedom requires some responsibility. So, when you're like saying burn the ... town down, you're out of your mind," said LeDuff. "You know that thing's ricocheting around town today."

"Well, as a student of history, I look at Saginaw, I look at Benton Harbor, I look at Inkster, I look at Flint, I look at Highland Park, I look at Detroit, all of the African-American majority populated cities are being taking over by emergency manager. But I see fascism being inflicted upon the peoples of the inner cities of Michigan," Shabazz responded.

"But what about this, look, I mean, people got to live in this, right?" LeDuff asked as he motioned to a decrepit home in Detroit. "So how is this white supremacy when finally white dudes want to help fix this?"

"Because -- and when I say white supremacy, that's not an assault on my white brothers and sisters -- I'm talking about institutions, power, financiers, bankers, they willfully, skillfully and purposely through subprime lending depopulated and deconstructed Detroit, which leaves us in this dilapidated blight," Shabazz explained.

"Do you agree it's time we did something here?" asked LeDuff.

---

[406] http://www.detroitnews.com/article/20120328/METRO01/203280441/

"We need to do something," Shabazz replied.

"Do you agree it's time to get a reign on our budgetary process here?" LeDuff inquired.

"I agree," said Shabazz.

"Do you agree that the people are suffering because the status quo won't work?" LeDuff further asked.

"This status quo is not working," Shabazz stated.

"So, tell the people what you want them to do," LeDuff said.

"What I want the people to do? I want you to unite -- black, white, blue -- unite, come together, deconstruct this wicked, reprobate-minded society and let's build a new one," Shabazz explained.

"And, don't burn it," said LeDuff.

"Don't burn it down," Shabazz said. "Don't burn the city, but burn evil and injustice and white supremacy, not white people."

"And you want to apologize?" asked LeDuff.

"No sir," said Shabazz.[407]

White supremacy had nothing to do with Detroit's collapse. It was, simply put, Black people who engineered the disaster that has been unfolding in Detroit since Coleman Young's election following the Black insurrection of 1967.

Johannes Spreen, who served as Detroit Police Commissioner from 1968 – 1970, co-wrote the book Who Killed Detroit with Diane Holloway. It's one of the more honest accounts of The Motor City's demise, with an exacerbated Spreen writing about crime in the city:

---

[407] http://www.myfoxdetroit.com/dpp/news/charlie_leduff/leduff-to-minister-malik-shabazz-burn-down-detroit-are-you-out-of-your-mind-20120227-msdk

The violence and hopelessness affects everyone. Almost all of the victims are black and are males in this now nearly totally black city. The cost to Detroit is enormous in dollars and perception. It makes me think of July 23, 1967.

According to the Detroit Free Press Special Report, "it's not uncommon to see a scene with multiple gunshots. The violence in Detroit has morphed into something new, something truly evil. The code of the street has changed. Ten or 20 years ago, there was morality to street violence. There were unspoken rules: Never kill children. Never kill family members. Take one persona t a time... But now, the killers shoot at anyone. They empty a clip into the crowd. They shoot in any direction."

What do the black militants say today? What do some of the white activists against police say today? What do the mayors and the city councilmen and women say today? Do they feel responsible for the parts they played? It's their city now, and Kwame's. It's a black city now. The police department is mostly black. It's black on black crime! It's a shame.[408]

Who killed Detroit? It should be obvious by now.

There's nothing to burn down in Detroit that hasn't been set into a mighty conflagration on Devil's Night or destroyed by highly flammable destroyer of working civil services known as affirmative action.

Detroit is the case-study for why this policy should be abandoned immediately. In fact, Detroit is a shining example of why freedom failed.

White People to the

---

[408] Spreen, Johannes F., and Diane Holloway. "Who Killed Detroit?." *Who killed Detroit: other cities beware*. New York: iUniverse, 2005. 174.

Rescue: Inc. Magazine dubs Detroit - The Black Metropolis of the Future - a "Start-up" city for business

The biggest news story in America right now is the impending collapse of Detroit, perhaps the biggest Black metropolis in the entire world. Under Black-rule, Detroit has become the poster-child for corruption in America[409], and as custodians of a city whose famous landmarks and buildings were all erected by white people, have watched them become the subjects capable of fueling the addiction of "ruin porn" aficionados from around the world.[410]

Once a symbol of economic might, the majestic Packard Plant ruins are a reminder of what *Life after White People* looks like. No Black developer nor outside investor ever converted these abandoned buildings into lofts, one of the hallmarks of a city seeking urban renewal by attracting bohemian white people there from the boring, lily white suburbs. Now the Packard Plant shall be demolished.[411]

Why couldn't Black entrepreneurs in Detroit convert these old buildings into something useful, as have their white counterparts in Pittsburgh (and many other cities where America's former manufacturing might is now the playground for Stuff White People Like - SWPL - whites)? Where once buildings produced the steel used by companies all around the world, now these buildings are lofts and residential space for the citizens of Pittsburgh, considered one of the best places to live in America.

---

[409] http://www.detroitnews.com/article/20120301/METRO/203010423/1409/FBI-unveils-public-corruption-task-force-Metro-Detroit

[410] http://www.freep.com/article/20090929/BLOG36/90928073

[411] http://www.freep.com/article/20120303/BUSINESS04/203030406/Dilapidated-Packard-Plant-reminder-of-Detroit-s-industrial-fall?odyssey=tab%7Ctopnews%7Ctext%7CFRONTPAGE

In the 1960s, Disingenuous White Liberals (DWL) like Detroit Mayor Jerry Cavanagh thought that massive spending programs - redistribution of wealth - could maintain a steady peace between the white and Black populations of the city. These dreams would spectacularly end in late July 1967 when Black people rioted, but the rest of the nation still clings to the belief that the government can redistribute money to the Black community to maintain the peace.

The August 4, 1967 issue of *Time* magazine produced this nugget of information for us to ponder. On p. 13:

> Fully 40 percent of the city's Negro family heads own their homes. No city has waged a more massive and comprehensive war on poverty. Under Mayor Jerry Cavanagh, an imaginative liberal with a knack for landing Government grants, the city has grabbed off $42 million in federal funds for its poverty programs, budgeted $30 million for them this year alone. Because many of the city's 520,000 Negroes (out of a population of 1,600,000) are unequipped to qualify for other than manual labor, some $10 million will go toward special training and placement programs for the unskilled and the illiterate. A $4,000,000 medical program furnishes family planning advice, outpatient clinics and the like. To cool an potential riot fever, the city had allotted an additional $3,000,000 for this summer's Head Start and recreation programs. so well did the city seem to be handling its problems that Congress of Racial Equality Director Floyd McKissick excluded Detroit last winter when he drew up a list of twelve cities where racial trouble was likely to flare.

All of this wasn't enough to keep Black people from burning down 1300 buildings and sacking 2700 businesses in late July of 1967 during the worst racial riot in American history.

Just like in the summer of 2011, when Black people engaged in riots all across the nation causing Newark, Chicago, Atlanta, Baltimore, Columbia, Philadelphia, Milwaukee, Peoria, and New Orleans to pass emergency curfews, Black people across the nation were rioting in 1967. The same types of activities used now to stop the violence were used then. From that same *Time* article (p. 14):

> Ironically, New York, - like Detroit - has launched a major

summer entertainment program designed to cool the ghettos by keeping the kids off the streets. "We have done everything in this city to make sure we have a stable summer," said Mayor John Lindsay. But after one of these stabilizing events, a Central Park rock-'n' roll concert featuring Smokey Robinson and the Miracles, a boisterous band of some 150 Negroes wandered down toward midtown Manhattan, heaved trash baskets through the windows of three Fifth Avenue clothing stores and helped themselves. The looters' favorite was a $56 Austrian alpaca sweater, which is a status symbol in Harlem. Among the 23 who police were able to catch; four Harlem summer antipoverty workers who earn up to $90 a week from the city.

The more things change, the more they stay the same.

It was after the Black insurrection of 1967 that white people surrendered the city of Detroit over to Black rule. In B.J. Widick's 1972 book *Detroit: City of Race and Class Violence*, we learn quickly that the Visible Black Hand of Economics was already proudly on display during the transitioning of power from white rule to Black rule. On p. 195:

> The limitations of black capitalism were especially visible in the city of Detroit, where in 1966, 65 percent of the inner-city population was black, but only 38 percent of the businesses were owned by blacks. Of these - mostly small retail and service operations - 60 percent had an annual net income of less than $8,000.

The concluding chapter of Widick's book is titled *Black Metropolis of the Future*. The Motor City indeed did become a Black Metropolis, a direct representation of what the Black inheritors (perhaps conquerors is the apt word?) were capable of producing, maintaining, and building. The "Ruin Porn" that is now one of the cities primary exports (no less than five books have been produced detailing the ruins of the white city under Black rule). Widdick points out in the early days of Black rule seeping into Detroit, businesses fled the city (p. 210):

> For every new business moving into the city, two more move out. There are over 7,000 vacant store fronts. Thousands of other small stores look like tiny military posts under siege

because of their wire or steel fronts and closed doors. Symbolic of the city's new look is the *Detroit News* building downtown, with its surrounding brick wall reminiscent of of a medieval fortress.

This was before Coleman Young was elected the city's first Black mayor. Libertarians always make the claim that people will innovate when businesses leave, because "free markets" dictate it, or some other nonsense.

Why have the descendants of those who conquered Detroit been incapable of creating new businesses and industry in the city? The white people of Pittsburgh - whose steel industry collapse in the 1980s took with it more than 100,000 jobs - have survived, and built a city considered the "most livable" in America.

Black people in Detroit? The honor bestowed upon the city under their custodianship is "most dangerous."

As Black-run Detroit limps to its death, *Inc.* magazine has dubbed the former Motor City a "Start-up City for Business." In the dying days of Black-run Detroit, the cost-of-living and starting a business in the city is so low, that entrepreneurs are flocking to the city.[412]

A city, mind you, whose death was sealed because Black people lacked the ability to innovate on their own. They lacked the ability to even sustain the city. Were it not for Coleman Young International Airport, one wonders where many of the Black people who actually work (and don't live off the government) would find employment?

At the Inc.com sub-site "Innovation Hotspots: Detroit"[413] we learn about those hip, SWPL white people who will build the next Detroit:

> For the most recent Startup Weekend in Detroit in mid-February, organizer Brandon Chesnutt cap attendance at 120, and still had people banging down his door.
>
> "We literally just ran out of space," Chesnutt says. "I can't go

---

[412] http://www.freep.com/apps/pbcs.dll/article?AID=2012120302025

[413] http://www.inc.com/innovation-hot-spots-detroit

an hour without getting e-mail from somebody wanting to attend."

The most popular Startup Weekend in the city's history took place inside the M@dison building, a modern five-story start-up Mecca that—as home to several VC firms and many of their portfolio companies—is part of the groundwork for a tech-centered rebirth of Detroit. The building is the brainchild of Dan Gilbert of Quicken Loans, who has been making it his crusade to reignite Detroit's downtown by buying property, seeding ventures, and moving thousands of Quicken employees into the area.

The M@dison is located on a stretch of Woodward Avenue that is poised to become Detroit's own Silicon Alley: Gilbert has dubbed it "Webward Avenue" for its burgeoning concentration of tech businesses and incubators. And with the neighborhood's surge in restaurants, bars, and entertainment options, Webward just might become the movement that is key to transforming Detroit back into a great American city.[414]

The seeds are being planted for the rebuilding of Detroit. Black-run Detroit is coming to an end, yet Black people nationwide will resist this usurpation of power by the state of Michigan. But even to the end, the only contributions of Black people will be more violence and more corruption from the elected officials. It will be up to white people to pull Detroit from the doldrums of Black-rule, the real lesson of the *Inc.* magazine expose on innovation in the city.[415]

Once you've hit bottom, there's only one place to go: up. The only hope for Detroit is for white people to flock to the city and utilize the existing infrastructure (repositioning it in the process) to rebuild and create a thriving metropolis that can eventually attract outside capital for renovation projects.[416]

---

[414]   http://www.inc.com/hot-spots-detroit/tim-donnelly/how-detroit-got-its-groove-back.html

[415]   http://detroit.cbslocal.com/2012/02/28/councilman-suggests-way-to-curb-violence-in-city/http://detroit.cbslocal.com/2012/02/28/councilman-suggests-way-to-curb-violence-in-city/

[416]   http://www.inc.com/hot-spots-detroit/nicole-carter/detroit-start-up-education.html

---

Such as the Grand Central Station, a dilapidated building whose past opulence is lost on Black people.

If this does not work, Detroit must be evacuated entirely and left to stand as a monument to DWL folly, a reminder of what the power of Black-Run America (BRA) did to *The Paris of the West*.

This is the lesson to draw from the "ruin porn" that people capture through photos and video of a decaying city whose current majority population can't sustain. And yes, downtown Detroit is more than 90 percent Black (the city is 82 percent Black).

The *Black Metropolis of the Future*... fitting that the city looks less like *The Jetsons* and more like a Black version of *The Flintstones*. That's the legacy of any city that reverts from being a majority-white metropolis (with a white government, regardless of political persuasion) to a majority-Black city.

We Shall Overcome

Can you feel it? It's in the air. You can almost taste it.

No, not the fallout from the Trayvon Martin racial-bomb that turned out to be a huge dud for Organized Blackness and those Disingenuous White Liberals (DWLs) foolish enough to believe that a "NO_LIMIT_NIGGA" was the rocket-fuel needed to propel the narrative into a different stratosphere.

No, it's not the sad story of 64 percent Black Baltimore (a city with one of the highest crime rates in America; 89 percent of those held in jail for their penchant for law-breaking are Black males), where the city is forced to sell-off landmarks and historic buildings - in hopes of meeting the budget - erected by a vastly different people than the Black population in charge of the city's future now, whose sons and daughters help make the Baltimore City Public Schools the worst in all of Maryland.[417] It's not poverty that causes horrifically low test scores[418] by these primarily Black students; it's that 87 percent of Baltimore City Public School students are Black.[419]

No, it's the soon-to-be biggest story in the world: the takeover of the 89 percent Black Detroit by the state of Michigan and the placement of a emergency financial manager in charge of the city's fiscal restructuring. Suzette Hackney of *The Detroit Free Press* reported that Michigan's white governor Rick Snyder met with a hostile crowd in Detroit today, with many of the Black people chanting "We Shall Overcome" as the news of fiscal Armageddon become ominously clear:

> Detroit's financial review team this afternoon declared that the city is under a financial emergency and no consent agreement between the city and state has been adopted, a move that forces Gov. Rick Snyder to appoint an emergency manager within the next 10 days under state law.
>
> State officials, however, are hopeful that an agreement can be reached before an emergency manager is named.
>
> "In that 10-day window, if a consent agreement can be adopted, that's an alternative for the governor and that's what he prefers to see," state Treasurer Andy Dillon said after the review team's meeting.
>
> Dillon said the financial review team, in a recommendation letter to Snyder, said they preferred to see the city and state enter into a consent agreement. He said there are three steps left in the process within the next 10 days: Mayor Dave Bing would have to accept the agreement, City Council would also have to vote to accept it and the governor would

---

[417]   http://articles.baltimoresun.com/2011-08-22/news/bs-md-co-school-buildings-inadequate-20110818_1_school-buildings-new-schools-schools-opening

[418] http://www.bsos.umd.edu/gvpt/stone/baltimore.html

[419]   http://crosscut.com/2011/01/24/education/20564/What-can-we-learn-from-the-struggles-of-Baltimore-public-schools-/

have to sign off as well.

About 100 Detroiters turned out, many of them defiant and outraged over what they considered a hostile takeover of a predominately black city.

As the meeting was about to begin at 3 p.m., most in the audience began chanting, "No takeover!"

The chanting and outbursts continued throughout the two-hour meeting, as security struggled to gain order.

For many in attendance, the state's threat to appoint an emergency manager stirs the bitter memories of unfair wages, forced segregation and other injustices against black people about a half-century ago.

"This is white on black crime," community activist and Minister Malik Shabazz said from a microphone during public comment. "This is white supremacy. Before you can take over our city, we will burn it down." [420]

"We will burn it down," Minister Shabazz said. Again? Come on Black people. This is why white people gave the city to you in 1967 - because for five days ten percent of Detroit's Black population tried to burn it to the ground - leaving to rebuild their lives in what are some of the most prosperous suburbs in all of America (with the highest test scores too!).

The Detroit News reported this:

> State officials say they hope to negotiate a consent decree with Detroit within 10 days after a raucous review team meeting concluded Monday with no deal in place.The team, which was required by law to report to Gov. Rick Snyder today, reiterated only that a severe financial emergency exists in Detroit and no consent decree has been adopted.

---

[420] http://www.freep.com/article/20120326/NEWS06/120326048/With-video-Financial-review-team-declares-emergency-Detroit-agreement-can-still-avert-takeover-10-days?odyssey=tab%7Ctopnews%7Ctext%7CFRONTPAGE

The team sent a letter to Snyder indicating that negotiations toward a deal continue.

Gov. Rick Snyder now has 10 days to rule on whether Detroit is in a fiscal crisis and say if a consent agreement has been adopted under Public Act 4, the controversial law that allows Michigan governors to appoint emergency managers with broad powers to run failing local governments.

Officials from the state and Detroit are moving closer to a consent deal, state Treasurer Andy Dillon said during the meeting.
An unruly crowd repeatedly shouted down Dillon as he attempted to explain the status of discussions. Crowd members chanted "no justice, no peace," "no takeover" and the song "we shall overcome."

" That was one of four conclusions it could report under Public Act 4, the controversial law under which emergency managers can be appointed to rule over finances of failing cities. Dillon said the review team could meet again Thursday and possibly Friday, with the hopes of getting an agreement approved by the city council and mayor by the end of the week. He said the proposed agreement would include a nine-member financial advisory board whose powers are still being debated, and the creation of a program manager position to carry out the city's financial plan.
During public comment to the review team, residents lined up to blast the state for taking away the rights of Detroiters. Activist minister Malik Shabazz said black cities are under attack all over the state."We understand we have financial difficulties," Shabazz said. "Give us the help we want, need and deserve, not the help you want to impose on us. We don't want an emergency manager or a consent decree. This is white supremacy and we will fight you.

"Before we let you take over our city we will burn it down first," Shabazz said.Ed McNeil, chief negotiator for AFSCME Council 25, said people have sacrificed and fought hard to bring the city back.
"There's no kind of way in this world you should be taking anything from Detroit and its residents," McNeil said. "We

intend to keep it our city. We intend to work in our city and progressing for our city."[421]

And here's a hilarious anecdote from Detroit's Fox Affiliate:

Conrad Mallett, one of the state's first black Michigan Supreme Court justices, came under pointed criticism for cooperating with the white treasurer as the review board shaped its recommendation.

"You sit up there and you fix it for him, just like a good colored person," former Detroit Public Schools board member Marie Thornton told Mallett, now president of Sinai-Grace Hospital.

Mallett dismissed the complaints as a "family fight" within the city, which is 80 percent black. He added he's not mad at his critics but said they need to realize the review board's goal it to create a stable financial future for Michigan's largest city.A final deal remains up in the air in part because Detroit Mayor Dave Bing is hospitalized after having surgery over the weekend on a perforated intestine, said Dennis Muchmore, Snyder's chief of staff.

Doctors said the mayor likely would remain hospitalized for five to seven days, but would be able to perform some duties of his office. Bing's chief of staff and deputy mayor in his absence, Kirk Lewis, is handling negotiations with the governor's office.Detroit faces a $200 million budget deficit and could run out of cash by the end of May. The governor has declined to offer any short-term financial assistance until some agreement is reached to deal with the city's ongoing financial difficulties and its long-term liabilities for pensions, health care and bonds. Two ratings agencies this month downgraded Detroit's bond ratings.

"Everyone knows Detroit's finances are in very difficult

421

http://www.detroitnews.com/article/20120326/METRO01/203260394/Review-team-Detroit-crisis-consent-deal-close?odyssey=tab%7Ctopnews%7Ctext%7CFRONTPAGE

shape," Snyder said.[422]

"We Shall Overcome,"Black people sang. What exactly, is difficult to discern. Black ineptitude? The Visible Black Hand of Economics? Black incompetence in virtually every level of the city government of Detroit? Black crime in Detroit, which makes the city inhospitable to investors and urban pioneers?

The Paris of the West in 1950, when the city was 80 percent white; The Mogadishu of the West in 2012, courtesy of an 89 percent Black population.

We Shall Overcome.

Yes, America will one day overcome the insanity of Black-Run America (BRA).

We Shall. Overcome.

It begins with admitting the reason Detroit failed. The collapse of Detroit is culmination of more than 40 years of uninterrupted Actual Black Run America (ABRA).

The lesson to other major America cities: *Don't Get Detroit-ed*!

Restrictive Covenants: The Only Hope in a Multi-Racial Nation

In 1943, as American troops battled German and Japanese troops during the heart of World War II, Detroit was engulfed in a war as well.

---

[422] http://www.myfoxdetroit.com/dpp/news/local/review-team-detroit-in-severe-financial-stress-20120326-ms

An influx of Black people from the south – part of The Great Migration – had more than doubled their population numbers in Detroit, immediately putting a strain on resources available to them. Housing, always a tenuous situation when dealing with Black and white relations, was an issue threatening to tear apart the city. Established white communities had no desire to integrate; established Black communities didn't want the new Black immigrants to the city moving into their neighborhoods either, as crime was a problem from day one.[423]

To mitigate the housing problems – considering that restrictive covenants were still constitutional – something had to be done.

The federal government decided to intervene on behalf of the growing Black population by building housing projects in the city:

> Even before the attack on Pearl Harbor, the federal government was concerned about providing housing for the workers who were beginning to pour into the area. On June 4, 1941, the Detroit Housing Commission approved two sites for defense housing projects--one for whites, one for blacks. The site originally selected by the commission for black workers was in a predominantly black area. But the federal government chose a site at Nevada and Fenelon streets, a white neighborhood.
>
> The Rev. Horace White, the only black member of the Housing Commission, stated, "As much as I disagree with the site selection, the housing shortage in Detroit is so acute, particularly among Negroes, that I feel we should cooperate."
>
> On Sept. 29, the project was named Sojourner Truth, in memory of the female Negro leader and poet of Civil War days. Despite being completed on Dec. 15, no tenants moved into the homes because of mounting opposition from the white neighborhood.

---

[423] Graham, Lawrence. *Our kind of people: inside America's Black upper class*. New York: HarperCollins, 1999. Print.

On Jan. 20, 1942, Washington informed the Housing Commission that the Sojourner Truth project would be for whites and another site would be selected for black workers. But when a suitable site for blacks could not be found, Washington housing authorities agreed to allow blacks into the finished homes.[424]

Understand that Detroit in the 1920 was only 4.1 percent Black; in 1930, were still only 7.1 percent of the population; by 1940, that number was 9 percent of Detroit's population.

Interesting, it was the practice of segregation that allowed the formation of a Black elite and the establishment of a Black business district, a fact Michael Goodin begrudgingly admits in *Our Kind of People*.

"The Black Bottom-Paradise Valley neighborhood was an entrepreneurial oasis for blacks. Black doctors and lawyers…car dealerships, the Paradise Theater, Sonny Wilson's Bar, Sidney Barthwell's drugstores, insurance office – all the black-owned businesses were there.[425]

Detroit in the 1940s was a period of intense racial animosity, with both legal and extralegal methods implemented to keep the exploding-in-population Black community in what Todd Shaw labeled overcrowded and unhealthy slums.[426] That entrepreneurs didn't arise from this community and come up with ides to improve sanitation is never explained. Were these Black people incapable of investing money into their community and bettering the lives for their families?

These conditions amounted to a powder keg for race relations in the city, and the fuse was quickly lit:

---

[424] http://apps.detnews.com/apps/history/index.php?id=185

[425] Graham, Lawrence. *Our kind of people: inside America's Black upper class*. New York: HarperCollins, 1999. Print.302-303

[426] Shaw, Todd Cameron. *Now is the time!: Detroit black politics and grassroots activism*. Durham: Duke University Press, 2009. Print. 42

By the 1940s Detroit already had a long history of racial conflict. Race riots had occurred in 1863 and as recently as 1941. By the 1920s the city had become a stronghold of the Ku Klux Klan, an organization committed to white supremacy. The industrial plants provided jobs but not housing. White communities militantly guarded the dividing lines imposed by segregation throughout Detroit's history. As a result, the city's 200,000 black residents were cramped into 60 square blocks on the East Side and forced to live under deplorable sanitary conditions. Ironically, the ghetto was called Paradise Valley.

These and numerous other indignities contributed to escalating racial tensions in June of 1943. In many cities the demands of wartime were manifesting themselves in outbursts of intolerance. Race riots had already erupted in Los Angeles, as well as Mobile, Alabama, and Beaumont, Texas. In 1943 the National Association for the Advancement of Colored People held an emergency war conference in Detroit and accused the nation of its hypocritical commitment to personal freedoms abroad and discrimination and segregation at home.

The Detroit riot began at a popular and integrated amusement park known as Belle Isle. On the muggy summer evening of June 20, 1943, the playground was ablaze with activity. Several incidents occurred that night including multiple fights between teenagers of both races. White teenagers were often aided by sailors who were stationed at the Naval Armory nearby. As people began leaving the island for home, major traffic jams and congestion at the ferry docks spurred more violence. On the bridge which led back to the mainland, a fight erupted between a total of 200 African Americans and white sailors. Soon, a crowd of 5,000 white residents gathered at the mainland entrance to the bridge ready to attack black vacationers wishing to cross. By midnight, a ragged and understaffed police force attempted to retain the situation, but the rioting had already spread too far into the city.[427]

Thirty-four Americans died and more than one thousand other were wounded in the streets of Detroit during the white-Black clashes of the week of June 20, 1943.[428]

While their relatives fought and died on overseas battlefields for "freedom," the home front in "The Arsenal of Democracy" was beginning to see that slow establishment of Black-Run America (BRA).

---

[427]   http://www.pbs.org/wgbh/americanexperience/features/general-article/eleanor-riots/

[428] Lee, Alfred McClung, and Norman Daymond Humphrey. *Race riot,*. New York, N.Y.: Dryden Press, 1943. 2

From 1940 – 1950, the share of the Black percentage of Detroit went from 9 percent to 16 percent of the total population. White homeowners, real-estate interests, and government appraisers used mechanisms to reserve the lion's share of Detroit's meager housing resources for white families. The rise of white neighborhood improvement associations is a story of how white homeowners resisted what they saw as their right to protect property values and to preserve racial homogeneity. Roughly 85 percent of all of Detroit's residential property was covered by racially restrictive covenants by the 1940s. White homeowners banded together and agreed not to rent or sell to Black people, though "blockbusting" occurred when real-estate speculators stoked whites' fears of new Black neighbors and profited from quick home sales.[429]

A restrictive covenant is a specifying legal agreement that property sold can't be owned or rented by a member of a designated minority group – often times legally-binding for forever, or for multiple decades or a century – which helped establish segregated neighborhoods in Detroit. Better, these helped establish a Black entrepreneurial class there as well that forced integration seemed to break apart.

When restrictive covenants made their first appearance in Detroit in 1910, Black leaders immediately contested them. It should be noted that Black people comprised 1.2 percent of the population of the city then. The state Supreme Court of Michigan upheld the validity of restrictive covenants in 1922 when they looked at a case involving a Black person in Pontiac who sought to buy property there.[430]

Today, Pontiac is 52 percent Black and only 26 percent white. It has been taken over by the state of Michigan, with an emergency manager now in control of the city's finances.[431]

Obviously, there was something to the concept of restrictive covenants.

---

[429] Lee, Alfred McClung, and Norman Daymond Humphrey. *Race riot,*. New York, N.Y.: Dryden Press, 1943. 42

[430] Farley, Reynolds, Sheldon Danziger, and Harry J. Holzer. *Detroit divided*. New York: Russell Sage Foundation, 2000. 147-148

[431] http://www.mackinac.org/16673

In 1926, the Supreme Court of the United States heard a case of northwest Washington D.C. white property owners who feared that a Black invasion would occur and agreed to write restrictive covenants into their deeds to maintain the value of their homes. However, one of the properties was sold to a Black person.

Voting 9-0 to approve restrictive covenants, the Supreme Court upheld their constitutionality. Justice Sanford argued that the issue of denying Black people the right to live in white neighborhoods was so insubstantial as to be without color of merit and frivolous.[432]

But it wasn't just Washington D.C. and Detroit white property owners fearful of what selling to Black buyers would inevitably bring into their neighborhood.

In Chicago, developers regularly added racial restriction as well: property owners could not sell their homes to non-white buyers. In Detroit, developers blanketed the new houses on the city's outskirts with restrictive covenants, turning this into a selling point. "We have carefully restricted this section to include only the kind of people you would be glad to have next door," one of the biggest firms proudly proclaimed as it unveiled its newest development. "Here you can feel free to make friends with your neighbors."[433]

The National Association for the Advancement of Black People (NAACP) had one of its largest branches in Detroit, and would wage a full assault on restrictive covenants after this ruling by the Supreme Court.

---

[432] Farley, Reynolds, Sheldon Danziger, and Harry J. Holzer. *Detroit divided*. New York: Russell Sage Foundation, 2000. 147-148

[433] Boyle, Kevin. *Arc of justice: a saga of race, civil rights, and murder in the Jazz Age*. New York, N.Y.: Henry Holt and Co., 20052004.144-145

In 1944 Orsel McGhee was a Black man who bought a home in a white area of Detroit where restrictive covenants were in full effect, even moving in, in the dead of the night. His white neighbor would seek a court order having him evicted with the local judge upholding restrictive covenants and ordering McGhee and his wife out. The NAACP would join the litigation, appealing this decision to the Michigan Supreme Court, who ruled unanimously two years later that restrictive covenants had legal standing and could be used to keep neighborhoods "Caucasian."[434]

Undeterred, the NAACP would take a similar case from St. Louis and the Detroit case to Washington, where Supreme Court would hear President Harry Truman's attorney general – Tom Clark – personally argue the case, stating that restrictive covenants violated the rights of Jews, Asians, and Blacks. In the summer of 1948, the Supreme Court ruled unanimously (in Shelley v. Kraemer)[435] that restrictive covenants violated both the Fourteenth Amendment and the Civil Rights Act of 1866.[436]

Now, 64 years after this ruling 89 percent Black Detroit is home to 12 of the 20 Zip Codes in America with the lowest property value.[437]

Detroit is the most dangerous city in America, though only 10 – 15 miles away, some of the safest (and whitest) suburbs in the nation are found.[438]

[434] Farley, Reynolds, Sheldon Danziger, and Harry J. Holzer. *Detroit divided*. New York: Russell Sage Foundation, 2000. 147-148

[435] http://en.wikipedia.org/wiki/Shelley_v._Kraemer

[436] Ibid. 152

[437] http://www.businessinsider.com/cheapest-zip-codes-america-home-prices-2011-10

[438] http://thelede.blogs.nytimes.com/2007/11/20/detroit-most-dangerous-or-most-disrespected/

The violence in so bad in Zip Code 48205 that the federal government has launched an initiative to curb high rates of crime there that comprise a disproportionate percentage of all crime committed in Detroit.[439]

Looking upon the actions of those white people who engaged the new Black migrants to the city of Detroit in 1943, and knowing how the future of Detroit would turn out under Black political rule, were their actions misguided?

Were restrictive covenants not the most important legal tool needed to keep the city safe and neighborhoods intact?

In 2012 Detroit, the FBI has declared fighting public corruption there its number one priority. No one seems to want to point out that almost every elected official in Detroit is Black. Well, almost no one.

The corruption in Detroit's elected officials is systemic, with the executive, treasury, school board, and police departments run all under some sort of investigation. But these elected and appointed officials are merely representative of the city's majority population, most of whom subsist on EBT/Food Stamps and TANF/Welfare.

To avoid any negative stereotyping, all children in Detroit get free lunches at school.

Police in Detroit have stopped responding to many 911 calls, leaving the majority Black population to fend for themselves in a city where Black criminals continually battle the Black criminals of New Orleans for the title of "Most Violent City in America."

For this reason, vigilante justice is rising in Detroit, with justifiable homicides up 2,200 percent above the US average. The violence is only getting worse, with task forces dedicated to restoring some semblance of law and order to the city.

---

[439]   http://www.freep.com/article/20110929/NEWS01/110929018/Feds-crack-down-crime-Detroit-ZIP-code-48205

The wealthy have taken to hiring out private security to patrol their streets, as a gated community isn't enough to guarantee safety anymore. Mercenaries now keep order, where the majority Black police force fails.

Social trust and social capital is non-existent in a city that is almost entirely populated by Black people.

Just this past week – taking a cue from majority Black Newark, which tried to pass a law mandating armed guards in all eateries - Detroit Councilman Kwame Kenyatta wants to pass a law forcing gas station owners to hire out security guards.

This is the cost of doing business in Detroit.

Strange that in a near homogeneous Black community, there seems to be so little social trust and social capital found in Detroit, which seems to fly in the face of Harvard political scientist Robert Putnam's study on diversity being the primary cause for a loss of civic engagement.[440]

Remember this story? Putnam was so embarrassed by his study and investigation that showed the harmful effects of diversity upon America, that he suppressed the findings for a number of years.

One has to ask: for an all-Black community like Detroit, the inverses of Putnam's findings appear to be true. The Blacker a community, the fewer people vote, the less they volunteer, and the less they work to better the community through projects. They don't even snitch to the police! Neighborhood trust appears to be low, especially in the 48205 zip code, the most violent in America.

Civic health is not only low in diverse communities, but it is especially low in nearly all-Black communities.

The Arsenal of Democracy. The Paris of the West. This is how Detroit was once described, when white people were more than 75 percent of the population.

440

http://www.mlive.com/news/detroit/index.ssf/2011/09/detroits_deadliest_neighborhoo.html

What do you call it now, after 40 years of uninterrupted Black rule? The Mogadishu of the West?

Restoring restrictive covenants is the only way to restore America and safeguard future cities from being *Detroit-ed.*[*]

Darrell Dawsey of Time reported that white people are beginning to move back into Detroit, a city that Black people have stood proud victors over since the 1967 ethnic cleansing riot:

> According to new studies, white people are moving back into Detroit proper in increasing numbers for the first time in nearly 60 years.
>
> The survey, more estimate than precise numbers, shows that the percentage of white, non-Hispanic Detroiters rose from 8.4% of the city's population in 2008 to 13.3% last year.
>
> Much of the rise can be pegged to younger white people -- along with some empty nesters -- moving to the city, even as African Americans continue to leave for the suburbs.
>
> Apparently, the city is "cool" again.[441]

Strangely enough, Detroit is attracting a Stuff White People Like (SWPL) community, attracted by the incredible low-rents found in The Motor City, with incentives and tax-breaks being offered by businesses and the local government desperate for actual talent to help save the city – a task that 89 percent Black Detroit can't perform.

The New York Times reported on this phenomenon:

---

[*] *Don't Get Detroit-ed – a warning to American Cities,* will be released in October of 2012

[441] http://detroit.blogs.time.com/2010/09/29/the-return-flight/

Recent census figures show that Detroit's overall population shrank by 25 percent in the last 10 years. But another figure tells a different and more intriguing story: During the same time period, downtown Detroit experienced a 59 percent increase in the number of college-educated residents under the age of 35, nearly 30 percent more than two-thirds of the nation's 51 largest cities.

These days the word "movement" is often heard to describe the influx of socially aware hipsters and artists now roaming the streets of Detroit. Not unlike Berlin, which was revitalized in the 1990s by young artists migrating there for the cheap studio space, Detroit may have this new generation of what city leaders are calling "creatives" to thank if it comes through its transition from a one-industry.

With these new residents have come the trappings of a thriving youth culture: trendy bars and restaurants that have brought pedestrians back to once-empty streets. Places like the Grand Trunk pub, Raw Cafe, Le Petit Zinc and Avalon Bakery mingle with shops with names like City Bird, Sole Sisters and the Bureau of Urban Living...

Part of the allure of Detroit lies in simple economics. Real estate is cheap by urban standards (Ms. Myles lives in a $900-a-month one-bedroom apartment with a garage), and the city is so eager to draw educated young residents that it is offering numerous subsidies to new arrivals. Ms. Myles, for instance, received $3,500 from her employer, which, like many companies in the city, is offering rent or purchasing subsidies to staff members who choose to live in the city.

Detroit Venture Partners is offering start-up financing to early-stage technology companies; Techtown, a business incubator, research and technology park associated with Wayne State University in Detroit, is providing support to entrepreneurs and emerging companies through its "Thrive" program. And Bizdom U, an "entrepreneurial boot camp" started by Dan Gilbert, the founder and chairman of Quicken Loans, is offering graduates of its four-month-long course financing opportunities of up to $100,000 if they base their start-up in Detroit.

"Downtown Detroit is quickly becoming a hotbed for both entrepreneurs and entrepreneurial companies," said Mr. Gilbert, who plans to fill two downtown office buildings he recently bought, as well as one he has a contract to buy, with tech and Web-based companies.

In addition, Green Garage Detroit, an incubator for environmentally friendly companies, plans to open its doors in August to lend support to at least a dozen start-ups. And there's the Detroit Creative Corridor Center, which supplies infrastructure, strategic counseling, consulting and resources for those wanting to start businesses in film, fashion, digital media, production or architecture. With all this help, the city seems like a giant candy store for young college graduates wanting to be their own bosses.[442]

Detroit can be rebuilt. The existing infrastructure, neglected by the Black political ruling class since they took over in 1973, can be refurbished. The old, crumbling buildings can be renovated and restored to their former glory, perhaps shining more illustrious than before.

The skyscrapers that once towered over all mankind and stood as beacons of hope for men, women and their families in search of a better life (remember, in the 1920s, Detroit's building were the tallest in the world) can be repopulated with a population capable of restoring a thriving local economy, sustaining a population off of revenues actually generated through work, instead of subsisting off of government aid and federal grants and doling them out to minority business owners.

America can be competitive again. Instantly. Overnight. It simply means rolling back the 20th century, one were progressives hoping to uplift an entire people inadvertently unleashed the most lethal force known to man: Black-Run America (BRA).

Detroit was ground zero for this weapon.

---

[442]http://www.nytimes.com/2011/07/03/fashion/the-young-and-entrepreneurial-move-to-downtown-detroit-pushing-its-economic-recovery.html?_r=1&src=ISMR_AP_LO_MST_FB&pagewanted=all

On March 8, 2012, *The Wall Street Journal* published an article confirming that Detroit has hope, only if "urban pioneers" continue to trickle into the city. You see, a Whole Foods is coming to the city:

> Whole Foods is locating in a section of Detroit rebranded Midtown. The neighborhood encompasses some important demographic anchors—Wayne State University, the Detroit Institute of Arts, and the Detroit Medical Center, among others. From that core, and fueled by business investment and economic-development incentives over the past couple of decades, a notable if nascent urban rebirth has taken root. It stretches piecemeal from Midtown to downtown and the river front.

> Refurbished commercial space has attracted companies looking for large facilities. Quicken Loans, for example, just relocated its Michigan staff—more than 3,000 employees— to downtown Detroit. Services and small shops have opened. New housing, clubs and restaurants have slowly drawn in more urban pioneers.

> "The opportunity to live downtown is really the most attractive factor in taking a job here," says Colm Fay, a graduate student at the University of Michigan in Ann Arbor. "It's a diverse and dynamic place from a lifestyle standpoint."

> Population may have declined in the city overall, but in the last several years it is up in parts of Midtown. That caught Whole Foods' eye, and so did income in the area. Mr. Bashaw says the chief hard metric in the company's calculations was education levels. "It's an indication of a person's willingness to consider a healthier diet," he says. Midtown scored well on that front too.

> Then there are those abandoned homes. I remember a Detroit fireman years ago telling me that arsonists had burned down so many empty houses in the city that Detroit had some of the best grouse hunting in Michigan. The birds loved hiding in the overgrown lots.

Today, there are many more vacant lots. But there are also more than 800 community gardens using some of that space to grow vegetables and fruit for home use. That also caught Whole Foods' attention. As did the city's bustling Eastern Market, one of the oldest and biggest farmers markets in the country. It draws in produce from throughout the region and sells it to supermarkets and restaurants. Up to 40,000 people shop at its Saturday Market. The new Whole Foods plans to buy there as well…

Ms. Stella's development agency gathered data from focus groups of Detroit shoppers and "psychographic" research that analyzed consumer behavior. The agency gave its findings to Whole Foods: A broad swath of Detroiters want a wider selection of organic food than they can get now, and Detroit consumers spend roughly $200 million a year at supermarkets in the suburbs, where Whole Foods already has locations. That "leakage" could be captured by the city. The new store will be close to freeways.

But the store's arrival in Detroit isn't really the big news. The big news is what's happened in this section of the city. After decades of incremental, three-yards-and-a-cloud-of-dust development work, Detroit has pieced together enough vitality to make a higher-end supermarket viable. Or at least worth trying.

That's the remarkable business story.[443]

"Urban pioneers." That term should have new meaning as you put down this book. Enough white people have moved back into Detroit to create an environment of hope in Black sea of despair. Whole Foods is moving in, the clearest representation of whiteness you can find.

Property value will begin to rise in this area; hope will return.

Restrictive covenants are the only way to ensure that this "urban pioneering" settlement is maintained.

---

[443]http://online.wsj.com/article/SB1000142405297020396120457726972377 68076382.html

—

It's the only way to save America.

There exists no greater freedom than that of Freedom of Association. From this, the allocation of all other freedoms can be discussed and established as they best serve to safeguard the future posterity of a community.

Who Wants to Live Forever?

April is the cruelest month, breeding Lilacs out of the dead land, mixing Memory and desire, stirring Dull roots with spring rain. – T.S. Eliot, *The Waste Land*

No city in America more represents the horrifying potential of Actual Black-Run America (ABRA) then Detroit. The collapse of Detroit is 100 percent racial. That so few people dare even discuss what the ramifications of the collapse of Black-run Detroit represent (on the heels of the collapse of Black-run Jefferson County - Birmingham - in Alabama) illustrates the power of Black-Run America.

Detroit isn't crap. Comparing the current state of the Motor City - a direct reflection of the majority population there (82 - 90 percent Black) - to fecal matter is an insult to fecal matter.

You can at least flush excrement down the toilet; with Detroit, all we can do is watch in horror as more and more taxpayer money is flushed down the toilet to... to what? So that gas stations can sell candy crack pipes?

No insidious plot hatched by a shadowy group of vigilantes destroyed Detroit. White people left, leaving Black people to enjoy the fruits of "Black Power," which in a mere 40 years has turned out to be nothing more than a silly chant by Black Marxists and Black Supremacists who have proved incapable of sustaining anything that evil whitey left behind.

Well, save the violence that forced whitey out to begin with.

The violence of Black people in Detroit is getting so bad that the Federal government is now intervening:

> Detroit's east side is being warned: The federal government is watching -- very closely.

> Responding to the latest spate of violence in the city, U.S. Attorney Barbara McQuade announced a federal crackdown Wednesday on the entire east side, saying the crime-plagued area has become the most violent section in the city and warrants federal attention. Homicides, in particular, she stressed, are "intolerably high" on the east side, where there was a 75% jump in homicides last year. The west side had a 27% drop last year.
> "I made it my personal resolution in 2012 to reduce homicides in the city of Detroit," McQuade said at a news conference, flanked by 15 uniformed federal, local and State Police officials. "We will not allow Detroit to be defined by violence and homicides."

> The city recorded 344 homicides in 2011, up from 308 in 2010. As of Sunday, Detroit has had 49 homicides this year, compared with 39 during the same period last year.

> However, overall violent crime was down 8% last year, with 7,300 fewer incidents.

> McQuade held the news conference to let the public know law enforcement isn't sitting idly by in the wake of the latest rash of violence.
> In recent weeks, Detroit has witnessed the shooting death of an infant, the slaying of a 12-year-old girl, a 14-year-old boy accused of killing his mother, and a 6-year-old critically injured after being shot with an AK47 during an attempted carjacking.[444]

Just like in the summer of 1967, when Federal troops patrolled the streets of a war-torn city - courtesy of a Negro Revolution that the first Black mayor of Detroit, Coleman Young, called an "Insurrection" - Black people have incapacitated the Motor City again.

---

[444] http://www.freep.com/article/20120301/NEWS01/203010529/Detroit-s-east-side-put-on-notice-Feds-are-cracking-down-on-rash-of-violence?odyssey=tab%7Ctopnews%7Ctext%7CFRONTPAGE

The reticence of people to speak out on Detroit's collapse is the real tragedy, but it's not unexpected. In BRA, publicly commenting on Black failure - no matter how minute - is grounds for career derailment and ostracism. To dare criticize an entire city of Black people (be it Baltimore, Atlanta, Memphis, Newark, Camden, Cleveland, St. Louis, Milwaukee, etc.)... Would you call that insanity?

No. What is insanity is our toleration of major city[445] (Black) police departments underreporting crime in their cities:

What's the murder capital of the nation? That depends on who does the counting.

Until this month, that dubious distinction for 2008 fell on Baltimore. But then, Detroit's police department conceded the city had 339 murders in 2008 rather than 306 -- making Detroit the deadliest city in the nation.

The disclosure followed newspaper reports that the city had consistently underreported its murder rate, leading to accusations that Detroit, along with other cities, was gaming the system to make the city appear safer.

"Figures don't lie, but liars sure do figure," former North Carolina Attorney General Rufus Edmisten, who used to announce that state's crime statistics, told ABC with a chuckle.

Was Detroit gaming the numbers to avoid an unpopular title? It's a common practice, Edmisten said.

"You have a lot of numbers manipulated, depending on what you want to achieve," he said. "If you need more help you say how bad things are. On the other hand no public official wants to say we're No. 1 in the number of murders."

According to the FBI, the total number of murders Detroit reported last year is 306. That put Detroit behind Baltimore in per-capita murders, at 36.9 murders per 100,000 residents. But Detroit Police Department spokesman Rod Liggons says that number undercounts the total.

---

[445] http://www.detroitnews.com/article/20090618/METRO/906180406

he higher number pushes Detroit's rate to 37.4 murders per 100,000 residents, making Detroit the deadliest city with more than 500,000 residents in the nation.

Abbe Smith, director of the Criminal Justice Clinic at Georgetown University Law School, agreed.

"I'd bet you this is highly politicized," Smith told ABC News, "especially that in places like Detroit, that are hard-hit by the recession, would do what they could to interpret the statistics in ways that are not quite so damning."

"Homicide is one of the more accurate crime statistics versus sexual assault, versus prop crimes, etc," said ABC News Consultant Brad Garrett, a former FBI agent.

In the 1990s, Philadelphia police routinely downgraded rapes to lesser crimes and portrayed the results as drop in crime, The Philadelphia Inquirer reported.

Detroit's disclosure came after an analysis of homicide cases by The Detroit Free Press found the city was undercounting homicides, in violation of FBI standards. The Free Press analysis found that among the deaths not considered a homicide were a fatal stabbing and a fatal beating.
Detroit isn't the only city that's had trouble with crime statistics. A recent audit of police practices in Atlanta, funded by the Atlanta Police Foundation, found that the "broken police department" routinely underreported crime, especially as the city prepared to welcome tourists for Atlanta's 1996 Summer Olympics.[446]

And you think crime is dropping around the nation? Police departments in majority Black cites routinely underreport crime as a means to try and convince businesses and entrepreneurs (and venture capitalists) to invest in their dying cities. This is a true act of criminality, jeopardizing people's safety for the illusion of protection.

---

[446] http://abcnews.go.com/US/story?id=7884362&page=2#.T0-xG4cgcm0

Even as elected officials philander, cheat, steal, and appoint corrupt police to "protect" the city of Detroit (who manipulate data), the citizens of this metropolis stand united behind these Black men and women, marching to keep Financial Martial Law from coming to Detroit:

> Emergency managers appointed by the state to run Michigan's financially struggling cities and schools soon could lose much of their sweeping power, at least temporarily, as an effort to overturn a controversial law moved forward Wednesday.
>
> A coalition called Stand Up for Democracy said it turned in more than 226,000 voter signatures to state election officials in hopes of giving voters a chance to overturn the law in the November election. If state election officials decide that at least roughly 161,300 of the signatures are from valid voters -- a decision which could be made within the next two months -- the law approved in 2011 would be suspended while awaiting the vote.
> That could have major ramifications in Benton Harbor, Flint, Pontiac, the Detroit public school system and a few other places that already have or could soon have state-appointed emergency managers in charge of their troubled finances. A review team is currently analyzing Detroit's finances to determine if an emergency exists.
>
> Gov. Rick Snyder's administration and Republican Attorney General Bill Schuette say that a suspension of the law would mean Michigan reverts to its previous law for emergency managers, adopted in 1990. Emergency managers would stay on the job, but wouldn't have the powers granted in 2011 revisions -- such as the ability to toss out union contracts and strip authority from locally elected officials.
>
> Snyder's administration is worried about the consequences of derailing the law, including the possibility it would become more difficult and take longer to resolve financial problems in locations where local leaders already demonstrated they couldn't fix the issues on their own. Snyder and other Republicans backed the 2011 changes in hopes of allowing emergency managers -- in the cases where they are needed -- to do their jobs more effectively and quickly.

"Unintended consequences could be severe and would not be in anyone's best interests," said Sara Wurfel, Snyder's spokeswoman. "The places where we're working right now, the whole reason we got there was that word `emergency.' Those communities and schools were in circumstances that in some cases hadn't been seen before because of how dramatic they were."

Critics of the law, including some labor unions and community groups, say the state is overreaching and undermining democracy. Some critics argue that if Public Act 4 is suspended, state-appointed emergency managers should be sidelined at least until the election -- leaving only locally elected leaders in charge of a community's finances.

"All the powers would rest with the democratically elected government," said Greg Bowens, a spokesman for Stand Up for Democracy, a coalition that opposes the law.[447]

Freedom has failed. It is in Wayne County, Michigan, home to the *Paris of the West-Mogadishu of the West,* America's true Atlantis - where the Black citizens of today look upon the crumbling white monuments and buildings of yesterday with a sense of wonder and open hostility - that the concept of "democracy" begins to die.

Charlie LeDuff, a reporter for Detroit's Fox affiliate, wrote a column deploring the moral decay and the crime rate in the *Mogadishu of the West.* Charlie[448]: it's the moral decay found in the Black residents of Detroit, just as it's the moral decay found in Black people in New Orleans, St. Louis, Chicago, and even Vermont.[449]

---

[447]

http://www.myfoxdetroit.com/dpp/news/politics/local_politics/emergency–manager-opponents-aim-to-suspend-michigan-law-20120229-ms

[448]   http://www.myfoxdetroit.com/dpp/news/charlie_leduff/moral-decay-is-not-the-only-reason-for-detroit%27s-out-of-control-murder-rate--dk

[449]

http://www.burlingtonfreepress.com/article/20120227/NEWS03/1202270 02/Vermont-race-crime-prison-data-troubling?odyssey=tab%7Ctopnews%7Ctext%7CFRONTPAGE

Hubert G. Locke, a Black man, wrote *The Detroit of 1967* only a few years after the Black insurrection transpired in that city. On p. 17 of the book, he writes:

> What all of this means for the future of Detroit is uncertain. there are simultaneously great possibilities and great dangers in the way in which the city is rebuilding itself, socially, economically, and politically. but that is a matter for the future; this book is concerned with Detroit's recent past and to some extent its chaotic present. It is a record of a week of terror in the nation's fifth largest city, of the quarter century of agonizing progress and abysmal failure that preceded it, and of a tension-filled year of dramatic shifts in power alignments, political loyalties, and social perspectives that emerged in its wake. It is, in essence, the story of contemporary urban America, as seen in the racial struggles of one city, but a city whose success or failure may well hold the key to the future of urban life in the entire nation.

Only a few years after this book was published, those great changes came to Detroit. The culmination of those changes are upon us. Detroit is not dying; it is dead. The epitaph on the grave of the city must be an answering of Locke's prediction.

Urban life in America, where a white settler participating in gentrification doesn't occur, isn't much of a life at all. It's Black people living in cities of their design (a city, town, or neighborhood is only a reflection of the majority population) that are more violent than war-torn cities around the world.

The failure of Detroit shows why any urban area hoping to have a "sustainable" future can't include Black people. One that does is an inherently unstable community.

And that is the lesson of Detroit; a city where fighting "public corruption" (remember, almost every elected position and city employee of Detroit is Black) is the number one priority of the FBI branch in the city:

> Federal, state and local officials will work more closely to uncover and prosecute public corruption in the Detroit area. The FBI announced Thursday the formation of a multi-agency task force.

Joining the FBI are the U.S. attorney's office, state Attorney General, Internal Revenue Service, Housing and Urban Development, Environmental Protection Agency, U.S. Department of Transportation, and Detroit and state police. For years federal prosecutors have been investigating corruption in Detroit city government. Among those already convicted are former City Council President Monica Conyers, her aide Sam Riddle Jr., former Detroit deputy mayor Kandia Milton, and Milton's brother, DeDan Milton.

Ex-Detroit Mayor Kwame Kilpatrick, longtime associate Bobby Ferguson, ex-city water director Victor Mercado, ex-mayoral aide Derrick Miller, and Kilpatrick's father, Bernard, have been indicted on federal corruption charges.[450]

This is a city that Black people destroyed. Capitalism didn't fail Detroit; Black people who inherited the city from the white people who created did.

Like the Titanic laying at the bottom of the ocean, the magnificent buildings and structures in Detroit that decay into nothingness is a reminder that a great people once lived there.

Unlike the Titanic, Detroit didn't hit an iceberg.

---

[450] http://www.myfoxdetroit.com/dpp/news/local/task-force-to-uncover-and-prosecute-public-corruption-in-metro-detroit-20120301-spb

Works Cited

Austin, Dan, and Sean Doerr. *Lost Detroit: stories behind the Motor City's majestic ruins*. Charleston, SC: History Press, 2010. Print.

Bergmann, Luke. *Getting ghost: two young lives and the struggle for the soul of an American city*. New York: New Press, 2008. Print.

Boyle, Kevin. *The UAW and the heyday of American liberalism, 1945-1968*. Ithaca: Cornell University Press, 1995. Print.

Chafets, Ze'ev. *Devil's night: and other true tales of Detroit*. New York: Random House, 1990. Print.

Colling, Herb. *Turning points the Detroit riot of 1967 : a Canadian perspective*. Toronto: Natural Heritage Books, 2003. Print.

Conot, Robert E.. *American odyssey,*. New York: Morrow, 1974. Print.

Darden, Joe T.. *Detroit, race and uneven development*. Philadelphia: Temple University Press, 1987. Print.

Farley, Reynolds, Sheldon Danziger, and Harry J. Holzer. *Detroit divided*. New York: Russell Sage Foundation, 2000. Print.

Fine, Sidney. *Violence in the model city: the Cavanagh administration, race relations, and the Detroit riot of 1967*. Ann Arbor: University of Michigan Press, 1989. Print.

Georgakas, Dan, and Marvin Surkin. *Detroit, I do mind dying*. Cambridge, Mass.: South End Press, 1998. Print.

Graham, Lawrence. *Our kind of people: inside America's Black upper class*. New York: HarperCollins, 1999. Print.

Ingrassia, Paul, and Joseph B. White. *Comeback: the fall and rise of the American automobile industry*. New York: Simon & Schuster, 1994. Print.

Ingrassia, Paul. *Crash course: the American automobile industry's road from glory to disaster*. New York: Random House, 2010. Print.

Jones, E. Michael. *The slaughter of cities: urban renewal as ethnic cleansing*. South Bend, Ind.: St. Augustine's Press, 2004. Print.

Keller, Maryann. *Rude awakening: the rise, fall, and struggle for recovery of General Motors*. New York: Morrow, 1989. Print.

Kilpatrick, Kwame M., and Khary Kimani Turner. *Surrendered: the rise, fall and revelation of Kwame Kilpatrick*. United States: Creative Publishing, 2011. Print.

Lee, Alfred McClung, and Norman Daymond Humphrey. *Race riot, Detroit 1943,*. New York: Octagon Books, 19681943. Print.

Locke, Hubert G.. *The Detroit riot of 1967,*. Detroit: Wayne State University Press, 1969. Print.

Marchand, Yves, and Romain Meffre. *The ruins of Detroit*. Goîˆttingen: Steidl, 2010. Print.

Maynard, Micheline. *The end of Detroit: how the Big Three lost their grip on the American car market*. New York: Currency/Doubleday, 2003. Print.

Millar, Mark, and J. G. Jones. *Wanted*. Los Angeles, CA: Top Cow Productions ;, 2007. Print.

Moore, Andrew, and Philip Levine. *Detroit disassembled*. Bologna: Damiani Editore ;, 2010. Print.

Rattner, Steven. *Overhaul: an insider's account of the Obama administration's emergency rescue of the auto industry*. Boston: Houghton Mifflin Harcourt, 2010. Print.

Spreen, Johannes F., and Diane Holloway. *Who killed Detroit: other cities beware*. New York: iUniverse, 2005. Print.

Sugrue, Thomas J.. *The origins of the urban crisis: race and inequality in postwar Detroit : with a new preface by the author*. Princeton: Princeton University Press, 2005. Print.

Taylor, Carl S.. *Dangerous society*. East Lansing, Mich.: Michigan State University Press, 1990. Print.

The Kerner report: the 1968 report of the National Advisory Commission on Civil Disorders. New York: Pantheon Books, 19881968. Print.

Widick, B. J.. *Detroit: city of race and class violence,*. Chicago: Quadrangle Books, 1972. Print.

Young, Coleman A., and Lonnie Wheeler. *Hard stuff: the autobiography of Coleman Young*. New York: Viking, 1994. Print.

Young, Coleman A.. *The quotations of Mayor Coleman A. Young*. New ed. Detroit: Wayne State University Press, 2005. Print.

15113427R00201

Made in the USA
Lexington, KY
08 May 2012